Digital Solidarity in Education

Digital Solidarity in Education is a book for educators, scholars, and students interested in better understanding both the role technology can play in schools and its potential for strengthening communities, optimizing the effects of globalization, and increasing educational access. The digital solidarity movement prioritizes the engagement and mobilization of students from diverse racial, ethnic, linguistic, and economic backgrounds, and with giftedness and/or disabilities, to utilize and apply technologies.

This powerful book introduces innovative technological programs including virtual schools, e-tutoring, and interactive online communities for K-12 students that can:

- increase students' knowledge and understanding of advanced concepts while reinforcing their basic skills;
- reinforce students' communication in their first language while introducing second and third language possibilities;
- nurture students' capabilities to think analytically, while using creative and innovative ideas to think simultaneously "outside of the box."

The experienced author team shows how collaborative partners from the private sector can assist public school systems and educators in creating access for all students to technological innovations, with a goal of increasing individual opportunities for future college and career success. Combining theoretical scholarship and research with the personal perspectives of practitioners in the field, this volume shares with readers both the nuts and bolts of using technology in education, and the importance of doing so.

Mary Kolesinski, Ed. D., is an online educator at Nova Southeastern University.

Evelyn Nelson-Weaver, Ed. D., is an online instructor at Nova Southeastern University and consultant for Weaver Worldwide Consulting.

Daryl L. Diamond, Ph.D., is currently the Intern Principal at Sheridan Technical Center in Broward County Public Schools in Fort Lauderdale, Florida; and an online instructor for Florida Atlantic University.

Digital Solidarity in Education

Promoting Equity, Diversity, and Academic Excellence through Innovative Instructional Programs

Mary T. Kolesinski,
Evelyn Nelson-Weaver, and
Daryl L. Diamond

 Routledge
Taylor & Francis Group

NEW YORK AND LONDON

First published 2014
by Routledge
711 Third Avenue, New York, NY 10017

Simultaneously published in the UK
by Routledge
2 Park Square, Milton Park, Abingdon, Oxon OX14 4RN

Routledge is an imprint of the Taylor & Francis Group, an informa
business

Library of Congress Cataloguing in Publication Data
Kolesinski, Mary T., author.
  Digital solidarity in education: promoting equity, diversity, and
  academic excellence through innovative instructional programs/
  Mary T. Kolesinski, Evelyn Nelson-Weaver, and Daryl Diamond.
  pages cm
  Includes bibliographical references and index.
  1. Educational innovations. 2. Multicultural education.
  3. Educational equalization. 4. Education and globalization.
  I. Nelson-Weaver, Evelyn. II. Diamond, Daryl (Daryl L.)
  III. Title.
  LB1027.K627 2013
  371.3028—dc23   2013007402

ISBN: 978-0-415-63613-1 (hbk)
ISBN: 978-0-415-63614-8 (pbk)
ISBN: 978-0-203-07526-5 (ebk)

Typeset in Bembo and Gill Sans
by Florence Production Ltd, Stoodleigh, Devon, UK

Printed and bound in the United States of America by
Edwards Brothers Malloy

This book is dedicated to the "have-nots" of our information society. The authors are committed to helping these underserved members of our community become fully engaged, digital citizens of the United States.

Contents

Illustrations

Figures

Tables

Foreword

Every so often a book of major educational importance and accomplishment is written. Such is the case with the publication of *Digital Solidarity in Education: Promoting Equity, Diversity, and Academic Excellence through Innovative Instructional Programs*. In this scholarly researched text, the authors have managed to bridge together an informative, factual, and comprehensive overview of the technological impact of distance learning and its effect on closing the digital divide, creating an environment of digital inclusion and promoting the principles of digital solidarity.

In Chapters 1 through 3, the authors trace the evolution of distance learning, the rapid expansion of technology choices in education, the design of innovative educational ideas utilizing information and communication technologies, and the overall implications each brings to the causes of digital solidarity. Chapters 4 and 5 continue the discussion of the "engagement and mobilization" of individuals, the general population, governments and corporations as they become active participants in the digital technology revolution. Chapters 6 and the Epilogue address the issues associated with bringing educational technology to a level of critical mass coupled with commentary focused on issues in education and society that continue to prohibit the achievement of the goals set forth by the digital solidarity movement.

Finally, this seminal work is a must-read for any individual, educator, or scholarly researcher engaged in the development and delivery of distance learning opportunities. Students at all levels of distance learning and digital education will be able to immerse themselves in a provocative and forward-thinking text.

John G. Flores, Ph.D.
Executive Director
United States Distance Learning Association
Program Professor and Administrator
Nova Southeastern University
Fischler School of Education

Preface

Digital Solidarity in Education: Promoting Equity, Diversity, and Academic Excellence through Innovative Instructional Programs posits that in today's world it is no longer acceptable for any of its population to be excluded from the global information networks that are the superhighways of economic, cultural, political, and social exchanges. With current research indicating that we are moving from a digital divide towards digital solidarity, it is imperative that schools prioritize the engagement and mobilization of students from diverse racial, ethnic, linguistic, and economic backgrounds with giftedness and/or disabilities to utilize and apply technologies so that they can compete academically with their global counterparts.

The mission of digital solidarity is to promote equity, diversity, and academic excellence through innovative instructional programs, thereby ensuring that underserved individuals and communities can access education and tools to improve the quality of their lives. The objective of digital solidarity is to promote an inclusive and sustainable information society by providing access to information and communication technologies and the advanced services, such as education and health care that these technologies can provide. Educators need to be aware of and advocate for new innovative instructional programs, including virtual schools, e-tutoring, and interactive online communities for K-16 students that effectively use technological tools while making appropriate linguistic, academic, and financial accommodations so that *all* students can experience equity of access through online participation.

Today many options are provided to school-aged children, adolescents, and adults using a variety of technologies that can increase their knowledge and understanding of advanced concepts while reinforcing their basic skills; technologies that strengthen their communication in their first language while introducing second and third language possibilities; and technologies that nurture their capabilities to think analytically, while using creative and innovative ideas to simultaneously think "outside of the box." While educators focus on issues of accountability and educational reform, we present innovative instructional programs and models that can provide the impetus needed to motivate students towards digital literacy, academic excellence, and global competitiveness.

The intention of this textbook is to provide students, parents, teachers, administrators, and community organizers with proven instructional practices and programs that have the potential to go to scale. As the authors, we discuss a variety of information and communication technologies that can be used by well qualified teachers to prepare diverse populations of young students to be successful consumers of knowledge while promoting equity of access as a concept to be realized throughout their childhood, adolescence, and adulthood. This effort requires awareness, aggressiveness, and advocacy. Readers "visit" a virtual elementary school and learn how diverse populations of students are provided with the necessary technological tools to succeed academically. Also, information is provided about collaborative partners from the private sector that assist school systems and educators in creating access for *all* students to technological innovations that ultimately improve and increase individual opportunities for college and career success.

The textbook is separated into six chapters and an epilogue. The first chapter, "The Emergence of Digital Solidarity and Competing Technologies," is designed to set the stage for the textbook by defining concepts such as digital divide, digital inclusion, and digital solidarity and placing these concepts along a digital literacy continuum. It details the origins of the global digital solidarity movement, tracing its inception as part of the 2000 United Nations Millennium Declaration, to the 2003 World Summit of the Information Society (WSIS), to the 2005 IFIP 8th World Conference on Computers in Education. The role of distance learning technologies in supporting digital solidarity is detailed. The chapter ends with identification of the specific digital generations, how each generation uses technology, and the implications these technologies and their use have for American education.

Chapter 2 takes a look at "Broadening Technologies in American Education" and offers increased student achievement and engagement as the rationale for increased technology usage in American schools. It details the expanding technology choices that are currently available to help school districts and post-secondary institutions "reimagine" schools and individualize the learning process.

Chapter 3 details various "Innovative Ideas in Education to Support Digital Solidarity." Topics covered include virtual schools, afterschool programs, online tutoring programs, and online communities. It specifically identifies afterschool and online tutoring programs for special populations that include: low income, gender-specific, and seniors. The chapter concludes with specific case studies of children with exceptionalities, medical problems, and those who speak another language other than English.

Chapter 4 details various "Accommodations and Adaptations" that promote digital access for all. Both global and American perspectives regarding the "haves" and have-nots" are reviewed through case studies depicting different types of inequalities ranging from racial, socio-economic, geographic, gender, language, and disability. Digital accommodations and adaptations are reviewed and technologies identified for use by at-risk students, English-language learners, students with disabilities, seniors, and the homeless.

Chapter 5 describes "Technology Activities to Support Digital Solidarity." It details how an effective action plan for innovative, technology-enhanced programs and activities needs to include adequate planning, funding, distribution, training and support, and evaluation. The chapter then goes on to examine proven technology-enhanced programs that include those for K–12 students, afterschool, post-secondary, community, and national technology programs.

Chapter 6 discusses how innovative technology-enhanced programs can be taken to scale. A differentiation is made between two concepts: "scaling up" and "going to scale." Where scaling up is defined as the replication of successful education reforms in more classrooms, schools, and districts, going to scale is seen as a much more complex endeavor, one to be characterized and analyzed across multiple layers including spread, depth, sustainability, and shift in reform ownership. The authors then utilize the concept of going to scale to evaluate the effectiveness of the No Child Left Behind Act, its role in education reform, and the impact it had in the digital divide. Also discussed are the expectations for the newly enacted Common Core State Standards and the relationship the standards have with promoting digital literacy and digital solidarity.

In the Epilogue, the authors conclude the book detailing some of the remaining obstacles that create barriers to achieving digital solidarity. These barriers include the lack of access to high speed and affordable Internet, the inability of teachers to effectively utilize technologies in their instructional practices, the high cost for school districts to maintain and purchase information and communication technologies, the training of students and staff on how to be good digital citizens in a digital world saturated with social media and improper Internet sites, and what is not being done to successfully advocate for digital solidarity in education.

Included in the textbook are numerous websites that will provide readers with an enormous amount of digital material that can be utilized within their schools and classrooms. Descriptions for the websites are provided so that readers are informed on the content prior to retrieving the site. A glossary is also provided, keyed to bold terms in the text, so that readers are aware of the definitions we are attaching to specific words and phrases.

Pedagogical Features

- An Instructor's Manual, which includes:
  - Chapter overviews
  - Chapter objectives
  - Student activities
  - Relevant websites
  - Questions for exploration
  - Teaching resources
  - Multiple-choice questions
- Chapter PowerPoint presentations
- Data bank of 100 multiple-choice questions

Acknowledgments

The authors would like to take this opportunity to thank those who have spent time and due diligence reviewing the chapters to ensure that the story we are telling is easily understood and provides relevant information that can be successfully implemented by practitioners in the field. Special thanks to John Flores for providing the foreword to this book. His knowledge, expertise, and leadership in the field of distance learning are unsurpassed. The authors appreciate the hard work and dedication provided by the Routledge editorial and production staff members in the compilation and completion of this textbook. Last, thanks to Roland Foulkes for his insight into the digital solidarity continuum and to all the individuals who shared their case studies with us so that we could provide the reader with stories about *real* individuals that digital solidarity serves.

Chapter 1

The Emergence of Digital Solidarity and Competing Technologies

Today it is no longer acceptable for much of the world's population to be excluded from the global information networks that are the superhighways of economic, cultural, political, and social exchanges. One need just recall the role played by the Internet and social media sites in both the 2011 Egyptian Revolution and the 2009 Iranian protests to emphasize this point. The Internet offered both opposition groups an intermediate space where they were able to disseminate information virtually that went beyond limited conceptual and physical spaces (Baiasu, 2011). This dissemination of information, currently referred to as "**viral marketing**," helped spread awareness through the network effects of the Internet. To productively live in today's society, it is apparent that both access to and knowledge of how to utilize information technologies are necessities that offer benefits to those who can.

Digital Solidarity Defined

Digital solidarity is the byproduct of multiple conversations currently taking place globally, and can be defined as a movement enabling the engagement and mobilization of individuals from *diverse cultural* and *linguistic backgrounds*, as well as *economic strata* to be active participants on the technology playing field (Voicu, 2004). Its mission is to promote equity, diversity, and academic excellence through innovative instructional programs, thereby ensuring that underserved individuals and communities can access education and tools to improve the quality of their lives. The objective of digital solidarity is to promote an inclusive and sustainable information society by providing access to Information and Communication Technologies (**ICT**) and the advanced services, such as education and health care these technologies can provide. The rationale for digital solidarity comes from two basic observations: (a) ICTs constitute powerful leverage for social development, and (b) the market cannot be the only way to provide universal access to digital goods and services (Madelin, 2008).

The Global Digital Solidarity Movement

Information and communication technologies (ICTs) include the Internet, the World Wide Web (WWW), online services, digital content, email, other Internet-related services, computer networks and devices, cell phones, and other applicable services or technologies either currently in use or to be implemented in the future. By widening access to ICT in developing countries, the digital solidarity movement plays an instrumental role in fostering access to education, training, and economic development. The origin of the digital solidarity movement can be traced to The Millennium Declaration of the United Nations (UN), a declaration that reaffirmed the UN Charter, the purposes of the UN, and Member States' commitment to the core values of freedom, equality, solidarity, tolerance, respect for nature, and shared responsibility. It was signed by global leaders in September 2000. In the Millennium Development Goals (MDG), the UN included as one of its goals (Goal 8) the improvement of access to Information and Communication Technology. Goal 8 of the MDG aspired to "develop a global partnership for development" and the last target of the goal (8f) stated that this can be accomplished in cooperation with the private sector, thereby "mak[ing] available the benefits of new technologies, especially information and communications" (Guillet, Diouf, & Haenen, 2009, p.10).

In 2003, the government of Switzerland, while hosting the first World Summit of the Information Society (WSIS) taking place in Geneva, started the dialogue regarding building an inclusive global information society. Its aim was to put into place the conditions that rally human, financial, and technological resources to enable every human being to be a part of the Information Society (WSIS, 2011). During the WSIS, the President of the Republic of Senegal, Mr. Abdoulaye Wade proposed the creation of the Global Digital Solidarity Fund (DSF) with the intent of providing the populations of the poorest countries with access to knowledge, to take part in the digital culture, and to acquire digital practices. The DSF was designed to further the commitments undertaken by the international community (national governments, local authorities, representatives of the private sector and non-governmental organizations) to facilitate change and gradually close the **digital divide**. Using an innovative financing mechanism called the "1% digital solidarity contribution" also known as the "Geneva Principle," the Digital Solidarity Fund is sustained through a voluntary commitment by the companies that win bids pertaining to the purchase of ICT-related equipment and services to pay a one percent contribution to the DSF (Madelin, 2008). The Digital Solidarity Fund can be seen as a concrete manifestation of the efforts to achieve the UN Millennium Development Goals and to help harness the power of ICTs to empower poor and marginalized people.

In July 2005, at the IFIP 8th World Conference on Computers in Education held in Stellenbosch, South Africa, a declaration was prepared entitled *ICT in Education: Make it Work* (Cornu, 2007). The declaration included all educational stakeholders (teachers, practitioners, researchers, academics, managers, decision-makers and policy-makers) and charged them with increasing the integration of information and communication technologies to improve teaching and learning in order to prepare our citizens for a knowledge society. According to the declaration, digital solidarity was one of the six major areas that will shape a beneficial use of ICT in education. The implication is that all stakeholders must guarantee the right of participation in the digital society for all students in the world. Going beyond the development of an information society, the declaration pushed to create a knowledge society where children and all people will not only be able to access and acquire knowledge, but they will also be able to derive benefits from being educated.

Therefore, a global effort is currently being made to identify and implement initiatives that address the uneven distribution and use of new information and communication technologies and enable **excluded people** (women, minorities, the elderly, and disabled individuals) and countries to enter the new era of the information society (Ginsburg, 2006). There are many examples of digital solidarity projects that are being implemented around the world. Global Cities Dialogue (GCD) (2011), an international network of mayors and high political representatives across the world, believe that the development of the Information Society should be for the benefit of all the citizens, communities, and peoples of the world. As a group, it is actively involved in creating projects that provide equal opportunities and access for all citizens. One program recommended by the GCD is the Sankore program, an educational digital solidarity program for Africa. It is defined as a "twinning program" between pairs of French and African cities, where up-to-date digital equipment and educational resources are offered to participating "twin" cities. French cities are invited to sponsor the program between the African city of their choice and one of their own schools. The twin classes receive the same equipment and are given the means to exchange teaching materials and concepts, thereby promoting an intercultural exchange between students through the use of information and communication technologies.

The Digital Solidarity Movement in the United States

Unique educational programs aimed at initiating digital solidarity are being implemented here in the United States. In 2009, as America faced social and economic challenges, the Digital Workforce Initiative, a summer academic and career program for young people interested in the game industry, was implemented in Louisiana (King, 2009). Forty middle school and high school students spent spring break at the Digital Workforce Initiative, working 12 hours per day creating games and virtual worlds that focused on Louisiana's core social problems of education, health care, coastal restoration, and pollution.

The intention of the project was to create an educational pipeline from middle school up through college and on to the workforce. In learning how to design the games, these participants also learned important 21st-century skills including creative collaboration and fluency with the digital culture. The premise of the Digital Workforce Initiative was to gradually grow an in-state game industry along with a trained workforce that will result in a more sustainable technology industry. The approach was unique in the fact that it addressed Louisiana's drop-out problem resulting from student disengagement with the educational system. By training the students on how to collaborate on the creation of games, they become better prepared for other collaborative opportunities, and are ripe to take advantage of the state's increasing involvement with the robust mixed media and film production industry and the creation of simulated virtual training environments.

Digital Solidarity Predecessors

Background Information

What separates the digital solidarity movement from its predecessors (digital divide and **digital inclusion**) is the ideal that individuals should be able to derive specific benefits (social, economic, political, and educational) from both the access to (bridging the digital divide) and the knowledge of how to use (digital inclusion) the available information and communication technologies. Recent history has demonstrated that the notion of the digital divide focused mostly on broadband infrastructure investment offering access to the Internet for the underserved. The concept of digital inclusion, in addition to focusing on infrastructure investment strategies, went a step further to focus "on activities and initiatives aimed at stimulating demand and generating relevant content, which increases the overall broadband market and generates more benefits to society" (Muente-Kunigami, 2011).

The Digital Divide

Some use the term digital divide to refer to the inequality of opportunity in respect to adequate access to information, knowledge, and communication networks that are transforming our lives (Brooks, Donovan, & Rumble, 2005; Dickard & Schneider, 2011). The great development of information and communication technologies (ICT) in recent years has given rise to a serious imbalance between information-rich and information-poor individuals, creating the "haves" and the "have-nots" of the information society. Global Cities Dialogue (2011) describes the efforts of two projects that reflect programs that answer the *access* need of the digital divide. The first project was found in Rufisque, Senegal and is in collaboration with Segrate, Italy, where an ICT youth center was created with a project aim to reduce the scarcity of available infrastructures and low capacity of ICT utilization. The center was equipped with 40 PCs and a wide-band connection enabling the people of Rufisque to be able to use the PCs and the Internet. The second project initiated between the city of Luxembourg and the Cape Verde Islands was aimed at providing three schools in Cape Verde, whose pupils are between six and 18 years old, with 150 refurbished computers and mobile devices.

An example in the United States of an individual meeting the demands of the digital divide by designing programs to eradicate it was broadcast on the NBC Nightly News program with Brian Williams on January 28, 2013. During the program, reporter Kerry Sanders profiled the 76-year-old daughter of migrant farm workers whose parents' education did not go past the fourth grade. Estella Pyfrom, though, went to college and obtained a master's degree to become an accomplished educator with a 50-year career. On a personal campaign to help level the digital playing field, she provided underserved children with access to technology aboard her "Brilliant Bus." The project aimed at bridging the digital divide was bankrolled by her $900,000 in savings and retirement money after working for decades as a teacher seeing the digital divide first-hand. She purchased the bus and converted it to a wired mobile learning center that goes out to find and help what she calls the "invisible" children. She did not forget from where she came and reached back to give these children a connection with a wider world through digital access.

Warschauer (2002) suggested that the digital divide issue was more of a gradation based on different degrees of access to information technology rather than, what he calls, a bipolar societal split of "haves" and "have-nots." He cited as an example of this gradation the difference between access for a professor at UCLA who has a high-speed connection in her office, compared with a student in Seoul who occasionally uses a cyber-cafe, with a rural activist in Indonesia who has no computer or phone line and relies on colleagues to download and print out information for her. This example demonstrates three varying degrees of possible access to online material that a person might have. In addition, he asserted that the digital divide is not only about the physical access to computers and connectivity, but also includes access to those resources that allow people to use technology well. He pointed out that the original sense of the digital divide term attached overriding importance to the physical availability of computers and connectivity, rather than to issues of content, language, education, literacy, or community and social resources. What has become more apparent over the years is that the digital divide is not only a barrier to accessing technology resources. It is increasingly an impediment to how the most vulnerable citizen receives vital social services (Wynne & Cooper, 2007).

Therefore, the digital divide has morphed into a two-pronged construct. On the one hand, it refers to the gap between those who have access to digital technology and those who do not. But this is no longer the whole story. The real issue is not merely about access to digital technology but also involves the benefits derived from that access (Smith, n.d.).

Digital Inclusion

Where the digital divide referred to the gap between those who have access to digital technology and those who do not, digital inclusion shifts the conversation away from the gap in technology access towards one of empowering people, organizations, and businesses to apply information technology in ways that result in greater participation in our growing knowledge-based society. Crandall and Fisher (2009) defined digital inclusion as technological literacy and the ability to access relevant online content and services. Wynne and Cooper (2007) asserted that those who have online access and are digitally literate are more likely to be economically secure and at less risk than those who do not. Therefore, the goal of digital inclusion goes beyond providing equity of access to information technologies, to include the need for developing both **digital literacy** and meaningful content. Digital inclusion moves past access to technology, and moves towards offering and training people on how to use tools and content that deliver meaning to their lives.

This is accomplished by first expanding access to critical information technologies and applications. In addition, end users need to develop the digital literacy skills required to utilize equipment and the Internet effectively for essential services, education, employment, civic engagement, and cultural participation. Meaningful and useful content and services must be made available for those in need, with culturally and educationally appropriate designs that are marketed and placed appropriately to reach underserved communities. Digital inclusion can be seen as social inclusion in the 21st century, ensuring that individuals and disadvantaged groups have access to and skills to use information and communication technologies; and are therefore able to participate in and benefit from our growing knowledge and information society. Digital inclusion offers strategies that address the barriers that underserved members of the community must overcome in order to be such participants. It is more than merely providing the infrastructure and access to technology. More so, it is the development of strategies that lead to social inclusion and empowerment through using technology.

What does digital inclusion look like in the real world? With the Internet as a vital tool in our information society, more Americans are going online to conduct many meaningful daily activities such as education, business transactions, personal correspondence, research and information-gathering, and job searches. "Each year, being digitally connected becomes ever more critical to economic and educational advancement and community participation" (U. S. Department of Commerce, 2000). Now that a large number of Americans regularly use the Internet to conduct daily activities, people who lack access to and knowledge of how to use these tools are at a growing disadvantage. Therefore, raising the level of digital inclusion by increasing the number of Americans *effectively* using the technology tools of the digital age is a vitally important national goal.

A program called Internet Essentials (Jackson, 2011) is one of the latest attempts to promote digital inclusion right here in the United States. Announced in August 2011, the program brings together the Miami-Dade County Public Schools (and other school districts across the nation) and the Comcast Corporation to address what research has identified as three primary barriers to broadband adoption: (a) a lack of understanding of how the Internet is relevant and useful, (b) the cost of a home computer, and (c) the cost of Internet service. Comcast offers discounted Internet access ($9.95 per month plus taxes) to low-income families living in Comcast's service areas with children who are eligible to receive a free lunch under the National School Lunch Program (NSLP). The goal of the Internet Essentials program is to help ensure more American families benefit from all the Internet has to offer. The program helps level the playing field for low-income families. About 60 percent of the over 300,000 students in Miami-Dade County Public Schools will qualify for the program to "help them connect with their teachers and their school's educational resources as well as enabling parents to do things like apply for jobs online or use the Internet to learn more about healthcare and government services available where they live" (Jackson, 2011).

Similarly, Milholland (2011) identified the We Are Now Connected initiative providing free Internet access and computer training to residents of affordable-housing projects throughout the state of California. The goal of the national program is to help low-income families use Internet resources to join the economic mainstream. One of the local partners helping to bring the program to San Diego said that "Internet access can be a powerful driving force for economic change" (para. 5). The program aims to provide free Internet access to 27,000 homes around the country, including nearly 600 in San Diego. Funding for the program comes from federal stimulus money, and the Internet service is donated by AT&T. Eligible households receive free Internet access for a while, and then pay about $10 a month after that.

Smith (n.d.) warned that extending non-meaningful access to digital technologies to certain sectors of emerging markets could be detrimental and actually widen the digital gap. He offered as an example, cyber-cafes. Years ago, many pointed to their spread into rural sectors of underserved areas as an example, demonstrating that the digital divide was shrinking. But when a local youth in a Cambodian village ignores his school work and instead spends his evenings playing violent video games with his peers, he is not really benefiting from digital technology. Gaming technology that has been designed for youth from wealthy families may actually add to the causes of poverty for children of families from poor, rural areas. For the positive potential of digital inclusion to be recognized, it needs to remain focused on how to use information and communication technologies in meaningful ways that result in greater participation in the information society.

Technology Trends

Distance Learning

Information and communication technologies, new media, and open and distance learning all include new ways for accessing knowledge and cooperating with others. Cornu (2007) recognized that a "knowledge society" is one in which knowledge becomes a valuable commodity necessary for human development where education is one of the most important investments in the future. In a knowledge society, new media and open and distance learning provide replicable innovative technology programs offering new possibilities for accessing and sharing information. Open and distance learning enables freedom from the constraints of time and space by allowing participants to be involved in learning activities at a distance through the participation in both synchronous and asynchronous activities. Cornu asserted that "open and distance learning gives the opportunity of new ways of collaborative work, of new ways of interactive learning activities" (p.49).

Distance learning has always been about affording access to, participation with, and deriving benefits from the given technologies of the day. Distance learning technologies have historically served in the delivery of innovative instructional programs, designed to bridge the gap of distance while reducing the imbalance of access to quality educational programs and instructors. As an educational delivery practice, it has developed over the past two centuries as an answer to specific educational needs of diverse populations requiring alternative means of access. Starr (1998) pointed out that "distance [learning] has historically generated a great deal of interest in areas where the student population was widely distributed" (p.157). Its advancement and further development throughout the years was in response to "those who could not attend regular school for reasons of geography, health, or complicated lifestyles" (Schrum, 2002, p.7). There are many benefits to offering the various options of distance learning. For students, it offers increased access to "flexible scheduling of personal time, convenient location, individualized attention by the instructor, less travel, and increased time to think about and respond to (via email or discussion board) questions posed by the instructor" (Mathews, 1999, p.57). Distance learning platforms expands access to "under-served populations; alleviates classroom capacity constraints; capitalizes on emerging market opportunities, such as working adults; and, serves as a catalyst for institutional transformation" (Singh & Pan, 2004, p.302). Furthermore, virtual courses enable students to have access to more and perhaps better learning resources than in the past. "Rural and inner-city students can take courses previously available only to students in suburban areas. Handicapped and disabled students have access to the same courses as everyone else—even if they are homebound or institutionalized" (Moore & Kearsley, 1996, p.15). What has developed, courtesy of the Internet, is "the possibility of learning on a scale more far-reaching than previously imagined" (Maeroff, 2003, p.4). Cavanaugh (2004) contends that "as we learn more about learning styles, brain-based learning, and differentiating instruction, we realize the value of technology, including distance learning, in meeting the unique needs of all learners" (p.vii). The development in distance learning can be structured into three generations of technological innovation: correspondence study, telecommunications, and computer mediated. In describing the development of distance learning technologies, the term "generation" is used to suggest a building upon previous capabilities. These generations of distance learning represent "a hierarchical structure with an increasing differentiation of technological capacity for integrating unique delivery systems" (Garrison, 1985, p.238). In this manner, new media can be combined with older media offering a greater range of choice for the design of effective distance learning delivery systems.

Correspondence Study

Historically, the practice of distance learning traces back to the 1800s. The pioneers of distance education used the best technology of their day, the postal system, to open educational opportunities to people who wanted to learn but were unable to attend conventional schools. People who most benefited from such correspondence education included those with physical disabilities, women who were not allowed to enroll in educational institutions open only to men, people who had jobs during normal school hours, and those who lived in remote regions where schools did not exist. "In 1840, Sir Isaac Pitman, the English inventor of shorthand, came up with an ingenious idea for delivering instruction to a potentially limitless audience: correspondence courses by mail" (Mathews, 1999, p.54). In 1850, the University of London offered distance courses and major fields of study to its inhabitants in far-away colonies like India and Australia. In Europe in 1856, Toussaint and Langenscheidt began teaching language courses by correspondence. By the end of the century in 1891, the University of Queensland in Australia offered complete programs at a distance. In 1926, the Ontario Department of Education established their Correspondence Courses providing elementary education for children living in isolated areas of northern Ontario. Mathews (1999) cited "before 1969, distance teaching had developed into an important sector of higher education in quite a few countries" (p.54).

In the U.S. during the 1800s we find the beginnings of distance learning curricula within the area of adult education. Nasseh (1997) reported "In 1873, Anna Ticknor created [a] society to encourage studies at home for the purpose of educational opportunities for women of all classes in society" (para. 4). Over a 24-year period, through correspondence instruction and volunteer efforts, over 10,000 members participated in this society. From 1883 to 1891, Chautauqua College of Liberal Arts in New York was "the first official recognition of education by correspondence" (para. 4) authorized to grant academic degrees to students who completed work at their summer institutes which was then followed by correspondence throughout the following academic year.

One of the first universities to deliver distance learning in an organized manner was Pennsylvania State University, establishing its first distance learning network in 1886. By the 1900s, the University of Chicago had created the first department of correspondence teaching. The Colliery Engineer School of Mines based in Wilkes-Barre, PA was also a member of the first generation of distance education. Its home study course on mine safety quickly became very popular after its formation in 1890. With the growing importance of railroads, the school became a very large institution. At one point, it offered courses to employees from as many as 150 railroad companies (Cobb, 2004). The International Correspondence Schools (ICS) evolved from the Colliery Engineer School of Mines. Today, ICS is the largest commercial provider of home study programs in the U.S. It also has a very large international presence (Moore & Kearsley, 1996). The U.S branch of the ICS is now known as Penn Foster Career School, although ICS still works under its original name in the United Kingdom and Canada. Students now access course materials via the Internet, rather than waiting on the U.S. mail.

As the concept of correspondence studies grew in acceptance, the National University Extension Association (NUEA) was created in 1915. Through this organization, the focus of correspondence learning broadened to such issues as "new pedagogical models and new national level guidelines, such as university policies regarding acceptance of credit from correspondence courses, credit [transfers], and standard quality for correspondence educators" (Nasseh, 1997, para. 10). Over time, increasingly more for-profit organizations began to offer correspondence courses. Moore (2003) asserted that "dubious sales practices by some of these organizations brought the method into disrepute" (p.6). To deal with this, in 1926 the more responsible schools set up a monitoring organization called the National Home Study Council.

As the development of and support for distance learning education programs increased throughout the country, new questions concerning its usage developed. These questions included "learners' characteristics, students' needs, effectiveness of communication, and value of outcomes in comparison with face-to-face study" (Nasseh, 1997, para. 13). Despite such concerns, by the 1930s there were "two million students enrolled every year in correspondence schools . . . Four times the number of all the students enrolled in all the colleges, universities, and professional schools in the United States" (Moore, 2003, p.6). Correspondence studies provided educational opportunities to vast numbers of people by allowing the freedom to choose when and where to study. Because the two-way communication between teacher and student was dependent upon the mail, the response rate was potentially slow and unwieldy. This slow rate of interaction between student and teacher placed the burden on the correspondence student who needed a strong desire to complete the course successfully. Considering these disadvantages, it is not surprising that distance education was quick to adopt other means of increasing the rate of interaction between the teacher and student. "The medium of mail was a dominant delivery system for over forty years, but new delivery technologies started to provide additional options for correspondence studies" (Nasseh, 1997, para. 7).

Telecommunications

Technology has always had an intimate relationship with distance learning because it mediates the separation between teacher and learner through the use of print, radio, telephone, television, audio and videotapes, and computers (Sumner, 2000). One of the most promising of all the modern technologies for distance learning was instructional radio. In the United States during the years between the two World Wars (1918–1946) "the federal government granted radio broadcasting licenses to 202 colleges, universities, and school boards" (Nasseh, 1997, para. 8). The use of radio in education spearheaded the development of educational television in the 1950s. In 1952, after World War II, the Federal Communications Commission allocated 242 of the 2,053 channels to educational purposes.

Gagne (1987) reported that "perhaps the most important factor to affect the audiovisual movement in the 1950s was the increased interest in television as a medium for delivering instruction" (p.17). The first educational television license was issued in 1945. In 1952, the Joint Council on Educational Television, a group of professional educators and interested parties, pressured the U.S. Federal Communications Commission to reserve a segment of the open TV channel spectrum for educational purposes. "Educational" stations began to spring up, and Instructional Television (ITV) was born. During the 1960s and 1970s, classrooms were privy to instruction via television. Still a relatively young medium at the time, television gave classrooms an avenue to receive instructional programming. Blakely, cited in Gagne (1987), claimed "By 1955, there were 17 such stations in the United States and by 1960 that number had increased to more than 50" (p.17). By the mid-1960s, the interest in using television for instructional purposes abated largely due to the "mediocre instructional quality of some of the programs that were produced" (Gagne, 1987, p.17).

In its place came the use of audio teleconferencing to facilitate two-way voice communications among three or more individuals at a distance. Although audio teleconferencing dates back to the 1930s, it was only since the late 1960s that serious efforts were made to use this technology in distance learning (Olgren & Parker, 1983). The use of audio teleconferencing marked a significant innovation in the delivery of distance education. With the introduction of teleconferencing technology, the agonizingly slow interaction of correspondence study was overcome dramatically. Audio teleconferencing built upon the foundation of correspondence study by enhancing the quality of the interaction between students and teacher. "The ability of the student to receive immediate feedback from the teacher as well as fellow students without a corresponding loss of independence is a significant development in distance education" (Garrison, 1985, p.240).

"Distance education is first and foremost a movement that sought not so much to challenge or change the structure of higher learning, but to extend the traditional university and to overcome its inherent problems of scarcity and exclusivity" (Mathews, 1999, p.55). From 1964 to 1968, the Carnegie Foundation funded the Articulated Instructional Media Project (AIM), which brought in a variety of communications technologies aimed at providing learning to an off-campus population. AIM impressed the United Kingdom Labour Government, which imported its ideas when establishing the University of the Air, which later became the Open University. With it came a new vision for distance learning as something separate from the traditional educational programs. The intent of the Open University was to "open opportunity for learning to any adult who wanted it. It set out to help those, particularly the working class, who had been denied entry to formal higher education, regardless of their geographic location within the United Kingdom" (Moore, 2003, p.3). The Open University initially relied on radio and television broadcasts for much of its delivery. Here in the United States, the first open university was started in 1971 at New York State's Empire State College, with its main purpose being to make "higher education degrees more accessible to learners unable to attend traditional programs, campus-based courses" (Nasseh, 1997, para. 12).

During the 1970s and 1980s, broadcast video and home video playback equipment provided another means of constructing a distance learning course and allowed the learning goals that could be addressed through independent learning to be expanded. At the college level, telecourses became a common distance learning format. Several major telecourse development projects were funded by the Annenburg Foundation, the Corporation for Public Broadcasting, and some community colleges and universities. Developed significantly here in the United States was "the application of DBS, direct broadcast by satellite, and other forms of teleconferencing, making possible group-oriented distance teaching by conventional universities, either alone or in consortia" (Moore, 2003, p.12). The merging of distance learning with telecommunication technologies brought about opportunities for interactivity and collaboration that were once only a dream (Schrum, 2002, p.7).

Cable television and satellite transmission offered an alternative method for delivering instructional television while offering themselves as new delivery medium for distance learning courses. Many cable companies picked up satellite transmissions of educational programs and broadcast them on public access channels. In the United States, by the mid-1980s "more than 300,000 students enrolled in university-taught distance education courses" (Mathews, 1999, p.56). This model of distance learning delivery was designed for group use, and therefore "fit in well with the view of education as something that happens in 'classes,' unlike the correspondence or the open university models which were directed at individuals learning alone, usually in 'home study'" (Moore, 2003, p.12). These systems provided instruction, but it was typically unidirectional, with little interactivity and very few feedback possibilities (Schrum, 2002).

Videoconferencing systems were first offered in Japan in 1984, and demand for them has grown rapidly ever since. Interactive videoconferencing poses many benefits to both the classroom and professional environments, allowing live interaction among users at various distant sites (Roblyer, 2006). Educators can provide a more interactive distance learning experience by delivering real time, multi-directional video, voice, and data communications to their distance students, rather than just the standard electronic media. There is much evidence to demonstrate that videoconferencing can provide enriching and enjoyable distance learning experiences to people of all ages and abilities regardless of where they live (Cole, Ray, & Zanetis, 2004). It addresses a wide range of intelligences and learning styles, while fostering educational collaboration and enhancing the experiences of learning communities. Students in one or many locations could watch and listen to an instructor, a subject matter expert, or other students in real time and maintain interactivity with those remote locations. "The real time, two-way visual and verbal interaction of the bricks-and-mortar classroom could be simulated by technology—creating a 'virtual classroom' whose boundaries were limited only by the extent of the videoconferencing network" (Greenberg, 2004, p.6). Mathews (1999) suggested that teaching based on videoconferencing is pedagogically close to traditional university teaching. There are some identified downsides to using videoconferencing technologies for distance learning classes. The most commonly cited issues include: (a) the difficulty of sustaining the interest of the remote learners, (b) the lack of specific training and guidance for teachers, and (c) concerns about the robustness and cost of the technology (Martin, 2005).

Computer Mediated

Whereas satellite and correspondence courses may have once been the primary means of distance learning for institutions of higher learning, Schrum (2002) concluded that over time videoconferencing, web-based learning, and completely online educational experiences took over. Starr (1998) indicated that with advanced computer technologies offering greater opportunities for desktop interactivity between teacher and student, both public and private universities were "moving beyond the rural connection and looking at distance education as a more efficient and cost effective means of educating a professional population in need of continuous training to remain competent and competitive in a rapidly evolving global market" (p.158).

Roblyer (2006) identified a shift in focus for the K–12 educational arena when the first microcomputers came into schools in the 1980s and transitioned districts from mainframes to desktop microcomputer systems. Introducing these locally controlled resources transformed the computers' role in education. Personal computers became common by the late 1980s. At first they were used mostly by distance learners as tools to type up papers to be submitted to correspondence teachers via the postal system, but very soon the Internet became popular and online Internet classes began to replace the postal system method of exchanging assignments (Cobb, 2004). Computer resources and their instructional applications enabled classroom teachers to decide what they wanted to do with computers. During the 1980s a wave of advocacy for computer literacy developed as a result of fears that students who would remain computer illiterate would be "left behind academically, further widening the gap between the advantaged and disadvantaged" (Molnar, 1978, cited in Roblyer, 2006, p.9). Computer literacy skills began to appear in required curricula across the country but were later dropped when they could not be linked to specific sets of skills. Roblyer (2006) affirmed a renewed interest in this topic in the 1990s, as school districts began requiring technology literacy skills.

Moore (2003) asserted that "in 1995, only 9 percent of American adults accessed the Internet, totaling 17.5 million users. By 2002, 66 percent of American adults were going online; a total of 137 million users" (p.16). The explosive growth in the access to and the use of the Internet and the resulting corresponding increase in the number of participants in online and distance learning courses at the start of the new millennium is exemplified by the following data:

- During the 1990s, universities started running web-based distance learning programs, with separate management units being responsible for online education.
- By the end of the decade, 84.1 percent of public universities and 83.3 percent of four-year public colleges offered web-based courses. Seventy-four percent of community colleges also offered online courses (Moore, 2003).
- According to the U.S. Department of Education about 12.2 million consumers enrolled in roughly 11,200 college-level distance-education programs during the 2006–2007 academic year. In addition, 89 percent of public four-year post-secondary institutions in the United States offered college-level distance learning courses (Taylor, 2009).
- Almost 3.5 million students were taking at least one online course during the fall 2006 term; a nearly 10 percent increase over the number reported the previous year (Allen & Seaman, 2007).
- The growth from 1.6 million students taking at least one online course in fall 2002 to the 3.48 million for fall 2006 represents a compound annual growth rate of 21.5 percent (Allen & Seaman, 2007).
- In 2009, online enrollments saw an increase of 21 percent over the previous year to approximately 5.6 million (Kaya, 2010).

History validates that adoption of these web communications increased faster than access to any previous information and communication technology. The Information Infrastructure Task Force created the "information superhighway" with a goal of increasing "access to high-quality education, to the best schools, teachers, and courses . . . without regard to geography distance, resources, or disability" (Moore, 2003, p.7). This technological wave, enabled by a convergence of the once distinct media of image, sound, books, and computer networks into digital multimedia, drove major changes in the way education was produced and delivered. Sumner (2000) indicated that computer technology provides us with "a unique opportunity in the history of distance education to create the conditions that foster communicative action—groups of people learning together to build the lifeworld" (p.271). Although universities were the first to apply these web-based technologies to distance learning, "nationally, politicians and policy makers soon came to notice this phenomenon and its implications for K–12 education and other government services" (Zucker & Kozma, 2003, p.7).

Virtual Schools

Clark (2001) defined **virtual schools** as "educational organizations that offer K–12 courses through Internet or Web-based methods" (p.1). At the beginning of the millennium, the virtual school movement was considered "the 'next wave' in technology based K–12 education, joining proven distance learning delivery methods" (p.i). His 2001 research study on virtual schools in the United States confirmed a continued developing trend from virtual universities, to virtual high schools, to virtual K–12 schools. The following reasons are cited for the creation and steady increase of the use of the virtual school environment: (a) to expand access to high quality or rigorous curricula, (b) to serve special learner groups, (c) to provide online college preparatory courses to high school students with the express purpose of increasing their eligibility to top-level universities, (d) to provide a bridge for students who left high school before graduating, (e) to serve students who cannot attend a regular high school in their home area, and (f) to meet the needs of students who could not be readily accommodated through the traditional classroom. Cavanaugh, Gillan, Kromrey, Hess, and Blomeyer (2004) claimed that "online virtual schools may be ideally suited to meet the needs of stakeholders calling for school choice, high school reform, and workplace preparation in 21st century skills" (p.4).

As a new way of delivering knowledge, virtual schools' addition into the K–12 educational arena had various implications for classroom-based education. It "altered the educational equation in fundamental ways . . . Learning has escaped the physical boundaries of the classroom and school, and students and teachers have become part of a virtual classroom they share with counterparts around the world" (Roblyer, 2006, p.192). The virtual school "injects fresh possibilities into the most extreme version of choice—school vouchers, raising the possibility of awarding vouchers to be spent for online education" (Maeroff, 2003, p.5).

The use of virtual learning environments in K–12 education began in 1994 in Utah at the Electronic High School, where courses were self-paced with some students taking as long as two years to complete a course; followed by the Virtual High School, a unique nationwide program providing online courses through a cooperative model to students in 27 states and 16 other countries. In 1997, the Florida Virtual School began offering courses and has experienced rapid growth ever since. Additional state-run virtual schools were established at the beginning of the new millennium, many as a continuation of previous distance learning programs (Diamond, 2007). The International Association for K-12 Online Learning, or iNACOL, estimates that more than 1.5 million K–12 students were engaged in some form of online or blended learning in the 2009–2010 school year. At the end of 2010, supplemental or full-time online learning opportunities were available in at least 48 of 50 states, plus the District of Columbia (International Association for K-12 Online Learning, 2010).

Web 1.0 and Web 2.0

Web 1.0 refers to the first stage of the World Wide Web released to the public in 1993 that merely linked webpages with hyperlinks. It could be considered as a "read-only web" (Getting, 2007) enabling us to search for information and read it. There was little user interaction or content contribution. Since 2004 the term **Web 2.0** has become popular and has been used to describe a more social web where users have the ability to contribute content and interact with other web users.

It is associated with the development of web applications that facilitate participatory information-sharing, interoperability, user-centered design, and collaboration on the World Wide Web. This is in sharp contrast with Web 1.0 (approximately 45 million global users in 1996) which was all about read-only content and static HTML websites used as information portals. When speaking about Web 2.0 (approximately 1 billion plus global users in 2006), one is making reference to a group of technologies—blogs, wikis, audio blogging and podcasting, RSS feeds and syndication, tagging and social bookmarking, and multimedia sharing—which have become deeply associated with the term. These technologies facilitate a more socially connected web where everyone is able to add to and edit the information space. The web is seen as a platform that focuses on the power of the community to create and to validate. Web 2.0 is about user-generated content and is a read–write web. People are consuming as well as contributing information in the Web 2.0 era where there is a blurred line dividing a consumer and content publisher.

But Web 2.0 is more than a set of cool new technologies and services. Web 2.0 is considered a new, improved, second version, user-generated web. It has at its core a set of powerful ideas that are changing the way some people interact. Second, these ideas are "not necessarily the preserve of 'Web 2.0,' but are, in fact, direct or indirect reflections of the power of the network; the strange effects and topologies at the micro and macro level that a billion Internet users produce" (Anderson, 2007, p.7). Anderson indicated that these ideas are building more than a global information space. Instead they are building something with much more of a social angle to it. Web 2.0 offers collaboration, contribution and community and "some think that a new 'social fabric' is being constructed before our eyes" (p.4). The advent of Web 2.0 brought dynamic content and rich interactive experiences, along with raised expectations for its use. Because of the functionalities inherent in the Web 2.0 tools, both educators and students are asking for more interaction in the virtual classroom.

Defining Digital Generations in the United States

Sociologists and the media have used titles to refer to different generations of people alive at the present moment. People have been broken down into generations characterized by similar qualities and attitudes. These generations normally span a 20-year period. Although it is impossible to generalize accurately and describe each individual in a group of people, it is uncanny how different generational attitudes can be discerned and specific characterizations can be made.

The Greatest Generation consists of those individuals who were born before 1928. Having fought and won World War II, it is this generation that was credited with saving the world. Rosen (2011) identified the Traditional or Silent Generation as those individuals born between 1925 and 1946 growing up through the Great Depression, World War II, and the Cold War. They have been characterized as having a belief in common goals and respect for authority. The youth of that day was seen as waiting for the hand of fate to fall on its shoulders, while working fairly hard yet saying almost nothing. The most startling fact about the youth of this generation was its silence.

Individuals born between 1946 and 1964 have been called the Baby Boomers and are characterized as being optimistic, idealistic, and communicative. They tend to value education and consumer goods. Williams (2011) noted that whereas the media and news tend to depict the Baby Boomers as deferring to **Generation Y** for technological know-how and use, this notion might not be accurate. He noted that Baby Boomers show a great deal of interest in purchasing consumer electronics, more than any other age group. In addition, they show a real interest in the continuing adoption of technology. Many believe that Baby Boomers will be a driving force behind the use of information technology in the next decade, particularly in the health care industry.

Coupland (1991) defined individuals born between 1965 and 1979 as **Generation X**, where the X was used to signify that Gen Xers are not as easily categorized as the previous generations. The letter X was meant to signify the generation's randomness, ambiguousness, and contradictory ways. These individuals are sandwiched between 80 million Baby Boomers and 78 million **Millennials**; while having just 46 million members amongst themselves. Stephey (2008) contended that the Gen Xers might be the most unsung and influential generation of all time, citing Gen-X icons like Quentin Tarantino and Jon Stewart, along with Gen-X triumphs like Google, YouTube, and Amazon as examples. This generation saw the inception of the home computer, the rise of videogames, cable television, and the Internet as tools for social and commercial purposes.

With the 1980s and the development of the World Wide Web came a new generation of web surfing learners. The label Generation Y was given to this group simply to signify them as the next generation after X. The timeframe for Generation Y can be stretched past 1999 to include the Millennials, the title given to the group of individuals born after the new millennium. Because this group can be referred to as the first true cyber-generation, some use the term Net Generation (Tapscott, 1999) to reflect the impact of the Internet on the lives of the Millennials. This generation is generally marked by an increased use and familiarity with communications, media, and digital technologies. These learners are tech savvy, with every gadget imaginable almost becoming an extension of their bodies. They multitask, talk, walk, listen and type, and text. Technology has always been part of their lives, whether it's computers and the Internet or cell phones and text pagers. They are used to working in groups and teams. In contrast to the lone ranger attitude of earlier generations, Millennials actually believe a team can accomplish more (Shaughnessy, 2009).

Rosen (2011) identified a separate generation of learners born in the 1990s and beyond who have been labeled as the **iGeneration**, where the "i" refers to the types of digital technologies used by these learners (iPhone, iPod, Wii, iTunes) and the highly individualized activities made possible by these technologies. These children are defined by the technology and media that they use, their engagement with electronic communication and their need and ability to multitask. Various research concluded that both the Net Generation and the iGeneration's older teen group are consuming massive amounts of media, with many children and teens spending nearly all their waking hours using media and technology (Lenhart, Ling, Campbell, & Purcell, 2010; Rideout, Foehr, & Roberts, 2010; Rosen, 2011).

These studies also found clear differences in what each generation does with its technology. The Baby Boomer generation tends to prefer face-to-face or telephone communication, although they commonly use email. Considered a transitional generation, Gen Xers appear to embrace the use of cell phones, email, and instant messaging. The Net Generation began to differentiate itself by using many available technologies, including social networks, instant messages, Skype, and texting. But it is the iGeneration, which has redefined communication usage. According to the Nielsen Company, the typical teenager in 2011 sent and received 3,339 texts a month. This translates into more than six messages every non-sleeping hour, while making and receiving only 191 phone calls during that same monthly period. This is in comparison with 2009, where teens sent and received about the same number of texts as phone calls (Nielsen Wire, 2010). The iGeneration members see the phone as a portable computer that can be used to do multiple tasks which can include tweeting, surfing the web, and texting.

This information has implications for how we teach the iGeneration students. Technology should be used to convey content more powerfully and efficiently. There is an enormous amount of curriculum content that can be accessed online, in audio and video formats that can be used to differentiate instruction and meet the multiple learning styles of our students. The iGeneration is immersed in technology anytime, anywhere and educators can use this love for technology to refocus education. Rosen (2011) indicated that with such a refocus "we'll not only get students more involved in learning, but also free up classroom time to help them make meaning of the wealth of information that surrounds them."

Implications for American Education

Technology trends in education run the gamut from increasing the technology infrastructure to the growth of social learning. Likewise, the organizations that posit these trends range from technology companies to the federal government. Educators, politicians, parents, economists, and digital designers all have their own ideas about how education should incorporate these technology trends. One fundamental idea upon which all stakeholders can agree is that equitable access to technology is essential in preparing students for college or career opportunities. Douglas Levine, Executive Director of the State Educational Technology Directors Association (SETDA), said, "We have an unprecedented opportunity and obligation to help all students succeed in the 21st century" (Nagel, 2010, para. 5).

Electronic Books and Mobile Devices

The 2011 Horizon Report focused on six emerging technologies that could feature predominately in the education arena in the near future: (a) electronic books, (b) mobile devices, (c) **augmented reality**, (d) game-based learning, (e) gesture-based computing, and (f) learning analytics (Johnson, Smith, Willis, Levine, & Haywood, 2011). Electronic books are increasingly available at affordable prices in the retail market. These books now offer color pictures with highlighting and bookmarking features. There is a growing market to attract young readers with interactive picture books and learning games. The

Horizon Report suggested that "electronic books are moving closer to mainstream adoption for educational institutions" while "resistance to mobile devices in the classroom continues to impede their adoption in many schools" (Johnson et al., 2011, p.5). Malamed (2011) disagreed and asserted that with decreasing educational budget dollars and improved cell phone infrastructure, we can expect a move towards using mobile operating systems and smartphones in education. This implies that we have hit a tipping point of readiness for increased use of mobile content.

Mobile devices offer reliable sources for information and communication. What this implies is that students can carry a single handheld device containing all of the materials needed for classes, including textbooks and other relevant reference materials. Students can download and interact with these materials by using software capabilities that allow bookmarking and content annotation, conduct quick searches, looking up of words in an integrated dictionary, and playing back phrases in synthetic speech. Students can do all of this connected wirelessly or through 3G to the Internet. All students are able to benefit from the ease and availability of mobile devices. However, students with disabilities will find the extra assistance from these products an indispensable part of their education. Apple promised that "the 32GB and 64GB iPod touch and the iPhone 3GS [and later models] come standard with features that accommodate people with physical impairments, visual and hearing challenges, and different learning styles" (Apple, Inc., 2011). Video chat can be used over some mobile devices enabling hospitalized or homebound children to participate in live sessions with their teachers. iTunes University sponsored by Apple offers more than 350,000 free course lectures or podcasts. In fact, "more than 800 universities have active iTunes U sites" (Apple, Inc., 2011).

Augmented Reality and Game-based Learning

Two more technologies already in use by some educators are augmented reality and game-based learning. "The expression augmented reality, often abbreviated to AR, refers to a simple combination of real and virtual (computer-generated) worlds" (Maxwell, 2010, para. 2). Students will soon be using textbooks that essentially come alive in front of their eyes. Imagine a third grader watching the development of a volcanic eruption in 3D or picture a kindergarten student who watches Jack climb the beanstalk as he hears the fairytale read to him. While game-based learning has been in our classrooms for many years, the future trend is to use computer games "to foster collaboration, problem-solving and procedural thinking" (Johnson et al., 2011, p.5).

In addition, we can expect an increase in the usage of 3D virtual world software replacing 2D PowerPoint-based virtual meetings. 3D virtual worlds offer an entirely new interface between meeting participants and the systems that they use at work. 3D worlds are multi-learner simulations thereby changing participation in simulations from a single-person to multiple-person collaboration. In addition to learning the material and information being presented in the 3D world, participants acquire the knowledge and procedures required to collaborate.

Gesture-based Computing and Learning Analytics

The final two technology trends discussed in the 2011 Horizon Report, gesture-based computing and learning analytics, remain four to five years away from widespread use. "Gesture-based computing moves the control of computers from a mouse and keyboard to the motions of the body via new input devices" (Johnson et al., 2011, p.5). The educational application of gesture-based computing offers teachers and students the opportunity for three-dimensional visualizations. This could be a wonderful aid in training through simulation of a task. Learning analytics offers another tool for teachers to use in gathering and analyzing data about their students. However, these technology tools are far more than just another arsenal of assessments. "Learning analytics goes much further than this, marrying information from disparate sources to create a far more robust and nuanced profile of students" (Johnson et al., 2011, p.27).

Web 3.0

Even the Internet is undergoing changes as new technologies provide wider availability of high-speed connections on a global scale. At the WWW2006 Conference in Edinburgh, discussions were held regarding expectations for the likely characteristics of a **Web 3.0**, and the potential benefits and impact these characteristics might have on the future of teaching and learning. Questions are arising pertaining to how information will be organized. Will individuals still do the "surfing" on the net or will the machine surf for us? Will the web look the same for each individual or will it be tailored to the individual? What technology will become commonplace or obsolete? It is believed that Web 3.0 will be about a semantic web that changes the web into a language that can be read and categorized by the system rather than humans, where search engines understand who you are, what you have been doing, and where you would like to go next. It will also include personalization that contextualizes the web based on the people using it; intelligent searches that extract meaning from the way people interact with the web; a portable personal web that offers everything, everywhere, all the time; and behavioral advertising where contextual advertising becomes more engaging and online purchase behavior turns users into brand advocates (Nations, n.d.).

It is thought that some Web 3.0 characteristics could include: (a) the integration of high-powered Scalable Vector Graphics (SVG); a family of specifications of an XML-based file format for describing two-dimensional vector graphics. The SVG specification is an open standard, widely deployed royalty-free graphics format that has been under development by the World

Wide Web Consortium (W3C) since 1999; (b) a focus on visualization, such as a system for displaying documents, including the links between them, in three dimensions; (c) creation of a 3D Internet which will take the best of virtual worlds such as Second Life and gaming environments, and merge them with the web; (d) the creation of software that "cleans up" after you, erasing your digital path through the information space, and (e) identity management services giving the user the ability to sell their attention span in blocks rather than giving it away for free (Anderson, 2007).

Electronic Learning

It is predicted that the expansion in K–12 electronic learning in the United States will continue to grow in the double digits at least through 2015 (Nagel, 2011). In the United States, PreK–12 will dominate all other segments, including health care and higher education, in the growth of annual expenditures on e-learning technologies and services. "The rate of growth in the PreK–12 segment is due to the relentless migration to online content formats and also due to the proliferation and success of for-profit online schools" (Nagel, 2011, para. 4). Self-paced e-learning products will be in demand and are defined as packaged content, custom content development services, learning platform and tool hosting services, authoring software and tools, and installed learning platforms. Higher education, meanwhile, will also continue to experience growth in e-learning expenditures, albeit at a much slower pace.

According to the International Association for K-12 Online Learning (2010), K–12 online learning is a field consisting of an estimated $507 million market, which is growing at an estimated annual pace of 30 percent annually. Supplemental or full-time online learning opportunities are available to at least some students in 48 of the 50 states, plus Washington, D.C. In school year (SY) 2012–2013, new fully online, statewide schools opened in Iowa and New Mexico, bringing the number of states with these schools to 31 (Watson, Murin, Vashaw, Gemin, & Rapp, 2012). The authors counted 619,847 course enrollments (one student taking a one-semester-long online course) in 28 state virtual schools in SY 2011–2012, an increase of 16 percent from the prior year. In addition, the authors found "state virtual schools continuing to diverge into those that are large and growing, and those that are small and may be fading—and for the first time some that are closing (Kentucky, Nebraska, and Tennessee)" (p.5).

According to the 2009 Sloan Consortium report, K–12 school district administrators cited "offering courses not otherwise available at the school," "meeting the needs of specific groups of students," and "offering Advanced Placement or college level courses" as the top three reasons they perceive online and blended courses to be important (Picciano & Seaman, 2009). Despite the growth of online and blended learning, "policy and access barriers still exist for many students who wish to take an online course or attend an online school" (Watson, Murin, Vashaw, Gemin, & Rapp, 2010, p.7).

With the explosion of social media sites affording people unlimited opportunities to connect and collaborate, educators can expect ongoing growth in social media technologies in the coming years. New social media services will likely emerge to meet the growing demands of professional development needs. Social media technologies enable non-structured learning opportunities as alternative learning approaches not requiring tracking mechanisms. This will change the current use of learning management systems (LMS), transforming them into a broader model that offers LMS platforms as just a small part of a larger learning community that enables collaboration, knowledge sharing, and social networking (Malamed, 2011).

Amateur videographers are using online formats such as YouTube to teach, demonstrate, and share their knowledge and expertise. Almost two billion videos are viewed on YouTube daily making the service the second largest search engine in the world. With this increasing and ongoing demand for video, it can be expected that new online services will be implemented that will change how videos are utilized for just-in-time tutorials and informal learning.

Concluding Thoughts

The world continues to play catch-up to the changes brought on by the great technological strides being made. As the world moved forward with technology innovations that changed how we live and conduct business, many people were excluded from the participation. Initially the issue was one of access—the digital divide. Programs were developed to assist in giving access to those individuals who did not have, such as computers in classrooms, offering free Internet connectivity, and one-to-one laptop initiatives. The lack of access to technology has abated and was replaced with issues of ability to use, and participate in, the activities that technology offers—digital inclusion. Digital inclusion places an emphasis on training specific **underserved populations** on how to use the hardware and software that is now available. People with disabilities are a key group requiring assistance in using ICT. They require assistive technology tools to help them learn, interact, and overcome barriers to accessing a computer and other ICT resources. Similarly, specific initiatives are required for the aging population to ensure the elderly are not left behind in the wake of digital progress (Ibrahim, 2011).

The digital solidarity movement focuses on additional issues besides access to and knowing how to use digital tools. Its focus is on enabling all citizens to derive specific benefits from the use of the technology. Digital solidarity is about creating initiatives that help the general population learn from, and experience the benefits of a digital lifestyle while improving their lives through the use of the information obtained from the technologies. Figure 1.1 depicts the digital continuum described in this chapter. It reaches across from those who are excluded and therefore remain digitally illiterate, to those who are included and are capable of obtaining digital literacy. What types of programs this might mean in practice, which digital technologies might make a significant difference, and for whom and with what resources, makes up the current discourse surrounding the digital solidarity movement. The challenge of digital solidarity consists in moving from words to actions, and in drawing lessons learned from pilot projects in order to scale up programs. The goal of digital solidarity within the *educational arena* is to identify and replicate those innovative technology programs and models that will provide the impetus needed to motivate students towards academic excellence and global competitiveness. This will require the involvement of all educators so that the actions taken can be both efficient and relevant. Cornu (2007) asserted that digital solidarity is "not only a technical issue and it is not only the development of infrastructure and equipment. It also includes pedagogical issues . . . in which all teachers and educators are invited to take part" (p.49).

When distance learning began in the 1800s, its primary purpose was to offer the underserved access to learning that was otherwise unavailable to them. These individuals included people with physical disabilities, women who were not allowed to enroll in educational institutions open only to men, people who had jobs during normal school hours, and those who lived in remote regions where schools did not exist. Few could have imagined the extent to

DIGITAL CONTINUUM

DIGITAL EXCLUSION	DIGITAL INCAPACITY	DIGITAL BLINDNESS	DIGITAL PRE-INCLUSION	DIGITAL INCLUSION	DIGITAL SOLIDARITY
Excluded from the "digitopia"/cyberspace for a variety of reasons that can include: economic, political geographic, socio-cultural, personal, residential, ethno-cultural, and personal avoidance.	Resulting from a disproportionate allocation of resources that can include: groups, lowered expectations for other groups, society prohibiting access to and utilization of digital resources. Not able to work digitally due to inaccessibility.	Two-fold problem – on the one hand individuals or groups feel uncomfortable with computers (i.e., the elderly population), and on the other hand there is a misinformed belief that the world's 7.0 billion citizens all have online access (i.e. 9.5 million students in the U.S. do not have home access to the Internet).	Delegate technology work to a certain mono-cultural group to the exclusion of others (i.e., women, minorities). Deliver quick fixes, packaged, short-term programs and initiatives that are not sustainable and do not go to scale thereby not enabling inclusion for all.	Advocacy for those who are excluded. Ongoing education of self and others enabling inclusion. Ongoing support, modeling and mentoring.	Full 24/7 inclusion in cyberspace. All individuals and groups benefit from a digital presence. Improvement in life by being able to access and utilize digital content, tools, and information. Inclusion of groups other than one's own.

DIGITAL DIVIDE → ← DIGITAL INCLUSION → DIGITAL SOLIDARITY

DIGITALLY ILLITERATE   DIGITALLY LITERATE

Figure 1.1 Digital Continuum and the Description of the Stages of Movement from Digital Exclusion through to Digital Solidarity. Adapted from a figure by Roland Foulkes (2011, personal communication). Reproduced with permission of the author.

which the distance learning concept and the technological mechanisms designed to implement that concept would evolve. From the postal service enabling the completion of correspondence courses, to the various teleconferencing tools, to videotapes, satellite TV, one-way and two-way audio, two-way videoconferencing, email, whiteboarding, interactive web-based courses, asynchronous learning networks, e-learning and multifaceted web conferencing, and open source access; the practice of distance learning has grown into a multi-pronged field designed to offer end users access to innovative educational opportunities and global information networks.

Information and communication technologies (ICT) increase the possibilities, resources and tools for distance education. In turn, distance learning has helped the cause of digital solidarity by developing the IT skills of its users and promoting an equitable information society. Distance learning technologies offer access to information and knowledge-sharing, thereby enabling the opportunity for all students in the world to participate in the digital society. Distance education is no longer perceived as merely a replacement for those who for one reason or another cannot attend a traditional school. It has become a core component of education, an acceptable alternative to traditional education, filling many of the needs for today's learners. A knowledge society "needs competencies linked to distance education, such as being able to learn at a distance, to learn through distant resources, to learn through digitized systems, and to learn through collaborative distant tools such as learning environments and learning platforms" (Cornu, 2007, p.46).

One of the most important aims for the next decade is to ensure that every child in the world has access to digital information and communication infrastructure, enabling all children and all people to access and acquire knowledge and to derive benefits from this knowledge base. Technology trends in education will bring today's electronic games and social networking devices into the classroom. The challenge for 21st-century educators will be to integrate these technologies into the curriculum and make them readily accessible and able to be used by all students. Electronic books, mobile devices, and computers will become replacements for textbooks, maps, and encyclopedias. Augmented reality and game-based learning will make stories and research come alive with interactive 3D pictures. Gesture-based computing will allow all students regardless of their age or disability to use computers. Learning analytics will allow teachers to combine a plethora of information, providing an individualized educational plan for each student.

The growth of the technology we presently use will be exponential. Web 3.0 will provide a 3D Internet with new and unique ways to communicate globally. Online learning will continue to expand reaching into the traditional brick-and-mortar schools. Hybrid programs with face-to-face instruction as well as virtual classes will be the norm. The 21st century will offer technologies not yet invented. Our goal is to offer educational opportunities that enable our students to be the technology designers of tomorrow.

Chapter 2

Broadening Technologies in American Education

The ability to access and work with information obtained through the Internet may well be the most important skill of the 21st century. If we are to prepare students to thrive in our rapidly evolving, technology-saturated world, schools must provide students with curriculum and exposure to a broader set of 21st-century skills (Jerald, 2009). Whereas a literate person was once defined as someone with the ability to read, write, and understand words; today the word "literate" has a tendency not to appear by itself. Digital literacy is at the center of these emerging literacies and describes the skills, expectations, and perspectives involved in living in a technological society. It includes the ability to locate, organize, utilize, understand, evaluate, and analyze information, and create content using information technologies and the Internet. Ohler (2009) posited that it is important to understand this evolving nature of literacy for two reasons. First, because it enables us to understand the emerging nature of illiteracy; and second, regardless of the literacy under consideration, the illiterate are left out.

Therefore, the goal of digital solidarity within the educational arena in the United States is to engage and mobilize students from diverse racial, ethnic, linguistic, and economic backgrounds with giftedness and/or disabilities to thrive as digitally literate persons who can utilize and apply technologies to compete academically with their global counterparts. As the integration of technology into our everyday life expands at a rapid rate, the need to infuse computer and technology applications into K-16 curriculum becomes more urgent (The Education Alliance, 2005). Computer-related skills and the knowledge derived from the ability to use computers and emerging technologies effectively are absolute necessities to function actively and profitably in the world today. Therefore, the purpose for any educational reform should be to create rich learning environments that offer a more equitable distribution of materials, expertise, and resources than what is currently available (Rose, 2010). The challenge educators now face is determining how to successfully provide educational opportunities for all students to practice and develop these important skill sets with a purpose of meeting three goals: universal digital literacy, a stronger workforce, and improved quality of life (Schaffhauser, 2009, June/July).

Academic Excellence: Increased Technology Usage, Increased Achievement

Rationale

The rationale for the continued use and support of technology in classrooms stems from research-based findings citing that its use improves student achievement. The International Society for Technology in Education (ISTE) members have monitored research on the effectiveness of technology in education on student outcomes for more than 20 years, and the emerging trend shows that when implemented appropriately, the integration of technology into instruction has positive effects on student achievement (International Society for Technology in Education, 2008; Nagel, 2009, April). Studies have shown that students with routine access to technology learn the basic skills of reading, writing, and arithmetic faster and better when they have a chance to practice them using technology. One reason cited for this improvement is that students are engaged by the technology. As a result, they spend more time learning and practicing the basic tasks than students who approach the same tasks in a traditional paper-and-pencil manner (Apple Computer, Inc., 2002).

Teachers who use digital media strengthen students' basic skills by incorporating pictures, sound, and animation. Multimedia significantly enhances students' ability to recall basic facts, as well as improves their understanding of complex systems. One reason for this improvement may be that digital media tools address each student's individual learning style, thereby enabling all students to achieve by using their preferred learning modality (Apple Computer Inc., 2005). Studies have shown that when technology is a routine part of their school experience, student attendance improves and dropout rates decline (Becta, 2006).

Organizations such as ISTE (http://www.iste.org), the State Educational Technology Directors Association (SETDA) (http://www.setda.org), the Partnership for 21st Century Skills (http://www.p21.org/), and 21st Century Schools (http://www.21stcenturyschools.com) suggest that access to technology for instruction and learning offers students more than just knowledge in core subjects. Educational technology provides students with opportunities to develop 21st-century skills which are needed to compete in a global market. Cummins, Brown, and Sayers (2006) found that technology tools such as the Internet and the World Wide Web contribute to the development of both a socially committed and an intellectually critical citizenry.

Positive results from the integration of technology into the classroom can also be found at the pre-school level. A study conducted by the Education Development Center and SRI International on behalf of the Corporation for Public Broadcasting found that educational videos and interactive games can have a positive effect on preschooler literacy when incorporated into classroom instruction (*T.H.E. Journal*, 2009, November/December). The study focused on economically disadvantaged children in both New York City and San

Francisco schools who were participating in the Ready to Learn program. According to the study, teachers who exposed students to digital media in the classroom as part of the program had children who came out with more advanced literacy skills and who were better prepared for kindergarten than those who were not exposed to such a program.

Reimagining Schools

With parents, policy-makers, educators, and students calling for educational change and choice, there has never been a better time than now to reimagine school and to improve it with innovative technologies. By using innovative technologies as part of the design and implementation of new instructional strategies, educators are creating opportunities for increased student achievement and engagement to prevail (Scherer, 2010). In the process, these new instructional strategies have the ability to change the conventional classroom learning model. For just such an example we can look at the phenomenon now known as the "**flipped classroom**." While teaching in a relatively rural school both Jonathan Bergmann and Aaron Sams found that many of their students missed a lot of school due to sports and activities. Since school was not nearby, students spent a lot of time on buses traveling to and from events, missing many classes and struggling to stay current with their school work. Unable to find the time to reteach lessons for absent students, the two decided to use software that would record a PowerPoint slideshow including voice and annotations and then convert the recording into a video file that was posted online. The core idea of the flipped classroom is to flip the common instructional approach through the use of teacher-created videos and interactive lessons. Instruction that once occurred in class is now accessed at home in advance of class. Class then becomes the place to work through the problems, and work in collaboration with other students and the teacher.

The "flip" includes students listening to the lectures at home at night where they would have time to review the recorded lecture as often as needed. While in class, the teachers are available to students and open up class time to provide help to them, as needed, while the students work on their assignments, which can include science labs (Schaffhauser, 2009, August). Since the teachers are requiring students to watch the video recordings, they have to ensure that every student has access. For students who do not have home computers, lectures are burned onto DVDs which the students play on a DVD player.

As a by-product, the process of recording their lectures made them rethink their role in the classroom. The two educators realized that flipping the classroom transformed their teaching practice. It is not the instructional videos on their own that are making the difference, but rather how they are integrated into an overall approach. They now implement a "mastery learning model" which allows their students to work through the material at their own pace, and when they are ready and have finished all assignments they take an exit exam to demonstrate proficiency. They identified that one of the greatest benefits of "flipping" is the increase in overall interaction, both with teacher to student and student to student. Both teachers asserted that using the flipped classroom approach allows them more time to work individually with students.

Technology and Individualized Learning

An example of an individualized learning program that technology enables can be found in New York City at the School of One (http://www. schoolofone.org). Levine (2009) asserted that the School of One individualizes student learning by tying instruction to each student's most effective learning style. Levine added that the "School of One turns the current model of education on its head, flipping the relationship between teaching and learning." The first pilot program began in 2009 costing $1 million to develop for the summer with most of the money coming from private donations. Those involved with the project indicate that the cost for running this type of program is equivalent to that of running a traditional school.

To date there are three middle school locations that offer this individualized middle school mathematics program. MS 131 with a student body that is 81 percent Asian, 6 percent Black, and 12 percent Hispanic piloted the first program in the summer of 2009 and is located in Manhattan's Chinatown neighborhood. IS 229 is the first in-school pilot that began in the spring of 2010 in one of the city's most racially diverse schools found in Brooklyn with 34 percent Asian, 16 percent Black, 23 percent Hispanic, and 27 percent White. The third school, IS 339, is located in the Bronx with a student population of 31 percent Black and 67 percent Hispanic.

School of One's first evaluation was a proof of concept for its use as a model. It was conducted on the 2009 summer school pilot at MS 131 by the Educational Development Center (EDC) Inc. EDC found a 28 percent rise in scores between pre-test and post-test for School of One summer school participants. The researchers concluded that these results, combined with positive qualitative data from the classroom, warranted the expansion of the program to serve students in after-school or in-school settings. A parallel evaluation of the summer 2009 pilot was conducted by the New York City Department of Education's Research and Policy Study Group (RPSG) to compare School of One's results to achievement gains achieved by their citywide peers. They found that over the course of the short summer school period, School of One students learned at a significantly higher rate than peers with similar starting scores and demographic characteristics. The statistical power of this calculation was limited due to the small sample size (n = 78) at School of One (Light, Reitzes, & Cerrone, 2009).

In spring 2010, School of One operated afterschool and in-school pilots, which were evaluated by RPSG. The study compared students who participated in the afterschool program and in-school program with those who did not.

They found that, on average, School of One students significantly outperformed those in traditional classes. They then adjusted variables such as fluctuation in afterschool attendance rates and the short duration of the pilot, and estimated that School of One students learned at a rate 50–60 percent higher than those in traditional classrooms. The effects were positive for all subgroups, but most pronounced for the two lowest-performing quartiles of students (Research and Policy Support Group, 2010).

Students work individually or in small groups on laptop computers accessing lessons in the form of quizzes, games, and worksheets. Each student takes daily quizzes that are then analyzed by a computer program to determine whether or not the daily lesson was mastered. This model, through its use of adaptive software, allows teachers to collect real-time data of student progress and design each student's learning plan around that data. This learning algorithm updates information in the student's profile to create a daily "playlist" of lessons for each student.

After learning about the specific academic needs of each student, the school then accesses a large bank of educational resources, and using the learning algorithm, recommends the best matches between students, teachers, and resources. Daily lessons can involve virtual tutoring online, computer worksheets, or small group lessons led by a classroom teacher. The learning algorithm takes into account factors such as each student's academic history and profile; the student's previous day's assessment data; and availability of content, space, staffing, and technology. With this information, the algorithm prepares a recommended schedule for each student and teacher based on the student's academic strengths and weaknesses. Each student's schedule is displayed on a large television screen that visitors liken to a flight schedule display at an airport (Medina, 2009).

The team behind the School of One has just launched a non-profit organization called New Classrooms that will allow any school to use its high-tech, personalized learning model. In addition to managing New York City's School of One program, including the expansion of the current participating middle schools to more than 50 schools in New York, New Classrooms will design new products that can be used by traditional public, charter, and independent schools (Barseghian, 2012, January). New Classrooms will bring Teach to One Math to public and charter schools in the Chicago Public Schools (financed through seed money provided by the Chicago Public Education Fund), and to Perth Amboy Public Schools and McGinnis Middle School in New Jersey.

There is real potential power in individualizing learning because it serves students with diverse needs, such as: students below grade level or at risk of being behind, students who might be performing at grade level but still need deeper learning in one or more key skills areas, gifted students needing accelerated instruction, students who have acquired the necessary skills outside the context of seat time and need a way to demonstrate proficiency in order to receive credit, and credit recovery for students who failed a course at first taking but who are missing just a few concepts. The real force behind individualizing instruction is that it increases student engagement and success because it targets individual students' needs and interests.

Barber (2012, January) proposed that educators will see an increased focus on individualization and personalization for student learning in the future and that technology will play a big role. Individualization will run the gamut from personalized learning environments to digital textbooks designed to connect students to the resources that work best for them. And with a growing number of students using handheld devices to access these learning tools, we can expect to see big pushes for faster innovation to tie everything together. Personalized learning environments tend to make learning more efficient and effective because they are more closely related to individual personal learning styles. Trends that will positively affect individualization of learning include the expansion of mobile devices, the improvement of digital content, and the use of social networking for learning. The resurgence in the idea of interest-driven learning is made possible by the advances in individualized learning technology and the new role of the student as collaborator in the creation of curriculum.

Individualized instruction can be delivered through the use of blended and online courses, and computer-based modules. But in some cases this access is limited, particularly for small or under-resourced schools, due to broadband and infrastructure issues (Zinth, 2012). Where the term "digital divide" used to refer to whether classrooms had computers connected to the Internet, it now refers to issues such as the inability to utilize newer software programs that require high-speed connections and WiFi-dependent devices such as iPads that are making their way into classrooms. It also refers to some schools having access to one-to-one laptop programs and other schools having old infrastructure that is barely functional so that students don't have access to the computers. In addition, technology spending in schools varies widely across the country, as some districts reap the benefits of grants and parental donations, while others tap local, state, and federal funding (Pandolfo, 2012). The result is that some students are neither able to develop technology skills nor access some courses and supplemental material that could help them to be more successful. Leveling this technology-rich playing field needs to be part of every school district's strategic planning process in order for all students to benefit from the individualized instruction that access to educational hardware, software, and web-developed tools can provide.

Equity and Diversity in American Education: The "Haves" and "Have-nots"

A major concern for many educators regarding educational technology is the inherent potential to exclude those who may not have access to it or may not be able to use it. Recognizing the positive effects on student learning that technology can provide for all types of learners, it will be of limited use in achieving educational goals if it is not available to all students (North Central Regional Educational Laboratory, 2005). Research has shown that minority students, those from economically disadvantaged neighborhoods, and students who live in either inner-city or rural (but not suburban) areas tend to have less access to computers, the Internet, and educational software than their middle-class and more affluent peers (Foss, 2002; Judge, Puckett, & Cabuk, 2004; International Society for Technology in Education, 2008). For many students the only access to computing devices and the Internet is that provided by their schools. Thus, they are reliant on schools, libraries, and community centers for their hardware, software, and Internet access. Yet, in a study conducted by Lenhart, Rainie, and Lewis (2001) it was found that more than half (53 percent) of teachers in public schools who have computers use them or the Internet for instruction during class. But in schools whose students are from higher-income families, 61 percent of teachers with computers use them in class compared with 50 percent of those teaching in schools with lower-income students.

Much of the debate regarding the digital divide centers on the issue of basic technology access. Yet another, equally important measure needing further examination involves the variation in pedagogical practices associated with technology used in different schools. Warschauer & Matuchniak (2010) reviewed a number of studies showing an emphasis on remedial or vocational use of new technology by low-income or Black and Hispanic students and more academic use of technology by high-income or White and Asian students. Economically disadvantaged students who tend to have lower grades and poorer test performance typically receive computer-based instruction only for drill-and-practice, traditional memory-based and remedial activities, and not for critical thinking skills or project-based learning. This is in stark contrast with schools serving wealthier communities that are more likely to focus on communication and expression.

A nationwide study examining the relationship between socio-economic status (SES) and teaching practices around technology found that teaching in low-SES schools correlated most strongly with using technology for "reinforcement of skills" and "remediation of skills," while teaching in higher-SES schools correlated most with analyzing information and presenting information to an audience (Becker, 2000) and for applications and simulations which are known to promote higher-order thinking (Warschauer, 2004). The accountability mandates of adequate yearly progress and high-stakes testing have created an atmosphere that promotes a pedagogical focus on teaching to the test in schools serving low-income and minority students. Cummins, Brown, and Sayers (2006) concurred: "Because drill-and-practice transmission pedagogy predominates in these schools, computer use tends to conform to the same orientation" (p.91). Schofield and Davidson (2000) detailed that 25 percent of teachers engaged in Internet activities primarily or exclusively with academically advanced students, yet only 5 percent carried out similar Internet activities primarily or exclusively with lower-achieving students. In addition, 70 percent of the teachers in their study allowed only some of their students to use the Internet, using it as a privilege for those who were already performing well academically or behaviorally. In this regard, Internet usage was given as a reward or special privilege for model students.

Warschauer (2004) warned that when we speak about the digital divide we should not place an overemphasis on the physical availability of technology (models of access) because it creates an inaccurate "binary" relationship between the "haves" and "have-nots." He found that there are limits to the models of access that are based on "devices" and "conduits," and proposes instead a model of literacy. Warschauer (2004) claimed that the device and conduit models are limiting because "what is most important about ICT is not so much the availability of the computing device or the Internet line, but rather people's ability to *make use* of that device and line to engage in *meaningful social practices*" (p.38). He posited that people who cannot read, who have never learned to use a computer, or who do not know the major computer languages supporting available software and Internet content will have difficulty getting on the computer, let alone use the Internet productively. The literacy model includes a variety of resources needed for literacy acquisition. These include physical artifacts in the form of books, magazines, newspapers, journals, and computers; exposure to relevant content transmitted through these venues; development of appropriate skills, knowledge, and attitudes; and the right kinds of community and social support. Such a literacy model supports the goals and objectives of the digital solidarity movement.

Expanding Technology Choices

School districts across the nation are utilizing an array of technologies in an effort to offer all students equity of access to knowledge and information that can be found online. Historically, school districts have utilized computer labs, computers in the classroom, wireless initiatives, one-to-one laptop initiatives, and most recently the implementation of handhelds and mobile devices. As new technologies are developed, school districts struggle with what to purchase, whether to purchase, when to purchase, and how to leverage dwindling school budget dollars against high ticket technologies.

The E-Rate Program in the United States (officially the Schools and Libraries Program of the Universal Service Fund) was authorized as part of the Telecommunications Act in 1996 and implemented in 1997. It was designed to address the technology gap between rich and poor schools. This was accomplished by allocating money from telecom taxes to poor schools without technology resources. Funding is requested under four categories of service: telecommunications services, Internet access, internal connections, and basic maintenance of internal connections. The discounts to school districts range from 20 to 90 percent and depend upon the socio-economic level of students in the community and whether the school or library is located in an urban or rural area. Though the program has faced criticism and controversy regarding how money was disbursed, E-Rate has been credited with: (a) increasing the overall number of public classrooms with Internet access from 14 percent in 1996 to 95 percent in 2005, (b) allowing 100 percent of public libraries to provide free Internet access to their communities, (c) enabling 90 percent of classrooms in rural, high-minority and low-income school districts to have Internet connections, and (d) offering 2,800 private schools funding from E-Rate dollars to support educational goals (Pozo-Olano, 2007). District technology plans need to include E-Rate strategies along with the manner in which these purchases will be allocated across district departments, schools, and grade levels. Creating such technology plans will be discussed further in Chapter 5.

Computer Labs and Computers in the Classroom

Taylor and Rudy (n.d.) described the computer purchasing practices of American school systems for administrative and teacher use during the mid-1980s as one where items were typically procured based upon best pricing or software bundled with promotional items. Student computer use was typically limited to the computer lab setting. As computers arrived in classrooms, educators with computer knowledge began to use the systems, and software was purchased based upon individual preference. By the 1990s, both lab settings and computers in the classroom allowed for technology-enhanced instruction and assessment and management of student progress via computer. In 2004, public schools had approximately one computer for every four students, up from 1:14 in 1994, and 95 percent of schools were connected to the Internet, up from 50 percent in 1994 (Reckles, 2007). Teachers provided appropriate interventions designed to improve retention and application of knowledge. As students' standardized test results were obtained, technology was used for remediation in conjunction with other instructional strategies.

A 1:5 computer-to-student ratio has been deemed as adequate access to computers in the classroom, with a computer-to-student ratio of even only 1:9 providing the level of access necessary to produce increases in student achievement (The Education Alliance, 2005). The problem with many computers in use in school systems today is that they are antiquated, in poor condition, have no battery life, and do not support the most up-to-date software. Compounding the problem is the lack of technology dollars available to districts and schools to fund new purchases, with those schools in the lower socio-economic strata faring far worse than their counterparts in the more economically advantaged neighborhoods.

One-to-One Laptop Initiatives

Rapid technological advances in the last decade have sparked educational practitioners' interest in utilizing laptops as an instructional tool to improve student learning (Gulek & Demirtas, 2005). One-to-one laptop initiatives were heralded as having the potential to close persistent technology gaps (Goodwin, 2011, February). According to Means and Penuel (2005), the large number of school districts that invested in laptop programs did so in order to increase equity of access to tools believed to be necessary for all students to master in the 21st century. They found that students in classrooms that provide all students with their own laptops spend more time involved in collaborative work, participate in more project-based instruction, produce writing of higher quality and greater length, gain increased access to information, improve research analysis skills, and spend more time doing homework on computers when compared with their non-laptop counterparts. Research has also shown that these students direct their own learning, report a greater reliance on active learning strategies, readily engage in problem-solving and critical thinking, and consistently show deeper and more flexible uses of technology than students without individual laptops. Shapley, Sheehan, Sturges, Caranikas-Walker, Huntsberger, and Maloney (2009) in a four-year study of 5,000 middle school students in Texas concurred that those who participated in laptop immersion programs were less likely to have disciplinary problems and demonstrated high levels of technology skills. After three years, low-income students in the laptop schools displayed the same level of technology proficiency as the wealthier students in the control schools.

Michigan's Freedom to Learn (FTL) is a statewide education program designed to help schools create high performing, student-centered learning environments by providing each student and teacher with direct, consistent access to 21st-century learning tools. The program was started in 2002 when the Michigan Legislature and governor dedicated state and federal (Title II, D) funds to a pilot demonstration phase that lasted two years. Seeing the positive early results, the state expanded the program in 2004. Michigan has allocated over $30 million in federal and state funds to include over 23,000 students in 100 school districts and 191 buildings, primarily in middle schools. The program provided laptops for students in a number of the state's middle schools along with extensive teacher professional development around technology integration and curriculum enhancement (eSchool News, 2005a, July). Evaluations show that students participating in FTL had significantly higher levels of engagement in their work and in using technology as a learning tool when compared with national averages (Lowther, Ross, Strahl, Inan, & Pollard, 2005). But a later study found mixed results. It examined eight matched pairs of schools and found higher achievement in four laptop schools, lower achievement in three, and no difference in the final pair (Lowther, Strahl, Inan, & Bates, 2007).

Goodwin (2011, February) indicated that most large-scale evaluations have found mixed or no results for one-to-one initiatives. Maine's statewide program was one of the largest in the United States, and after five years of implementation, evaluations found little effect on student achievement—with one exception, writing (Silvernail & Gritter, 2007). One rationale for no measurable improvements in other subjects is that the state assessment test does not measure the 21st-century technology skills that laptop initiatives promote. Currently, some school systems that had high expectations for their one-to-one initiatives have begun to eliminate them due to budget cuts (Lemagie, 2010, November); mushrooming maintenance costs (Vascellaro, 2006, August); and concerns about how students are using the computers (Hu, 2007, May 4).

Wireless Networks

Reckles (2007) suggested that the reach of the computer networks in most schools is unable to satisfy the necessary requirements of the increased usage of computer technologies. Schools have a growing need for and reliance on network-based resources and technologies. In addition, these technologies and resources need to be made accessible to more people, more often, in more places. For many the solution to the problem is to install wireless local area networks (WLANs). A **wireless network** is an infrastructure for communication "through the air" that allows an electronic device to exchange data wirelessly where no cables are needed to connect from one point to another over a computer network. These connections are used for email, Internet access, audio, video, and mobile telephones. With the deployment of the WLAN comes the need for network administrators to be extremely careful in regards to deployment costs, investment protection, network management, and security. The problems with the first generation of WLAN technology caused expensive and risky implementations, but with newer technology these issues were resolved. Reckles (2007) contended that with the advances in security, management, and investment protection of the equipment, schools are now able to roll out wireless networks that deliver economic and technological benefits for many years.

Wireless Networks: A Case Study

In 2003, the Broward County Public School District in Fort Lauderdale, Florida approved a Digital Learning Environment Study (DLES) to determine the feasibility of deploying wireless networks district wide to support the incorporation of web-based instructional tools for learning for every student (Cisco, 2006). As part of the study, the district installed wireless overlay networks in two high schools, one middle school, and one elementary school, and distributed wireless laptops to all teachers and students at each location. The district's challenge was to implement a wireless environment that could be managed and monitored at a central site with minimal responsibility by on-site school-based staff. If successful, the district would then implement this wireless solution in every other school.

In an effort to expand the successes evidenced by the DLES at an affordable cost, the district began a five-year project to deploy and manage wireless networks in all schools. The district determined that all students would receive an equitable technology-rich teaching and learning experience through distribution of 2000 mobile carts in the remaining schools during the 2005–2006 school year, each loaded with 20 wireless-equipped Dell or Apple laptop computers, a Cisco Aironet 1000 Series lightweight access point, and a printer. The six-wheel carts were moved from classroom to classroom and were available for teachers to use as needed. The wireless network was designed to enhance the way that students learned and how teachers educated. Many teachers planned entire course units using lesson plans accessed on the district's online teacher web portal. These lessons included assignments and research that students accessed via the Internet.

The Open Source Movement and its Role in Digital Solidarity Efforts

Wikipedia (2012a) defined the **Open Source Movement** as a "broad-reaching movement of individuals who support the use of open source licenses for some or all software." As such, open source software is available for anyone to use or modify. Open source software promotes learning and understanding through the dissemination of information. The Open Source Movement has allowed smaller businesses to participate in the global economy. Prior to this availability, smaller businesses could not acquire the software needed to participate and compete in the global market. As such, the movement has created equal opportunities for people all over the world to participate in the global economy.

The equal access philosophy of the Open Source Movement has extended into the development of free access to educational material and innovations that help promote student achievement while developing 21st-century skills. In 2001, the Massachusetts Institute of Technology (MIT) first announced their OpenCourseWare (OCW) program. The OCW program, completed in 2008, is a free and open educational resource (OER) for educators, students, and self-learners around the world. The OCW "provides open access to course material for up to 1,550 MIT courses, representing 34 departments and all five MIT schools" (Online Education Database, 2007, para. 1). Open source and open access resources have changed how colleges, organizations, instructors, and prospective students use software, operating systems, and online documents for educational purposes. OCW courses are not meant to serve as distance learning initiatives since credits, degrees, and access to university faculty are not offered through them. Johnstone (2005) stated that OERs should not be perceived as a degree-granting system nor should they be considered a substitute for institutionally supported open and distance learning materials. Rather, they should be considered as a means of providing access to resources that have some educational value, particularly for those with limited or no access to educational resources.

In addition to open course ware, we have seen an influx of what has been termed **Massively Open Online Courses**, or MOOCs. These are online courses that institutions are offering totally free of charge. The term MOOC was coined in response to Siemens and Downes's 2008 "Connectivism and Connective Knowledge" course where an initial group of 25 participants registered and paid to take the course for credit. Then the course was opened up to nonregistered learners to participate in the course lectures, discussion forums, and weekly online sessions (Cormier and Siemens, 2010).

A MOOC provides a way of connecting distributed instructors and learners across a common topic or field of discourse. Roscorla (2012) indicated that since they began on college campuses in 2008, large numbers of people are taking them. In July of 2012, 12 additional top universities announced that they will be offering some of these online courses. These 12 institutions signed an agreement with a company called Coursera (a company started in 2012 by two computer science faculty members from Stanford University) to provide courses to anyone totally free of charge through partnerships with various universities. The scale of interaction among MOOC participants has been likened to that of massively multiplayer online games. Where the gaming environment has large numbers of people coming together online to play, self-organize, develop skills, strategize as a group, and execute strategies, MOOCs "facilitate learning about or the development of a particular knowledge domain at a participation scale ripe for diversity" (Atkisson, 2011).

There are two main types of MOOCs: "x MOOC" and "connectivist MOOC." Companies such as Coursera, EdX (an MIT and Harvard partnership), and Udacity (a new venture founded by three roboticists) fall under the category of x MOOC. This type of MOOC "emphasizes content mastery, centralizes courses on one website and uses automated grading tools to support hundreds of thousands of students" (Atkisson, 2011, para. 12). The connectivist MOOC (a model developed by George Siemens, Stephen Downes, and Dave Cormier in 2008) is "more social and focused on deriving meaning of the learning experience with others" (para. 11). Participation in a MOOC is usually free except for those seeking some form of accreditation. It should be noted that most free MOOCs do not qualify students for college credit at the affiliated institution but may instead provide participants with a certificate of completion. However, students who pay tuition may qualify for college credit if they demonstrate mastery of the course material (Wikipedia, 2012d). What is exciting about these approaches is the possibility of opening up classroom doors to off-campus students who can bring different perspectives to the class while exposing anyone in the world to the best professors at the best universities. The downside of this involves designing the open online courses in a manner by which students can be accurately assessed in a scalable way while also being motivated to participate successfully (Roscorla, 2012).

Moodle is an open source Learning Management System (LMS) or Virtual Learning Environment (VLE) that provides documents, graded assignments, quizzes, discussion forums, and other basic online features and functionalities to students. Moodle 1.0 was developed in 2002 and continues to grow through a worldwide effort of over 75,000 students, faculty, and staff at over 6,500 institutions around the world, coordinated by the main site at https://moodle. org/. As a global development project, it is designed to support a social constructionist framework of education. Moodle is designed to help educators create online courses with opportunities for rich interaction. Its open source license and modular design means that people can develop additional functionality.

The Sakai Project (Bradley, 2005) was formed in 2004 from several college and university projects and led to the development of a free open source learning management system. Sakai is a community of academic institutions, commercial organizations, and individuals who work together to develop a common Collaboration and Learning Environment (CLE). The Sakai CLE is a free community source educational software platform distributed under the Educational Community License, a type of open source license, and is used for teaching, research, and collaboration. As an online collaboration and learning environment, it provides a framework of pluggable tool modules for managing, delivering, and assessing student learning. It is designed to bring students and instructors together for knowledge-sharing, discussion, and shared learning. Users of Sakai deploy it to support teaching and learning, ad hoc group collaboration, and research collaboration.

In 2012, Blackboard officials announced that the company purchased both Moodle and Sakai as part of the company's newly announced Blackboard Education Open Source Services Group (Young, 2012). In addition, Blackboard has hired one of the founders of the Sakai project to lead its efforts to support colleges using open-source software. In the past, Blackboard has disbanded its purchased competitors, such as what was done with Prometheus, or merged the competing product with its own, as it did with WebCT. According to Blackboard, it plans to leave these companies alone and allow them to continue under their current brand names with existing staff.

The Khan Academy is a non-profit educational organization (http://www. khanacademy.org) whose mission is to "provide a high quality education to anyone, anywhere." The website offers a free online collection of more than 3,300 lectures via videos that are stored on YouTube. Videos deliver content in mathematics, history, health care and medicine, finance, physics, chemistry, biology, astronomy, economics, cosmetology, organic chemistry, American civics, art history, macroeconomics, microeconomics, and computer science. The Khan Academy began with Salman Khan remotely tutoring family members by using software programs such as Yahoo Doodle images, Wacom tablet, SmoothDraw3, and Camtasia Studio. All YouTube hosted videos are accessed on the Khan Academy website. The project is fully funded by donations, now with significant backing from both the Bill and Melinda Gates Foundation and Google. Funding was also made available through individual private donations, as well as by revenue collected through advertising up until 2010 when the Khan Academy ceased to accept advertising.

HippoCampus (http://www.hippocampus.org) is a project of the Monterey Institute for Technology and Education, and instead of providing free written content it offers free educational multimedia. The goal of HippoCampus is to provide high-quality, multimedia content on general education subjects to high school and college students free of charge.

Games and Virtual Simulations

Virtual simulations in education use 3D multi-user environments to immerse children in educational tasks. Educational games and simulations use strategies from the commercial gaming environment with lessons from educational research on learning and motivation. Strangman and Hall (2003) described the various types of virtual simulations. There is the desktop virtual reality environment that is presented on an ordinary computer screen and is usually explored by using a keyboard, mouse, wand, joystick, or touchscreen. Web-based "virtual tours" are examples of commonly available desktop virtual reality formats. Total immersion virtual reality environments are presented on multiple, room-size screens or through a stereoscopic, head-mounted display unit. Specialized wired equipment such as a DataGlove can be worn enabling participants to interact with the virtual environment through normal body movements.

Aldrich (2009) differentiated the nuances between games, simulations, and virtual worlds. He described games as fun, engaging activities usually used purely for entertainment. They may also allow people to gain exposure to a particular set of tools, motions, or ideas. Simulations, though, use rigorously structured scenarios carefully designed to develop specific competencies that can then be transferred to the real world. Finally, virtual worlds can be massively multiplayer, three-dimensional, persistent social environments with easy-to-access building capabilities. Although they are three-dimensional environments like games and simulations, they do not have the focus on a particular goal, such as advancing to the next level or successfully navigating the scenario.

Prensky (2007) positioned computer-simulation technology as a way of looking at situations and encouraging learners to wonder "what would happen if," and then try out various alternatives in a virtual environment to see the consequences of their actions. Learners, in this way, gain experience about how things behave in a virtual world. Students can observe and manipulate normally inaccessible objects, variables, and processes in real-time. Strangman and Hall (2003) cited the ability of virtual reality and computer simulations to scaffold student learning and individualize instruction as additional characteristics making them useful to a wide range of curriculum areas. There is quite a bit of empirical evidence proving that simulations are of great teaching value. Prensky (2007) offered a few basic examples of their current practical use: NASA's astronaut training program using simulated events, airline pilots practicing in simulators prior to actually flying, and medical students learning about the anatomy and how systems of the body work through physical simulators. Although virtual learning environments had mainly been used in such applied fields as aviation and medical imaging, these technologies are now being used in the traditional classrooms (Strangman & Hall, 2003).

Many schools and universities are employing virtual labs to supplement classroom instruction or serve online students. The Center for Digital Education (2012) reported, "Virtualization uses digital technology to provide virtual training for students to help them master any number of fields within which they might find future employment" (p.10). There are many exciting examples of **virtualization** already being employed in the United States today. For instance, Prince William Sound Community College has set up a variety of virtual labs to serve their students living in remote areas of Alaska. Students can virtually use "wet labs" to run experiments through "the virtual 3D world of Second Life" (p.10). At Duke University, students study neurology using a "virtual reality simulation environment built on the 'Unreal' gaming engine" (p.10). Students go through training exercises using a "patient avatar to perform medical procedures and become familiar with the clinical environment" (p.10). Virtual labs are allowing students to work in real-life simulations to prepare them for 21st-century careers.

Prensky (2007) believed that simulations can be extremely powerful educational tools and offered three reasons why they are not being used more in education: (a) a lack of time, (b) a lack of knowledge on the part of the teachers, and (c) a lack of technology. Although the cost of simulations is often cited as an issue, educational simulations are readily becoming free tools for use by teachers and students. Sadly, the continued focus on accountability, standardized tests, and antiquated pedagogy do not leave enough room in the teaching schedule for the use of games and simulations. The best technology-based simulations available require relatively modern computers or handhelds, as well as global-positioning-system technology and broadband connections. These are items that not all schools have. Last, as is too often the case with teaching with technology, many teachers have not experienced learning through games and simulations and therefore do not recognize their potential as an educational tool.

A new term, "**gamification**," has evolved from the gaming and virtual world environment and relates to the use of game design techniques, game thinking, and game mechanics to enhance non-game contexts (Wikipedia, 2012b). Currently practiced in the business world, gamification is applied to non-game applications and processes in hopes of encouraging people to adopt them or to influence people on their use. Gamification works by making technology more engaging and encourages users to participate in specific behaviors by showing paths to mastery and autonomy, and by helping humans to solve problems through their psychological predisposition to engage in gaming. It has been called one of the most important trends in technology and is seen as having the potential to be applied to any industry and almost anything to create fun and engaging experiences.

Mobile Learning, Handheld Devices, and Smartphones

Over the past few decades we have moved from the desktop computer, to the laptop, and now we are going mobile. Students are able to walk around with full curriculum content in their pockets due to, in large part, a faster and smarter Internet, and a marketplace ready to help support these new platforms. Because they are inexpensive when compared with laptop computers, many schools are finding that a mixture of desktop, laptop, and handheld devices can be used to meet a variety of educational needs. The key to the handheld device is its portability. It is ideal for the classroom, field trips, home use, and anything requiring quick information access and recording. These devices can be used without the hassles of heavier technology and without the need to be tethered to the Internet.

A current trend is "the **app**" and the one tablet that seems to be driving the market is the iPad. A mobile application (or mobile app) is a software application designed to run on smartphones, tablet computers, and other mobile devices. They are available through application distribution platforms, such as the Apple App Store, Google Play, Windows Phone Marketplace and BlackBerry App World. Some apps are free, while others have a price (Wikipedia, 2012c). With the help of smartphones students not only in America, but across the entire globe are suddenly able to access massive amounts of educational materials.

The development of a mobile device capable of delivering multiple applications for web browsing, information, and entertainment is the primary reason for the continued success of the smartphone revolution. The changes began when both the iPhone and Android smartphones were released in 2007–2008 and their use has quickly skyrocketed. With low-cost, pre-paid and no-contract cell phone plans ranging in price from $30 to $50 a month, the smartphone revolution is democratic in character (Hood, 2011, August). Smith (2011) found that 46 percent of American adults in 2011 owned a smartphone of some kind, up from 35 percent in May 2011. Hood (2011, August) asserted the smartphone revolution enables people to take matters into their own hands and can be an effective approach in narrowing the digital divide.

According to the Pew Internet Report on smartphones, under 30, non-White, low-income and less-educated smartphone users report going online mostly through the use of their phones (Smith, 2011). Eighty-seven percent of them sometimes use their mobile phones to browse the web, but 38 percent use their handsets as their primary means to access the Internet. The Institute for Communication Technology Management (CTM) at the University of Southern California found some similar statistics regarding smartphone ownership and use. More than 60 percent of Latino, Black, and young smartphone users often, or even always, use smartphones for their Internet connections. This use of smartphones for Internet browsing is far more extensive than by Whites. According to the CTM surveys, Latinos and Blacks are disproportionately higher users of data services, with the two minority groups being twice as likely as the average user to access health information via smartphones. In addition, the use of smartphones to purchase items (m-commerce—where the "m" stands for mobile) is 50 percent higher among Blacks and Latinos (Smith, 2011).

Since the rise of the Internet there has been a worry amongst government officials and educators about the creation of a digital divide between those who could connect and those who could not. They have been struggling with identifying mechanisms that could bring broadband to rural communities and to poor urban residents who could not afford laptops or a broadband connection at home. The smartphone might be just such an affordable and capable tool enabling access to valuable information and capabilities.

Concluding Thoughts

Society began using the term "digital divide" in the mid-1990s. As a nation we have made some strides to bridge the chasm between the digital "haves" and "have-nots" through the design and delivery of inexpensive computers and the explosive growth in the use of smartphones as a digital platform, both here in the United States and in other developing nations. But, more than a decade since the phrase was coined, we still find a wide gap between those who have access to technology and the skills to benefit from that access, and those who do not. Wilhelm, Carmen, and Reynolds (2002, June) asserted that because 21st-century technology literacy is so important, governments, industry, and philanthropic organizations must make it a top priority to support programs that provide access and training to underserved communities, particularly to young people. So we will end this chapter detailing some of the innovative community, business, government, and societal programs that embrace the goals of the digital solidarity movement.

Because broadband is the great infrastructure challenge of the early 21st century, in 2009 Congress directed the Federal Communications Commission (FCC) to develop a National Broadband Plan to ensure every American has access to broadband capability. The plan was directed to include a detailed strategy for achieving affordability and maximizing use of broadband to advance "consumer welfare, civic participation, public safety and homeland security, community development, health care delivery, energy independence and efficiency, education, employee training, private sector investment, entrepreneurial activity, job creation and economic growth, and other national purposes" (National Broadband Plan, n.d.). The FCC believed that, like electricity a century ago, broadband is a foundation for economic growth, job creation, global competitiveness, and a better way of life. Broadband is changing how we educate children, deliver health care, manage energy, ensure public safety, engage government, and access, organize, and disseminate knowledge. According to the FCC, the number of Americans who have broadband at home has grown from eight million in 2000 to nearly 200 million in 2011. But approximately 100 million Americans do not have broadband at home.

eSchool News (2005b, September) cited a study that found that while 87 percent of young people use the Internet, there are also three million who remain without Internet access. Many of those without access come from financially disadvantaged backgrounds, and a disproportionate number are Black. Microsoft claimed that about 9.5 million students in the U.S. do not have home access to the Internet. According to the Federal Reserve, those students have a high school graduation rate six to eight percentage points lower than those who do have home access. To tackle this problem, Microsoft, in 2011, launched a three-year program to ensure that a million students from low-income families in the U.S. will have access to computer software, hardware, and the Internet. They work with city, state, nonprofit and private organizations to develop and accelerate programs and policies that include Windows-based PCs for students, broadband Internet access, Microsoft education software, and jobs skills training (Tu, 2011, September). Seattle is one of the first cities to be involved with the program through their Great Student Initiative.

The Great Student Initiative is the city's effort to establish partnerships with technology companies and financial institutions to provide Internet access to the most vulnerable students in the Seattle Public Schools. This program provides high-speed Internet service for $9.95 a month (through Comcast's Internet Essentials program), 75 percent reduction from the average Internet cost, to students in the Seattle Public School District who are eligible for the free lunch program. This commitment made by Microsoft is part of the company's global Shape the Future program, which has provided technology and access to over ten million students around the world over the past five years.

Afterschool programs across the nation serve about 8.4 million children each afternoon (Peterson, 2012). While most programs are located at schools, other places such as community and recreation centers, Boys & Girls Clubs, local YMCAs, libraries and housing projects all serve as viable locations. When the afterschool programs are of high quality, they serve as true school–community partnerships that provide staff, volunteers, materials, and other resources. To create such programs, the FCC is considering a proposal to spend $200 million to create a digital literacy corps to advance broadband adoption by low-income people through digital literacy training in our nation's public libraries and schools (Newman, 2012, June). This group of potentially thousands of trainers would be sent to schools and libraries to teach how to productively use computers for parents, students and those who are seeking employment. In addition, the commission will send digital literacy trainers to such organizations as the Boys & Girls Clubs, the League of United Latin American Citizens, and the National Association for the Advancement of Colored People. More information pertaining to afterschool programs will be discussed in the next chapter.

Chapter 3

Innovative Ideas in Education to Support Digital Solidarity

Innovation means something new or novel, whether it's an idea, process, or a product. It entails the qualifiers of performing "on the cutting edge" or "ahead of the curve"; that "one step beyond" everyone else. Being innovative requires the unique ability to combine the artistic dreams of a Picasso with the scientific realities of an Edison. Although many humans seek to be innovative, few possess the innate attributes that allow their innovative ideas to be realized.

A true innovator must be intuitive, having that internal vision of knowing something instinctively without perceiving it consciously. A true innovator is a risk-taker who is still able to move forward when most people around him or her are not fully appreciating the idea conceived, the problem solved, or the product created. A true innovator must be an inventor, a creator who is able to predict what humans need before they fully conceptualize the need. In the 15th and 16th centuries, Leonardo da Vinci demonstrated his innovative qualities through his theme of "knowing how to see." His creative genius was displayed through his graphic representations as an artist, sculptor, architect, anatomist, writer, cartographer, and engineer. As archetype of the Renaissance Man, his diverse talents along with his curiosity and imagination epitomized the humanist ideals of the times.

In the United States, we have benefitted politically, economically, and socially from the historical ideas and creations of innovators like Franklin, Jefferson, Edison and Beulah Henry, "the Lady Edison" (Bedi, 1999). Today, one of the greatest venues for innovators appears to be the information technology realm, with individuals like Apple's Steve Jobs, Yahoo founders Jerry Yang and David Filo, social media's Facebook creator Mark Zuckerberg, and Truenorthlogic's visionary president and CEO, Jeanette Haren (PRLog, 2012, October 2).

Recognizing the global implications of supporting and valuing American ingenuity in the 21st century, the White House's National Economic Council, the Council of Economic Advisors, and the Office of Science and Technology Policy developed *A Strategy for American Innovation: Securing our Economic Growth and Prosperity* (2011). This document identified political priorities for improving "America's economic growth and competitiveness" (p.2). The strategy includes a Wireless Initiative to assist businesses in providing high-speed wireless access to all Americans, a patent reform agenda that will provide for new initiatives and improved product quality, and provide the start-up for an Advanced Research Projects Agency-Education (ARPA-ED) to provide financial support for innovative technologies that enhance learning (p.2). Ongoing initiatives include financial support for adoption of comprehensive reforms by school districts through programs such as Race to the Top and public–private partnerships that nurture excellence of science, technology, engineering, and mathematics (STEM) in females and other underrepresented groups in American society.

The creation of an Office of Innovation and Improvement at the U.S. Department of Education has reinforced the political initiatives through strategic investments, using more than 25 discretionary grant programs to financially support innovative educational programs and practices (United States Department of Education, 2013). Among these innovations can be found educational and technological models that will not only move American students "to the top" but ensure America's role as a global competitor and investor in the concept of digital solidarity. Some of these innovations include virtual schools that enroll students representing diverse linguistic, cultural, and socio-economic backgrounds, afterschool technology-based programs and online tutoring programs designed for underserved and underperforming groups, and online communities developed to improve skills and competencies for academic achievement in special populations.

Virtual Schools

A Day in the Life of an Elementary Virtual Student: A Case Study

Let's take a look behind the scenes into the workings of an elementary level virtual school. Elementary virtual education offers students the ability to work from home under the guidance of an adult learning coach. Usually this coach is one of the child's parents. Certified district teachers offer **differentiated instruction** that extends learning opportunities for students to work at their own pace. This virtual public school contracts a provider of online education for the curriculum for students in kindergarten through twelfth grade. However, the district employs its own local teachers to deliver the curriculum. The curriculum materials are shipped directly to each virtual school family. The shipment includes a wide range of children's literature, textbooks, teachers' guides, workbooks, writing paper, science equipment, and art supplies: everything the learning coach needs to provide academic instruction in a home classroom.

Students spend no more than 20 to 25 percent of their time working on the computer, especially in the primary grades. Interactive lessons engage every learning style and students are challenged to use the computer as a research tool. The provider's online program includes over 120,000 interactive animations, games, audio files, and videos. Blending the provider's curriculum with the expertise of the district school offers students a comprehensive educational experience. Students meet with their local teacher in grade level electronic classes (eclasses) every week and face-to-face classes once a month.

Our journey begins with a visit to one of our virtual school families. In this home the mother is the primary learning coach and she works directly with her children every day. The learning coach downloads an academic schedule for her children every week. This schedule has been set up through teacher/parent conferences where each child's academic progress is discussed in detail. The virtual school offers an individualized program for each student at all academic levels. The provider's curriculum was designed to let students find the pace and learning style that work best for them. Gifted students have the opportunity to work ahead of pace with an engaging and challenging curriculum, while students working below grade level receive remedial instruction to bring them quickly up to the appropriate academic standing. Students spend from four to six hours a day working independently and with their learning coach. Learning activities range from worksheets or essays to hands-on experiments and interactive assessments. Let's eavesdrop on the interaction between this learning coach and her children.

> **Learning coach:** Today's science lesson is asking you to investigate the properties of matter. What is the definition of matter?
>
> **Johnny:** Matter is what everything is made of.
>
> **Learning coach:** OK, that's a good start. Can you name the properties of matter?
>
> **Judy:** The types of matter are solid, liquid, and gas.
>
> **Learning coach:** Your textbook gives you a neat experiment to do that combine two types of matter to create a third property of matter. Here are two different types of matter. Please label each with the appropriate property.
>
> **Judy:** I know . . . the baking soda is a solid.
>
> **Johnny:** And the vinegar is a liquid.
>
> **Learning coach:** That's correct. Johnny, please put two teaspoons of baking soda in the empty balloon using this funnel. Judy, pour one cup of vinegar in the empty bottle. Alright, now I will carefully place the balloon over the neck of the bottle. When we combine the baking soda and the vinegar what do you think will happen?
>
> **Judy:** I bet the balloon will blow up.
>
> **Learning coach:** That's a good hypothesis. Johnny, go ahead and empty the baking soda from the balloon into the bottle.
>
> **Johnny:** Wow! The balloon is inflating!

Learning coach: What was created when the solid baking soda combined with the liquid vinegar?

Judy and Johnny: A gas!

Learning coach: You are correct! Now please spend the next 30 minutes reading the rest of the chapter about matter and answer the questions at the end of the chapter. You may move to the computer to complete the chapter assessment when you think you are ready.

Another event during the day is an eclass taught by the virtual school teacher. This is a class delivered over the computer using Blackboard Collaborate, a web conferencing tool offering audio and video communication. Students are able to use on-screen controls to raise their hands, select a multiple-choice answer or indicate their feelings through emoticons. Both teachers and students use microphones to speak with each other in real time. There is also a chat box into which older students can type their questions or responses. Often the learning coach sits in with his or her primary children to assist them with the chat feature. Blackboard Collaborate also offers students an opportunity to read along as written material is presented via a document camera directly to their computer screen. Students eagerly look forward to their weekly eclass.

Each week the teacher presents five 30-minute eclass sessions as she meets the students by grade level. The kindergarten and first graders are taught together and today they will be following along as their teacher reads a book about graphs. Let's listen to some of the interaction between the teacher and her students.

Teacher: Good morning students. Click on the smiley face on your computer screen if you are ready to begin our eclass. Great, everyone is ready to go. Today we are going to learn how to make a graph or chart. If you have already studied about graphs with your learning coach, click on the green check. If you haven't studied about graphs yet, click on the red X. OK, most of you have not reached this part of your math text so we will read a book to introduce you to different types of graphs and charts. Pay close attention because I will be stopping on each page to ask you a question. Cassie, I see your hand is raised so you have permission to click on your microphone button and ask your question.

Cassie: I just want to read the first page of the book.

Teacher: All right, you may begin reading as soon as I place the book on the document camera and you see it on your computer. Everyone else follow along on your computer screen, too.

Cassie: We can make graphs. On Monday we made a graph about our shoes.

Teacher: Thank you, Cassie. Let's all click on the clapping-hands button to give Cassie applause for reading so well! Now look closely at the picture and tell me what kind of shoes did the students use in their graph? Justin, I see your hand is raised so you can use your microphone to give us the answer.

Justin: Buckle shoes, laces, Velcro, and other.

Teacher: You read each category correctly. Let's give Justin a clap! Now who would like to read next? Wow, so many hands are raised. Let's see, Amy, you may read the next two pages.

Amy: On Tuesday we made a graph about our birthdays. On Wednesday we made a graph about our fa . . . fav . . .

Teacher: Sound it out . . . fa-vor . . .

Amy: Fa-vor-it . . . favorite colors.

Teacher: Good job! Let's give Amy a clap. Now students look at the graphs on both pages. The first graph is a pie chart. Raise your hand if you can guess why it is called a pie chart? Maxwell.

Maxwell: It's called a pie chart because it is in a circle, just like a pie.

Teacher: That's correct! We'll give you a clap! Now if you look at the graph on this page (pointing to the next page on the document camera) you can see the green and blue pieces of paper that make up each bar. This is called a bar graph. Today we are going to create a bar graph about our favorite type of ice cream. Let's do that now before we finish reading this book. I will take away the book and place this chart on the document camera. You will see that the title of this bar graph is *Our Favorite Flavor of Ice Cream*. At the bottom I have written the three flavors of ice cream. Who would like to read those flavors? OK, Lola, read the flavors, please.

Lola: Chocolate, Strawberry, Vanilla.

Teacher: Very good reading. Let's give Lola a clap! Now everyone needs to decide which of these three flavors you like the best. Johnny, do you have a question?

Johnny: My favorite ice cream is cookies and cream!

Teacher: I understand that there are many other flavors that you might like better. In fact Rebecca's learning coach just wrote in the chat box that Rebecca likes peach ice cream the best. My all-time favorite is mint chocolate chip but today we have to decide which of these three flavors we like the best . . . chocolate, strawberry, or vanilla. Now when I call out your favorite flavor, give me a smiley face. Remember that you may only vote for one flavor of ice cream. Now if you like chocolate the best, give me a smiley face. I count eight students voted for chocolate. On this graph I will place eight brown blocks of paper in the column above the word chocolate. OK, now I'll clear your smiley faces and those of you who have not voted can give me a smiley face if you like strawberry ice cream the best. I counted three students who like strawberry the best. On the graph I will place three pink blocks of paper in the middle column above the word strawberry. Now give me a smiley face if you like vanilla ice cream the best. I count five smiley faces. Whoops . . . there are only 15 students participating today. What do I get when I add all the smiley faces together . . . 8 + 3 + 5? Maribeth?

Maribeth: 16.

Teacher: Good job, Maribeth!! I'll give you a clap! This means that one person voted twice. I'll clear the smiley faces and you can vote again for the vanilla flavor. OK, vote now if you like vanilla the best. Now we have the correct number of votes . . . four smiley faces for vanilla. 8 + 3 + 4 = 15. I will now place four white blocks of paper in the column above the word vanilla. So now, looking at our bar graph, what ice cream flavor is most popular in this class today? You or your learning coach may type in the answer in the chat box. Oh my, I am reading a lot of correct answers. If you said "chocolate" you are correct. The bar above the word chocolate is taller than the other two bars. Which flavor was the least popular as shown in the shortest bar? Please type your answer in the chat box. If you wrote strawberry, you are correct. There are only three blocks in the strawberry column. I hope you have had fun helping me make a bar graph today. Here is your assignment for next week. I'll place it on your screen while I use the file share to send you a copy of the assignment. Make sure you accept the download or ask your learning coach to help you. Your assignment is to create some type of graph or chart with your learning coach. I have included some websites with ideas that might help you get started on this project. Make sure your learning coach uploads your completed assignment to the Blackboard Collaborate website. Learning coaches can scan your graph or take a digital picture of it. I look forward to sharing your graphs on the next eclass so make sure you get your assignment posted before the end of this week. Now let's go back and finish reading the book about graphs before we end the class.

We will leave the live eclass now and find out what is planned for the rest of the grade levels. The second grade eclass is about force and motion. The class begins with a short video clip which the teacher "sends" to the students using the "web push" feature of Blackboard Collaborate. Students access the video on their own computer and the teacher signals when everyone should return to the eclass home screen. Then the teacher reviews the concepts of force and motion by conducting a demonstration with a little toy truck being pushed or pulled across the document camera. Students are encouraged to use their microphones to describe other examples of a push and pull force of motion. The eclass ends with the teacher reading a short book that summarizes the day's lesson. Students are asked to make a list of examples of force and motion at work in their home or neighborhood.

Third graders are in the next eclass session. They are preparing for an Antonym Bowl game that will be held on next month's Terrific Tuesday. This will be like a spelling bee where students will give the correct antonym for a word. Today the teacher reviews the definition of an antonym and reads a short book where students must give the antonyms for familiar words. Next, students listen and then sing along to the "Antonym Rap." The words to this song are displayed on the home screen using a PowerPoint presentation. Finally, the teacher sends a document to every student using the file-sharing feature of Blackboard Collaborate. This document is an Adobe Portable Document Format (PDF) containing the words and their corresponding antonyms that will be used for the Antonym Bowl. The rest of the eclass session is spent practicing the antonyms on the word list. Their assignment is simply to study their antonym word list.

The next eclass session is with the fourth graders. These students are preparing for the state writing assessment. Three students begin by sharing the essay they wrote last week. The teacher displays the essay on the document camera while the student reads aloud. Students are selected to read as a reward for creating a good writing sample. Next, the teacher reads a picture book while the students view the pages via the document camera. Today's book gives excellent examples of the writing trait: word choice. Students are asked to make a list of these examples as the teacher reads the book. Then students will type their examples in the chat box. Next, students are asked, "Which way is the best way to say this? Which way makes a clear picture in your mind?" Then the teacher shows the students this *stripped-down* sentence: The car is green. She tells the students "get a picture of the car in your mind." Then the teacher shows them this descriptive sentence: The shiny new 2005 Volkswagen was painted the color of a green Granny Smith apple. The teacher asks, "So which sentence painted the clearest picture in your mind?" The students all indicate that the second sentence was better. Students are then presented with other stripped-down sentences. They are to replace each stripped-down sentence with a descriptive sentence. Using their microphone, students read their descriptive sentences to the rest of the class. The homework assignment is for each student to write five stripped-down sentences about a single topic. Then students will exchange their sentences with a writing buddy using the discussion forum in Blackboard. Finally, all the students will enhance the sentences and add more information to create an entire essay.

The last eclass of the day is for the fifth graders. Today they will be reviewing mathematical transformations. Students will interact with a variety of games from Compass Learning Odyssey, an educational website to which their virtual school has a subscription. The first game asks students to identify whether the shapes are congruent or similar. Students type their answers into the chat box directly to the teacher so that she is the only person to see their answers. In this way the teacher can also privately write back a response to each student as necessary. Once the teacher reveals the correct answer they move on to the next question. This procedure is continued throughout all the Odyssey trans-formation activities with the exception of multiple-choice questions. Then the students click on one of the four choices (A, B, C, D) listed at the top of their home screen. Once again the teacher will be the only one to view the answers. The students are very enthusiastic about the transformation games. Their homework assignment is to complete all these games on their own computer. The difference is that they must make a score of at least 80 percent to successfully complete their assignment. If they score below 80 percent then they must repeat that activity. The teacher will have access to their scores and can monitor each student's progress.

Now that the eclass is finished, let's see if we can ask these parents some questions about their virtual school experience.

Interviewer: Excuse me; do you have a few minutes for some questions?
Parent 1: I would be delighted to talk with you.
Interviewer: What do you like best about a virtual school?
Parent 1: I like the one-on-one instruction. This is the most excited I have ever been about my child's education.
Interviewer: What do you think about the virtual school curriculum?
Parent 2: When I investigated the curriculum that was used, I spent a lot of time looking through all the materials and the samples. I realized that both my kids could do really well with this curriculum and learn quite a bit at their own speed. That was important for both children because one was struggling to keep up and the other was struggling to find enough work to do. So it has really worked out well for both of them. I just think that this virtual school curriculum builds very strong foundations.
Interviewer: Why did you decide to enroll your children in a virtual school?
Parent 3: I've tried other schools. I've tried private school. I've tried charter school. The virtual home school is the perfect school for my children. I love the program because I can also keep up with my children's education. I know where they are and I know what level they need help in. So this virtual program is a perfect school for myself and my family.
Interviewer: How about the children? May we ask them a few questions, too?
Parent 1: I know they would like to speak with you.
Interviewer: What do you like best about the virtual school?
Samuel: I like Terrific Tuesdays because I actually get to know other people and Dr. Weaver makes it fun! (Smiles)
Interviewer: How is the virtual school a better fit for you than a traditional school?

Tamika: The virtual school is a better fit for me than a traditional school because the time schedule is much more flexible than the regular school.

Interviewer: Thanks for speaking with us today.

Terrific Tuesdays are an opportunity for direct interaction with the teacher and other virtual school students. The virtual school provides a group of portable classroom buildings where district teachers can meet their students individually, in small groups or by grade level. The children work on projects together, share their assignments with each other as well as hone their skills with specialists from the school district. Terrific Tuesdays are a key ingredient in this virtual school blended educational experience.

On the first Tuesday of this month, Kindergarten and first graders completed a mural of ancient Egypt as a backdrop for their individual models of the pyramids. Second graders brought their lunch for a social time before beginning their art activity. These students completed a shadow box for their projects about the Roman Coliseum. Today third graders are working on their cursive writing so each student sits at a desk to write a short story. Then students sit in small groups at tables to share art materials while they illustrate their stories. Next week fourth graders will be reading their essays to the rest of the class before participating in a spelling bee. The fifth graders sharpen their math skills with a curriculum specialist from the district office. Their favorite activity is the math jeopardy game. Now let's visit another virtual school's educational center . . . the teacher's home office.

A virtual teacher uses many types of technologies to teach and track students' progress, from phone conferences to eclasses, using the curriculum provider's online school platform and district assessment databases. But there are still person-to-person interviews with parents and teachers that make the virtual school's differentiated curriculum a success. Let's see if we can interrupt the classroom teacher, Dr. Weaver, for a short discussion.

Interviewer: Excuse me, Dr. Weaver, can we ask you a few questions?

Dr. Weaver: Certainly, step into my home office and have a seat.

Interviewer: Why is online learning the best educational situation for some children?

Dr. Weaver: Many children in a traditional school setting do get *left behind*. The virtual school setting provides an individualized approach allowing gifted students the opportunity to take accelerated courses while at the same time students below grade level can take advantage of remedial courses.

Interviewer: Is your virtual school open to all students?

Dr. Weaver: Our virtual program is part of the public school system. It is free to any student who meets our basic requirements and lives within our school district's boundaries. Our basic requirements are set to provide students with the optimum educational setting for their skills. Students are required to have a passing score on the year's previous state reading assessment. We have found that this is an important requirement when so much of our material is presented online or in textbooks. However, our school is set up to provide all the learning coaches the tools they need to help their children be successful. We provide translators when necessary for parents who are still struggling with English. School counselors are readily available to work with students who need special services. If a student qualifies for free or reduced lunch, he or she will receive a school laptop computer to use at home. Our virtual school is anxious to meet the needs of the "haves" and the "have-nots."

Interviewer: What do you think of the online academic curriculum?

Dr. Weaver: The academic curriculum offers a rigorous course of study beginning with kindergarten. Students have computer courses developed by our virtual curriculum provider. These courses allow students to move quickly through a skill they have already mastered or if they need more practice, alternative lessons are provided. This mastery-based curriculum is a win–win situation for all learners. However, the virtual school also offers workbooks and manipulatives that provide hands-on learning. The virtual curriculum is also very comprehensive. In addition to the core subjects, a full year of history, science, and art are offered for each grade level.

Interviewer: What are the challenges of assisting parents in their role as a learning coach?

Dr. Weaver: Working with the parents is very rewarding. We are a team! I consider each learning coach as part of my faculty. With that in mind, I offer teaching strategies and instructions to improve their home learning experience. The online curriculum provider also offers many virtual seminars and videos to assist the learning coaches.

Interviewer: Thank you, Dr. Weaver.

Well, that concludes our brief look at a typical day in the life of an online student. Our virtual school offers equitable access to high-quality, individualized education. The virtual environment provides flexibility of time and location, and promotes development of the skills, the attitudes, and the self-discipline necessary to achieve success in the 21st century. Come join us today!

Online Career and Technical Education (CTE) Programs: A Case Study

Sheridan Technical Center (STC) is the oldest of Broward County's three technical centers. As a Broward County Public School located in Hollywood,

Florida, STC offers post-secondary workforce development programs affording students the opportunity to gain skills in high-wage, high-demand occupational fields and compete successfully in the local employment marketplace. Its mission is to promote excellence in academic, career, and technical studies in order to prepare students to enter and remain competitive in a global workforce. STC provides students full- or part-time training using the latest industry-approved technology and equipment. The instructors are licensed and certified teaching professionals. To meet the needs of students preparing for occupations, 37 workforce development programs are offered, including three applied technology diploma programs in Medical Coder/Biller, Medical Records Transcribing, and Medical Lab Technician. The Career and Technical Departments include: Adult General Education; Automotive Technology; Barbering, Cosmetology, and Spa Services; Business, Marketing, and Real Estate; Construction, Energy, and Gaming Machine Repair; Culinary Arts; Education and Training; Graphic Arts and Information Technology; and Health Science.

Executives say they need a workforce fully equipped with skills beyond the basics of reading, writing and arithmetic (the "3 Rs") to grow their businesses. Skills such as critical thinking, communication, collaboration, and creativity (the "4 Cs") are becoming even more important to organizations. To flourish in a dynamic, global economy, STC believes that every student deserves an education that culminates in 21st-century readiness for college, careers, and civic participation. It recognizes that how students learn has a decided impact on what they learn. Teaching and learning environments matter. Many students learn more when schoolwork is connected to their interests, to real-world problems, and to the worlds of work. Experiences outside the classroom, variation in the school day, and the ability to use technology and other hands-on tools engage students in learning and help them discover new interests and passions. Instructional strategies that foster higher-order thinking and personalize learning to meet students' specific needs are critical as well. Confining education to traditional classrooms severely constrains both the opportunities and time for learning.

Sheridan's e-Learning Broward began in July, 2005 when the convergence of online resources, multimedia, and digital capabilities afforded educational institutions such as STC the ability to alter the manner in which teaching and learning unfold. The mission of e-Learning Broward was to transform the instructional culture of workforce education. This would be accomplished through the re-engineering of curriculum delivery methods as it expanded learning opportunities for post-secondary (and selected secondary) students enrolled in career, technical, adult and community education programs and courses through an online distance learning environment.

STC offers online courses to equip students with the skills needed to be successful and stay competitive in today's job market. These courses can fit around individual student schedules, enabling them to succeed, and helping them reach their full potential. The use of an online platform to deliver training to STC students enables the school to focus on increasing student enrollment while being a landlocked school. Since there was no room to build additional "brick and mortar" buildings to house additional students, the only logical solution was to offer robust, flexible virtual courses that could fit into the busy schedules of its students.

Sheridan's Career and Technical Education (CTE) online programs enable freedom from the constraints of time and space by allowing its students to be involved in learning activities at a distance through the participation in both synchronous and asynchronous activities. Online courses offer its students opportunities for new ways of collaborative work and new ways of interactive learning activities. There are many benefits to offering the option of online and blended courses. For the students, it offers increased access to flexible scheduling of personal time, convenient locations to complete coursework, individualized attention by the instructor, less travel, and increased time to think about and respond to (via email or discussion board) questions posed by the instructor. Its online courses expand access to underserved populations; alleviate classroom capacity constraints; capitalize on emerging market opportunities, such as working adults; and serve as a catalyst for institutional transformation. Furthermore, the online courses enable students to have access to more and perhaps better learning resources than in the past. As more is understood regarding learning styles, brain-based learning, and differentiating instruction; the value of technology, including online learning, is recognized as a solution to meet the unique needs of all learners. In addition, Sheridan's online program is ideally suited to meet the needs of stakeholders calling for school choice, high school reform, and workplace preparation in 21st-century skills.

Since the rise of the popularity of online courses, more tools have been added to facilitate communication. Email, websites, chat rooms, streaming video, and web-conferencing are all incorporated into the technical center's online course delivery. Utilization of these various applications of the Internet enables the distribution of classroom materials and helps students and teachers interact with one another. Specialized software packages that provide easy access to these functions are used to facilitate these classes.

In addition to its online programs of study, STC offers online workshops for the Adult General Education students to augment and reinforce the material taught in its adult education online programs (i.e., GED, ESOL, ELCATE). Online workshops were originally launched because attendance at a series of similar face-to-face workshops was not high, regardless of location or the time they were offered. While many students expressed interest in attending these sessions, they often couldn't do so because of issues involving child care, transportation, or scheduling conflicts. Being that workshop locations and times had to be planned around existing school locations and their hours, the flexibility in workshop scheduling was also limited. Therefore, it was decided to try offering the same sessions online to broaden their reach.

In 2009, STC was recognized as an Elluminate Center of Excellence for significantly increasing attendance of live and recorded online workshops that included thousands of adult students; enabling them to improve academic skills, increase proficiency and confidence with technology, and increase the number of diplomas earned. This series of online, subject-specific adult education workshops that complement and reinforce the content provided in the adult education online courses was also recognized as a promising practice by the Florida Literacy Coalition.

Common Core State Standards and STEM (Science, Technology, Engineering, and Mathematics)

With a significant decline of college students selecting majors in the science or technology- related fields, the current outcry for the United States to become more scholastically competitive with other global nations, and the building and delivery of the new **Common Core State Standards** to help achieve this for our students, STEM programs can help train our students for the jobs being created in the future that will require math and science skills. STEM is the acronym that stands for Science, Technology, Engineering, and Mathematics; and the innovative programs that are being implemented are designed to support digital solidarity in our country. In 2009, the Obama Administration launched the Educate to Innovate campaign designed to improve both the participation and performance of our nation's students in STEM courses. Involved in this campaign is the Federal Government and leading companies, foundations, nonprofits, and science and engineering societies working together to help students excel in math and science. The goals of this program are to: (a) increase STEM literacy enabling all students to learn deeply and think critically in science, math, engineering, and technology, (b) move American students to the top of the global scholastic chart within the next decade, and (c) offer STEM education and career opportunities to underrepresented groups including women and girls. As part of the Educate to Innovate campaign, a non-profit, CEO-led organization called Change the Equation has been launched as an effort to mobilize the business community to improve STEM education in America (The White House, 2012). The STEM approach to education changes the way that mathematics and science are being taught by incorporating both technology and engineering into the curricula. In addition, STEM education is attempting to transform the traditional teacher-centered classroom by delivering content and developing skills through a problem-solving instructional design. By incorporating a STEM philosophy, science, engineering and mathematics are made complete by integrating the technology component in creative and innovative ways that assist students in problem-solving and applying what they have learned.

One such innovative program can be found in Memphis City Schools where the STEM Virtual High School was built. Recognizing that by 2020 our economy will require 15 million new engineering and technical jobs, this STEM virtual experience provides "all students, including often underrepresented minorities and female students, the opportunity to compete for these jobs locally, nationally, and globally" (Council of the Great City Schools, 2012, March, p.5). The virtual school offers students self-paced online assignments, on-site individual and group activities, and real-world application of material being taught. The way the program is designed, the first cohort of 70 students start with an initial course in the principles of engineering and if they maintain a "B" average, they are allowed to continue with the program. Students participate through a co-enrolled status where they do their lab studies and STEM content virtually and participate in other coursework such as art, humanities, physical education, and competitive sports at their home school. Students are expected to participate in weekly labs, summer programs, and internships. There is no fee to attend the STEM Virtual High School, but there is an admission's process which includes identifying student and parent interest, test scores, grade point averages, and interviews. If satisfactorily completed, the student is invited to enroll in the school. Funding for the STEM Virtual High School comes from the state, as well as federal Race to the Top dollars.

The current challenge is to spotlight high-quality STEM programs and scale up those efforts for underserved communities. To properly prepare students for the increasing number of future STEM jobs "high quality programs are needed to increase STEM literacy for underrepresented groups, including female and minority students" (Mohan, 2012, para. 2). It is imperative that all students have an understanding of scientific and mathematical principles, a working knowledge of computer hardware and software, and the problem-solving skills developed by STEM courses. Therefore, STEM education is an enormous and pressing national need (STEM Education Caucus, n.d.).

Afterschool Programs

Educators have found that the more time students spend learning, the more they achieve and excel. Parents have discovered the importance of keeping their children motivated to learn outside of the classroom. One of the ways to address ongoing learning beyond the classroom is through afterschool programs. Afterschool programs can provide acceleration (going above grade-level studies) and enrichment (going more indepth into on-grade-level studies) for students who are ready for those educational options. For many students who need tutoring to reinforce concepts and skills learned in day school or remediate skills that have not been learned thoroughly, afterschool programs provide a viable solution. If the afterschool program is designed to address the technological needs of a specific population, such as students from rural poverty areas, underserved populations, students whose native language is not English, gender-specific students, or students with learning disabilities, then it becomes a venue for nurturing digital solidarity.

A Sampling of Afterschool Technology-enhanced Programs for Special Populations

In 2007, the Afterschool Alliance reported that afterschool funding under the 21st Century Community Learning Centers federal grants program is less likely to happen for rural students than for their urban or suburban counterparts. High illiteracy rates, lack of transportation, and at-risk behaviors, including attempted suicide and alcoholism in rural communities, add to the challenge of involving rural students in afterschool experiences. However, afterschool programs can provide the necessary instructional support for students to meet grade-level expectations and specific emphasis on teaching the latest technologies can improve the specialized skills needed to compete in a global workforce. The availability of programs in rural areas is also an issue, but partnering with the business sector, such as the MetLife Foundation, the Bill and Melinda Gates Foundation, the Annenberg Foundation, and the Wallace Foundation has proven to be a successful venture.

The Community Access to Technology (CAT) Program (http://cat.slco.org/), funded by the Bill and Melinda Gates Foundation, has provided greater access to digital technology for four rural communities in the state of Washington. Findings from this multi-year project indicated the positive impact of technology as a learning tool for low-income, rural populations. This program has been redesigned to expand technology access to underserved populations in Washington State, including at-risk youth, persons with disabilities, homeless persons, immigration populations, Native Americans as well as rural areas to improve lives and communities (MGS Consulting, 2008).

The Computer Clubhouse Network™ (http://www.intel.com/content/www/us/en/education/computer-clubhouse-network.html), sponsored by Intel and MIT Media Lab, has been designed for underserved populations and brings together, through the use of state-of-the-art technology, groups of youth to think about and apply new technologies to enhance their learning. The network has expanded to 15 countries, providing a virtual clubhouse to network participants and the use of the **Intranet** to facilitate the interchange of language other than English. Although there have been some challenges, the network shows how innovation can spawn creative and productive solutions to problems.

In New York City there are afterschool programs designed specifically for homeless children. With almost half of the children suffering from social anxiety disorders and lack of constancy due to life in a homeless shelter, Bound for Success Afterschool Program (http://www.coalitionforthehomeless.org/programs/bound-for-success) offers the stability that is needed as well as opportunities for educational and social development. In addition to individual tutoring and homework assistance, students are engaged in innovative computer programs.

Digital WAVE (http://www.miamisci.org/~digiwave/), sponsored by Miami's Science Museum and the National Science Foundation, is a technology-based afterschool program for high school students. Seventy-five percent of enrollees in Digital WAVE are non-English native speakers and 100 percent of the participants are on free or reduced lunch programs in their day schools. In addition to learning about digital technologies and related careers, the students use computers to create 3D models. A survey of enrollees indicated that 77 percent planned to major in science or technology fields in college as a result of their participation in the program (Afterschool Alliance, 2011).

Foundations Inc.'s Center for Afterschool and Expanded Learning (http://www.foundationsinc.org/expanded-learning) has assisted school districts with professional development, technology assistance, and program design to create innovative afterschool, summer, and extended learning opportunities for children and youth. The Center has developed programs and materials, including digital games, to support English Language Learners (ELLs) in informal afterschool settings. It has also developed enrichment activities for afterschool learners that lets them explore and apply technology to real world experiences.

Build IT (Koch, Gorges, & Penuel, 2012, Fall) is an afterschool and summer program designed for middle school girls to develop their fluency in technology and increase their knowledge of careers in technology for women. Educational researchers and practitioners have worked together to formulate an afterschool program model that has successfully focused on improving girls' attitudes towards technology and strengthening their technology fluency.

A variation of this program is Project IT Girl that has been designed in Austin, Texas for female middle school students, 93 percent of whom are African-American and Hispanic and 91 percent of whom are eligible for free or reduced lunch. The afterschool activities have resulted in the participants' increased knowledge in web design as well as improved teamwork and communication skills (Afterschool Alliance, 2011).

In Oakland, California, TechBridge is an afterschool program that has been designed for girls in grades 5 through 12. Activities are focused on the girls visiting tech companies and using new computer programs. The students learn to use teamwork for problem-solving and gain skills in using varied technologies (Afterschool Alliance, 2011). For elementary-aged students, the afterschool TECHie Club was developed so that participants could learn about and use digital media tools so that they could become more confident in knowing how computers work and increase their interest in computer careers (Afterschool Alliance, 2011).

Case Studies for Afterschool Programs

Luis is a 14-year-old native of El Salvador who is at high risk for dropping out of school before he graduates. He wants to go to college, become a productive citizen, and aspires to becoming a doctor. To attain these goals, Luis spends several days a week in an afterschool program at a local magnet high school involved in computer-related activities, college-preparedness skills, and homework help. In addition to facing the transition challenge from country to country and culture to culture, Luis faces the challenge of not reading on grade level in both his native language of Spanish, as well as in English. Financed by the Kellogg Foundation and sponsored by the Hispanic Apostolate of Catholic Charities, the afterschool program focuses on teens like Luis who are from families where there has been little or no formal education and college is not an option from a financial standpoint. For Luis, this afterschool experience has given him more confidence about his schoolwork as well as more As and Bs on his report card (Bronston, 2009, November 22).

Trenton is a high school student with dual exceptionalities; he is gifted and he is disabled. He has not let his disabilities prevent him from succeeding in his schoolwork. As a participant in the Sarasota High School/High Tech Program, funded by The Able Trust (http://www.abletrust.org/planned_giving/impact/foundation.shtml), Trenton works closely with program staff members who understand his special needs and help him to excel in his high school studies and prepare for the transition to college where he plans to major in the fields of science and technology. With the aid of adaptive and assistive technology tools, Trenton has achieved self-confidence and academic excellence (Afterschool Alliance, 2004).

When he was a baby, Luigi was involved in a serious car accident that left him with visible scars and his coordination skills severely damaged. As he continued through school, he had problems keeping up with his lessons and homework; he also disrupted class frequently and was often teased by his classmates. The afterschool program, LA's BEST (Better Educated Students for Tomorrow) was his mother's solution to the problem. At LA's BEST, Luigi learned to use every computer program at the center, to read fluently in Spanish and English, and to dance Ballet Folklorico for a community performance. Luigi has gained confidence and the respect of his classmates and has become a risk-taker for new adventures (LA's BEST, 2012).

For two years, Shakira has been living in homeless shelters with her mom. Like any seven-year-old, Shakira enjoys drawing and new challenging experiences, like using a computer. However, Shakira is shy, withdrawn, and anxious, as are many homeless children. To "draw her out of her shell," homeless shelter personnel recommended that Shakira's mom enroll her in an afterschool program at the shelter. One of the first important lessons that Shakira learned in the afterschool program was to finish her homework before participating in computer activities and art. As a result of her involvement in using computers, Shakira has learned the importance of good work habits and on-task behaviors. She is finally realizing her potential for success and life is looking more positive to her.

Afterschool Videoconferencing Teacher

I am a videoconference instructor for one of the largest school districts in the United States. My job is to teach weekly classes through video-conferencing to students enrolled in afterschool programs. Most of these programs are delivered to underserved populations who are struggling with their schoolwork. My classes offer remediation in basic skills taught through the arts. Teachers and daycare workers guide the students in responding to the class activities. These activities range from answering questions to sharing their drawings or performing simple folk dances. I try to make learning fun!

I remember one afterschool teacher who loved the arts integration in my classes, so she followed up throughout the week with supplemental books, music, and art projects. Her students always had amazing things to present during our sharing time. Another teacher who taught special needs students said her students always looked forward to the videoconference classes. The students loved to participate and interact with children in the other schools. Many other teachers felt that it was a good idea to have something special for their students to do in the afterschool program and the video-conference class was not only connected to the curriculum but lots of fun, too!

Afterschool Programs Designed for Students with Disabilities

In addition to providing an array of social benefits to disabled students, partici-pation in afterschool programs benefits their academic needs. The Children's Aid Society (http://www.childrensaidsociety.org/) and Boys and Girls Clubs of America (http://bgca.org/Pages/index.aspx) address disabled children's and teens' developmental needs through a variety of afterschool programs, including the operation of technology centers. In Harlem, Club Tech and Intel Computer Clubhouse™ "bridge the digital divide" by providing computer access to children, including the disabled, who may not have home computers or Internet access. The Club Tech program (http://www.bgca.org/whatwedo/Specialized Programs/Pages/ClubTechDAF.aspx) offers experiences with web and graphic design, digital film editing, and digital music composition. In addition to emphasizing the application of technical skills, Club Tech nurtures critical thinking, project management, and problem-solving skills. For teens, Club Tech has created The Instructional Zone where youth learn technology fundamentals and The Exploratory Zone where teens work on teams using advanced skills to become experts in using technologies (The Children's Aid Society, n.d.). At the Intel Computer Clubhouse (http://www.computerclub house.org/) sponsored by Boston's Museum of Science, teens learn to use technology tools to express themselves through a variety of media, including digital music production, video editing, and three-dimensional modeling. Working with professionals and student mentors, the teens use advanced computer technologies to inspire and motivate themselves and others (Intel Computer Clubhouse Network™, 2013).

LA's BEST afterschool program (http://www.lasbest.org/) for both abled and disabled children has designed KidTech as an eight-week computer basics program in which students create documents, edit photos, conduct Internet research, and give presentations. After completing the program, students are given refurbished desktop computers to take home. A culminating workshop for the students and their parents focuses on how to set up, manage, and use the free computer.

Florida High School High Tech (http://www.abletrust.org/hsht/), funded by The Able Trust, is designed for teens with all types of disabilities. The program focuses on post-secondary education leading to careers in technology-related fields. With 36 projects across the state of Florida, the program has increased the self-esteem of its disabled participants and has decreased the high school dropout rate. At the post-secondary level, programs like Disabilities, Opportunities, Internetworking, and Technology (DO-IT) Center at the University of Washington use technology to create successful experiences for students with learning and other disabilities. This international program provides access to the web for individuals with disabilities, access to distance learning opportunities for individuals with disabilities, as well as information on adaptive and assistive technologies available to individuals with disabilities. The DO-IT Center also has a teen component that seeks out high school sophomores with disabilities to help prepare them for college that includes a summer program on the University of Washington's Seattle campus. DO-IT connects these teens and post-secondary students with each other and adult mentors year-round, using computers, assistive technology, email, and social media. The DO-IT Center is funded by the National Science Foundation, the U.S. Department of Education, the State of Washington, and many other sources (DO-IT Center, University of Washington, 2013).

Assistive and Adaptive Technologies for Students with Disabilities

In order to participate in afterschool computer-based programs, students with disabilities need adaptive and assisted technologies. These technologies provide the tools for disabled individuals to compensate for their disability so that they can demonstrate their level of intelligence and conceptual understanding. Finding appropriate adaptive and assistive technologies for individual disabilities may require some trial and error testing, but ultimately the selected technologies should enable the disabled person to participate actively in computer-based learning experiences (National Center for Technology Innovation and Center for Implementing Technology in Education, 2006). For individuals with dyslexia, a language-based processing disorder that can hinder reading, writing, spelling, and sometimes speaking (National Center for Learning Disabilities, 2012), a word-processing program that includes a spell checker and grammar checker and color-coded text options may prove to be a low-priced tool solution. In addition, tools such as an mp3 player for audiobooks (like Playaway that can be checked out from a public library, or a computer with Windows Media Player), audiotextbooks from Learning Ally (https://learningally.org) for the blind and dyslexic, text readers and scanners (Intel Reader, Kurzweil's Universal Design for Learning tool) and talking devices, (such as Livescribe's WiFi smartpen, Franklin's talking spell checker, and Fusion Writer Learning's talking keyboard) can provide the necessary individual accommodation for learning. For individuals with dysgraphia who have problems with spelling, poor writing, and putting thoughts on paper, devices such as the Franklin Electronic Dictionary and portable spelling PDAs assist people with dysgraphia and dyslexia by spelling words phonetically. Integrated software, such as Kurzweil's 3000-firefly, provides a digital environment for dysgraphic students' note-taking, essay-writing, and test-taking.

For individuals with a wide range of learning disabilities, speech recognition products provide the ideal solution. Such products include: Window's Speech Recognition, Nuance's Dragon Naturally Speaking (both can be checked out from the library), and Sensory Inc.'s embedded speech technologies for various consumer products. Individuals with dyscalculia have difficulty in understanding and interpreting mathematical concepts and symbols. For them, large key or talking calculators provide input assistance. They also may be a solution for low-vision or blind individuals working on math problems (e.g., Freedom Scientific's Braille 'n Speak). Electronic math processing software, such as Intel's Math Pad and Math Pad Plus can assist individuals with basic math functions and Microsoft's Equation Editor and Design Science's Math Type can be used for higher-level math operations. Individuals with dyslexia or non-verbal learning disorders may need specific compensatory tool assistance with organization and management skills. Accommodations can be made for these individuals with Personal Information Managers (PIMs). Free online plug-ins are available from Plaxo Contacts (http://www.plaxo.com/) and Google Calendar (http://www.google.com/calendar). EssentialPIM is a free download for Windows (http://essentialpim.com/) and freeware is available for PIMs at http://www.freedownloadcenter.com/Information_Management/Personal_Information_Managers/index3.html. Matchware Education developed Mindview, a software that enhances disabled students' ability to visualize, organize, and present, and is based on the principles of mind-mapping and includes templates, timeline activities, and project management. Students with disabilities can use screen readers to research Internet topics and participate in Internet scavenger hunts and Webquest activities that provide disabled learners opportunities to use innovative assistive technology devices.

Online Tutoring Programs

What better way is there to keep active preschoolers engaged in learning than through an online educational experience? Since computers have "endless patience," interactive, online learning activities can provide the challenge and stimulation that young minds need and want. For grade school children, online tutoring, like afterschool programs, can provide enrichment as well as remediation experiences. For some teens, whose lack of academic progress places their ultimate graduation from high school in jeopardy, online instructional programs provide an alternative to attending summer school classes. Online tutoring in particular subjects, such as English 101 and Math 101, are also popular with undergraduate students who are trying to maintain a passing grade point average or avoid academic probation in college. Senior citizens have also utilized online tutoring options to provide them with the necessary skills for pursuing second-career-choice jobs after first-career-choice retirement. Also, seniors looking for lifelong learning opportunities find online tutoring to provide the ideal optional experience. Whatever the age level or educational goal, afterschool and tutoring online options provide individually paced, sequentially designed programs that meet the personal needs of most learners. Also, since today the issue of safety in schools is a priority for parents, online instructional opportunities have a particular magnet effect.

Sampling of Online Tutoring Programs

One online program for the littlest elearners can be found at Time4Learning (http://www.time4learning.com/preschool-games.shtml), which uses a combination of technology, games, animation, fun, and music to "inspire" preschoolers' love of learning. Through developmentally appropriate, thematic curriculum, preschoolers learn important skills in emergent literacy and numeracy. In addition, by participating in an online learning experience, preschoolers learn how to respond to simple auditory directions and interact with the computer by using interface buttons. Most importantly, the programs are designed for children with minimal attention spans, minimal vocabulary development, and minimal fine motor control skills. As educators know, these are essential components for educational programs for students with special needs. In addition to learning basic concepts about the alphabet, colors, shapes, numbers, patterns, etc., preschoolers are exposed to lessons on feelings, manners, self-awareness, and staying fit while learning skills such as memorizing, ordering, matching, locating, planning, measuring, counting, and creating. It should be mentioned that Time4Learning is also designed for homeschool students and summer school students at the elementary and middle school levels.

Another online option for parents of preschoolers is the creation of their own homeschool program. Cullen's Abcs (http://online-preschool.cullensabcs. com/) provides a series of video-based learning activities that are correlated with preschool curriculum. The attraction to this online experience is that it is offered for free to parents who want to get their child ready for school. This program also includes a religious component for those parents who seek a Christian focus in their preschool child's early education.

For elementary, middle, and high school students, there are a number of online sites that charge fees for access to tutoring activities, such as SmartTutor Education Programs (http://www.smarttutor.com), but there are some free resources that are made available to parents and educators. It is just a matter of looking for the "freebies." For example, SmartTutor provides free educational games, sample math and reading lessons, printable flashcards and stories for children to read.

At Teacher's Café (http://www.theteacherscafe.com/Teacher-Directory/Free-Reading-Activities.htm), parents, teachers, and students can find Story Online, which provides free stories on streaming video read by members of the Screen Actors Guild with lessons and activities designed to get children excited about reading. Similarly, Starfall is provided as a free learn-to-read through phonics and phonemic awareness website, although there are low-cost fees for some online activities. Parents and educators can access free online tutoring, practice, and games. Starfall was specifically designed for primary-aged children (kindergarten to grade 2) as well as children with special needs and English-language Learners (**ELL, ESL, ELD**). The Starfall research-based, field-tested curriculum is aligned with the Common Core State Standards. Also, found at the Teacher's Café (http://www.theteacherscafe.com/Teacher-Directory/Free-Math-Activities.htm) for students who are "bored with, confused by or hate" math, there is Cool Math (kindergarten through grade 12) that includes math lessons and practice for geometry, pre-algebra/algebra, and pre-calculus/calculus in addition to math games, puzzles, and online calculators. Math Cats provides online opportunities for students to explore the World of Mathematics through thought-provoking mathematically related questions, discovery problems, and real-world math applications. For children who need online basic math facts practice, there is Kids Numbers that includes a free worksheet generator. Finally, for kids who generate their own math questions, and enjoy interacting with a mentor/expert-in-the-field, there is Drexel University's Math Forum and Ask Dr. Math.

Last, e-Learning for Kids (http://www.e-learningforkids.org/aboutus.html) is a global, non-profit foundation providing free learning on the Internet for children ages five through 12. This site provides courses in math, science, and reading.

Sampling of Afterschool and Tutoring Online Programs for Special Populations

Gender-specific: Girls

For gender-specific programs, The Girls Initiative Network (http://www.girls initiativenetwork.org/onlinelearning.html) is designed for girls from diverse cultural, social, and economic backgrounds. In addition to offering a variety of tutorials, educational games, and virtual libraries, The Girls Initiative Network provides online learning tools, including online forums, live chat sessions, webinars, and interactive blogs to connect girls from around the world in educational discussions and collaborations.

Low-income

A free online math tutor is available at http://aimiuwu.com/algebra/index.htm for low-income students from elementary school to college and focuses on providing tutorial assistance with grade school math, geometry, algebra, and trigonometry. The tutors also provide help to pre-college/college students, especially single mothers, preparing for college-admission exams such as the SAT, ACT, GRE, and GMAT.

Seniors

Free Computer Internet Tutoring (http://www.computerinternettutoring. com/) specializes in helping seniors learn how to navigate the Internet as well as learn about terms like browser and acronyms like FTP, HTTP, HTML, URL, and IP. Meganga (http://www.meganga.com) also offers free, online computer lessons for seniors and beginners, using Microsoft Office Word and Excel. The program combines the use of online tutorials and videos. For free classes and courses, the Goodwill Community Foundation (GCF) offers more than 750 lessons to seniors as well as an opportunity to learn on your own time at your own pace. Although it is a blog or forum for sharing learning experiences, Get Seniors Online (http://www.getseniorsonline.org/2011/07/why-did-we-create-this-website-and-blog/) is an innovative effort to "bridge the divide" between seniors who are online and those that are not, particularly seniors who are residents of government-assisted (Housing and Urban Development) public housing.

Senior Case Study

I am 88 years young but confined to a nursing home. The computer is my lifeline to the outside world. The nursing home provides computers and computer training sessions for the residents. If I can't remember how to do something on the computer, there is a staff member or volunteer available to help me. Since my stroke I only have the use of one hand but I can still use the computer mouse to direct the cursor. So with just a click I can connect with my family.

My daughter lives over eight hundred miles away and she is very busy raising three daughters of her own. Although they try to visit as often as they can, I rarely see them in person more than a couple times a year. However, I can use the computer camera and microphone to connect with my family over Skype. It is so much fun! I actually watched my granddaughters open their Christmas presents last year. These are precious memories that I cherish until I can hug them in my arms.

Developing Online Communities

In order to develop an **online community**, it is first necessary to define it and identify its various components. An online community can be defined as a site on the Internet where learners meet virtually for the purpose of sharing information and communicating with others of similar interests and/or collaborating on projects. In his research of online community practice, Johnson (2001) defined an online community as "a group separated by space and time (i.e., geographic location and time zone). The other key concept behind virtual communities is the use of networked technologies in one form or another to collaborate and communicate" (p.52). The "networked technologies" include chat rooms, instant messaging, electronic mailing lists, and discussion systems, such as Usenet, Weblogs, and forums.

Online communities have been developed for business, society, and education. In the business sector, the HSBC Business Network and Bank of America's Small Business Community are examples of online communities that provide business/financial advice and opportunities for networking to both global and local customers and non-customers. In such communities, business/financial expertise is intermingled with non-expert peer advice. In the retail industry, Walmart's Elevenmoms is an online community based on a simple idea, moms blogging about money-saving ideas. Customers having input in the business was another simple idea that was the basis for creating Starbuck's online community, MyStarbucksidea, which began in 2008 (Rhodes, 2009, February 23). In the telecommunications industry, Sprint's Buzz About Wireless addresses customer service issues in an online community forum, while T-Mobile's Sidekick Wiki uses the wiki format so that customers can exchange ideas and tips about T-Mobile products (Rhodes, 2009, March 24). The Mayo Clinic's online community that uses simple tools, such as blogs and podcasts, to engage stakeholders, is a prime example from the health care industry (Rhodes, 2009, April 8).

Social networking sites, such as Facebook, Twitter, and MySpace, are examples of societal online communities. Initially limited by founders Mark Zuckerberg and his college roommates to Harvard students and then expanded to students at other colleges and eventually high school students, Facebook, as a social networking service, began in 2004 and now claims more than a billion members as participants in its online community. Twitter, another online social networking service that was created by Jack Dorsey in 2006, enables its over 500 million active users to send and read text-based messages, known as "tweets." Officially launched in 2004 as a competitive social network by eUniverse founder Brad Greenspan, MySpace uses widgets, such as YouTube, boasts having more than 125 million users, and seeks to broaden the online network under new ownership (Specific Media) and creative direction.

In education, there are prolific examples of online communities sponsored by U.S. community colleges and four-year colleges and universities, such as Professional Learning Communities, designed to focus on collaborative teacher planning (Hord, 1997). The Professional Learning Communities are developed by and for public and private schools/school systems from preschool to high school, such as Learning Circles that has created virtual communities for elementary and secondary school students to exchange ideas with students in other places about various school subjects and personal beliefs (Riel, 1993). Others are created by professional associations that represent educators and researchers from a variety of disciplines, such as the National Education Association's (www.nea.org) Online Social Networking for Educators that emphasizes collaboration among America's educators. ASCD, formerly the Association for Supervision and Curriculum Development (www.ascd.org), offers Professional Interest Communities that provides a forum for participants to identify and solve collaboratively problems within the educational sector. The Council for Exceptional Children (www.cec.sped.org/) has its SharePoint Networking Community which engages educator-members in focused educational discussions, blogs, and surveys.

There are many advantages to developing online learning communities. They become the forums for supportive as well as collaborative communication. Online learning communities can be designed for any interest or any age group. They motivate learners to immerse themselves in the discussions, becoming interactive participants in the learning process. Ultimately, online learning communities provide the mechanism for learners to connect with other learners in the construction of new knowledge. The ability to access online communities, participate meaningfully in them, and derive benefits from that participation is the goal of digital solidarity.

Tools for Building Online Communities

Looking for innovative ways to use online communities to support digital solidarity means looking for readily available, low-cost or free tools for developing online communities for *all*. In order to participate in an online community, there is a need to have readily available web access. This doesn't mean just having appropriate equipment such as computers or mobile devices, but having fast, reliable equipment and the necessary computer skills to participate successfully in the online community experience. For some, it may also mean having the necessary language skills to communicate effectively with other members of the online learning community.

Hart (2011) has identified some inexpensive or free, innovative tools as pathways to creating successful online learning communities. These can be found in Table 3.1, "Tools for Creating Online Learning Communities."

Although there are a number of websites that provide invaluable information for developing and maintaining online communities, including helpful guidelines and the characteristics of successful online communities, there is one website, The Online Community Portfolio (http://buildinglearningcommunitiesol. wetpaint.com/page/Useful+Tools), that encourages its community members to post and evaluate information about online tools that can be helpful in developing online communities and addressing the specific needs of community members. Among this list found in Table 3.2, "Free Tools for Online Learning Sites," are resources that educators can use in their development of online learning communities.

Skills in Building Online Communities

From an administrative or managerial perspective in building online communities, there are a number of skills needed to successfully maintain an online

Table 3.1 Tools for Creating Online Learning Communities

Tool and examples	Description
Social Learning Platforms Sophia (http://www.sophia.org)	Sponsored by Capella University, provides multiple tutorials for different learning concepts
Social Networking Sites Ning (http://www.ning.com/)	An online platform for people to create their own social networks
Edmodo (http://www.edmodo.com)	Designed for teachers and students to share ideas, files, events and assignments
Facebook (https://www.facebook.com)	Free, easy to use and well-known to millions of learners
Course Management Systems Moodle (https://moodle.org/)	Free application for educators in creating online learning communities
Wikis Wikispaces (http://www.wikispaces.com/)	Designed for free educational use for teachers and students to collaborate and share resources
Blogs Edublogs (http://edublogs.org/)	Facilitate discussions, blog postings, podcasts, and class publications

Table 3.2 Free Tools for Online Learning Sites

Tool	Description
ANVILL (https://anvill.uoregon.edu/anvill2/frontpage)	National Virtual Language Lab, developed by the University of Oregon, allows teachers to record and place audio files in a lesson; a free, open source site for language teachers and language learners
Audacity (http://audacity.sourceforge.net/)	Free, open source software for recording and editing sounds
Geogebra (http://www.geogebra.org/cms/)	Free mathematics software for all educational levels
Google Suite (http://google.com)	Includes Google Docs (word processing, spreadsheets, presentations), Google Sites (creating web sites), Google Calendar, and Google Talk (chat) that can be used for student group collaborative projects
KompoZer (http://www.kompozer.net/)	A free HTML editor for creating HTML files for course content
Open Office Suite (http://www.openoffice.org/)	Designed for students to collaborate on projects
PodOmatic (http://www.podomatic.com/login)	Free account for creating podcasts
Sound Cloud (http://soundcloud.com/)	Captures voices, music, or sounds that can be embedded into online content; great tool for ESL, foreign language, and Music teachers
Survey Monkey (http://www.surveymonkey.com/)	Creates surveys to solicit student feedback and collect data
Tooble (http://tooble.tv/)	Free download that converts videos (from YouTube) into portable movie files
Zamzar (http://www.zamzar.com/)	Free, online file conversion

learning community. These include the management of the online community's projects, organizing events that successfully engage members of the community, and creating effective management processes that assist in maintaining and enlarging the online community. In his *Online Community Manifesto* (http://richchallenge.typepad.com/files/communitybuildingmanifesto-1.pdf), author and consultant Richard Millington stated that building online communities "requires the skill of motivating and bonding human beings like ourselves" (n.d., p.2). His point was that developers of online communities tend to know too much about technology and not so much about human nature which is an important element in creating online community membership. Millington asserted that knowing about human motivation, group interaction, and how humans react to certain influences plays a significant role in nurturing online community membership and experiencing ongoing success. Having effective people skills, as well as clear communication skills, creative problem-solving skills, flexible conflict resolution skills, and reasonable negotiating skills appear to be important skillsets for successful, online community managers. Similarly, Volkman (2012) noted that it is important to understand why people choose to participate in online communities by asking "why they are there and what needs it fulfills" (para. 2).

From the online community member's or learner's perspective, there are an increasing number of skills needed to participate successfully in the online community experience and this is where the digital inclusion becomes all too evident. Just as in any learning community, some learners have basic skills and other learners possess advanced skills. For online community learners, basic skills might include the ability to communicate with others in a mutually agreed-upon language, some level of proficiency in using a variety of technological skills, and the ability to utilize various tools for online community navigation.

Depending on the age, level of cognitive development, training, and/or background of experiences of the learner, the basic skills may be further subdivided into pre-basic skills, including computer skills (ability to do word processing, open a program, use menus, copy, cut and paste, save, open, move, and delete files); electronic communication skills (ability to send and receive email messages, post and respond to messages on a discussion board or blog); and Internet skills (ability to connect with the Internet, accurately enter a URL, search the Internet, download and save a file from the Internet). More advanced skills for this group of learners may include the ability to create webpages or websites, create discussion boards, blogs, wikis, listservs, and demonstrate the ability to integrate animation, audio, and video in their online as well as offline experiences.

In their case study of online communities of practice, Carvajal, Mayorga, and Douthwaite (2008) identified as significant the need for online community participants to "begin to share, listen to others, show interest in the discussions, and debate ideas and concepts" (p.78). Even though their study was conducted among participants from some third-world nations, it is important to understand that some of their findings are relevant to some populations in the United States. These include participants who are deficient in communication skills, who do not possess a wide range of experiences in understanding and using virtual tools, and involve seniors as participants who prefer "face-to-face communications and meetings, instead of virtual encounters" (p.76). So using innovative, online communities for a variety of learners with differing levels of proficiency and deficiency requires training on how to effectively participate in the community. This training, and subsequent development of the skills necessary to derive the benefits from participation in an online community, clearly aligns with the goals of the digital solidarity movement.

Online Communities in Higher Education

The concept of online communities in higher education institutions began in the 1980s and the practice of developing different kinds of online learning communities for students in U.S. colleges and universities has been evolving ever since. A number of factors have been found by researchers to be significant in the success of students' participation in online learning communities, including a sense of connectedness, trust, and rapport (Chapman, Radmondt, & Smiley, 2005; Veseley, Bloom, & Sherlock, 2007) and an indepth level of student interaction (DiRaimo & Wolverton, 2006). Rovai's Classroom Community Scale (2002) has incorporated many of these factors in analyzing the successful elements of online learning communities in higher education.

Recently, there has been an emergence of novel ways to support online learning communities at the post-secondary level, including blended courses (a combination of face-to-face and online activities), flipped classroom formats (using lecture videos from other institutions combined with the home institution's class discussions and research collaborations), and the blossoming of massive open online courses (MOOCs) through Ivy League (Harvard) and other prestigious research institutions of higher education (Stanford, MIT, University of California, Berkeley). The MOOC concept has created a mechanism for expanding online learning communities to low-income populations in the U.S. and around the world by allowing indefinite numbers of participants to take online courses without paying fees. The MOOC concept, as it currently functions, is an important link in the chain that enables digital solidarity.

The Associated Press (2013) reported that students who participate in MOOCs may be able to receive college credit. At the time this book was going to press, the American Council on Education was recommending degree credit for five entry-level courses offered by Coursera (Algebra, and Pre-Calculus from the University of California, Irvine; Introduction to Genetics and Evolution, and Bioelectricity: A Quantitative Approach from Duke University; and Calculus: Single Variable from the University of Pennsylvania). This is seen as an important step in determining the long-term potential for MOOCs both nationally and internationally. The article posited that "allowing students to get credit for the massive online courses could help make it easier to earn a college degree" (para. 6). The article indicated that this would all be possible so long as there were mechanisms in place that could assess and ensure quality. If that could be obtained then offering college credit for participating in MOOCs is "one more way that students can receive an education at an affordable cost" (para. 7). The courses themselves are offered for free, but students who want college credit need to pay between $100–$190 to "verify their identities, take exams monitored by webcams and receive transcripts with the council's credit recommendations" (para. 9). Coursera currently offers more than 200 open courses and is hoping to get the council's recommendation to offer more classes in the future.

Innovation in Online Communities in the United States

In U.S. education, online communities are supported financially and nurtured at the federal level through the U.S. Department of Education (DOE). Through the DOE's Connected Educators website (connectededucators.org), designed to strengthen the connection between online communities in education and its Connected Online Communities of Practice (COCP) Project (connected educators.org/about/), online participants can join the Education Online Community Managers Network, add to the Online Community Directory, and conduct and report on research design experiments and case studies that will ultimately result in "improving teacher and leader effectiveness and enhance student learning" (COCP, para. 2). Emphasizing the value of peer-to-peer professional learning among educators, the U.S. Department of Education has been investing and supporting "communities of practice," a term coined by Wenger (2006) and defined as "groups of people who share a concern or a passion for something they do and learn how to do it better as they interact regularly" (para. 4). Ultimately, the Connected Online Communities of Practice project will provide the mechanism for researchers, policy-makers, and practitioners to address educational reform at a faster pace. Real-time resources will be provided to educators across various disciplines for facilitating approaches to collaboration, knowledge-sharing and solving problems related to schools (Tackett & Cator, 2011). In identifying these federally funded exemplary projects as potential avenues for leading to digital solidarity, we must recognize that one of our greatest educational challenges is determining how to bring these successful innovations to scale thereby including new participants in additional locations (Kahn, 1999). To add to Kahn's statement, it is also critical to ensure that the new participants include those who have been unable to participate in online learning experiences because of age, lack of skills, lack of training, or limited background of experiences due to linguistic, cultural, racial, economic differences, or cognitive disabilities. Kahn (1999) has identified new basic skills that are needed by online community developers in creating effective online learning communities of knowledge:

- social networking skills
- conceptual skills
- simulation/modeling skills
- creative skills
- researching skills
- process- and project-management skills
- reflection skills.

Although these skills are taught at various educational levels and at various levels of intensity, there needs to be a greater value placed on their becoming an integral part of every learner's cognitive domain. "Because human talent is ultimately our most important resource, finding key people (through online learning communities) that have the right kinds of ideas, talents, or resources you need just at the right time is a huge challenge" (Kahn, 1999, para. 18). In Table 3.3 there are examples of some thriving, innovative online learning communities that are designed to address the special needs and interests of participants.

Just as Kahn (1999) identified basic skills for online community developers, Harris (2001, May) discussed how to use online collaboration tools in new and exciting ways with learners and make the online experience not only innovative, but worth the learners' time and effort. Also, she identified important higher-level thinking skills that need to be emphasized with learners in the online community experiences relating to the general curriculum as well as specific areas of research. These include:

- understanding multiple points of view, perspectives, beliefs, interpretations, and/or experiences
- comparing, contrasting, and/or combining similar information collected in dissimilar locations
- communicating with a real audience using written language
- expanding global awareness
- accessing information not available locally
- viewing information in multiple formats (e.g., text, graphics, video)
- comparing and contrasting differing information on the same topic
- considering emerging and very recent information (e.g., interim reports of research studies in progress)
- delving deeply into a particular area of inquiry (para. 24; para. 25).

As educational institutions in the United States (public/private, home schools at the pre-kindergarten to grade 12 level or public/private universities and colleges) develop more online learning communities, these should become the basic skills for all online learners. By providing the necessary skills to our youngest learners to become active, successful participants in innovative, virtual online experiences, we ensure their successful experiences as adult participants in yet-to-be-created online opportunities.

Case Studies

Virtual School Parent of Children with Exceptionalities

I am the mother of ten-year-old twins who both qualify for special programs in the public school. My daughter, Michelle, is a highly gifted student

Table 3.3 Innovative Online Learning Communities

Learning Community	Special Population
The Art, Science and Technology of Design Learning Environment for the 21st Century (http://www.csmh.org/about/lib/WhatIsPBL.html)	Elementary students in a low socio-economic community in San Jose, CA
Ohio State University's Online Community for Adolescent Bereavement (http://digitalunion.osu.edu/r2/summer08/agibson/index.html)	Grieving adolescents
Storybook Online Community (http://www.storybookonline.net)	Pre-schoolers
Scholastic's Community Club (http://teacher.scholastic.com/commclub)	Primary-aged students (K-3)
Gifted Haven Online Community (giftedhaven.net)	Gifted students
VetKids Online Community (http:// (vetkids.com)	Children of veterans
Senior Online Community (http://Senior.com)	Senior citizens
SeniorNet Online Community (http://SeniorNet.com)	Senior citizens
AARP Online Community (http://www.aarp.org/online_community/)	Senior citizens
MySpaceLatino (http://latino.myspace.com)	Latinos/Latinas
Migente Online Community (http://www.migente.com)	Latinos/Latinas
Native Web Online Community (http://nativeweb.org)	Indigenous people
Native Americans Online (http://native-americans-online.com/index.html)	Native Americans
Powwows.com Online Community (http://www.powwows.com)	Native Americans
Online Rural Community of Practice (http://www.schoolturnaroundsupport.org)	Rural Educators
Disabled Online Community (http://disabledonline.com)	Disabled individuals
Interactive Autism Network (http://www.ianproject.org)	Individuals with autism
Disabled World Online Community (http://community.disabled-world.com/)	Disabled individuals
Kid's Cancer Corner Online Community (http://yoursphere.com/KidsCancerCorner_UCDavis)	Children with cancer
TuDiabetes (http://www.tudiabetes.org)	Individuals with diabetes
Centerstone Online Community (http://www.centerstone.org)	Individuals that live in rural areas and have mental illness and/or addictions
JoinMyVillage (http://joinmyvillage.com)	Females

who made a perfect score on the third grade state assessment tests. While in a traditional classroom Michelle finished her work early and would resort to reading the dictionary to occupy her time and mind. She was successful but not challenged. My son, Michael, is a high-functioning autistic student who was enrolled in an Exceptional Student Education (ESE) program. In his traditional school Michael received one hour a week of intervention in a small group setting. While in the classroom Michael didn't disturb other students, but was often left alone to just sleep in class. Michael eventually fell below grade level in most of his subjects.

After researching all the public educational options provided locally, I decided to enroll both of the twins in an online elementary school. The virtual school option permitted customization of curriculum to meet each of my children's needs. Michelle was able to take advanced history and math courses. She had ample opportunities to explore history, literature, and art history in depth. Michael quickly mastered the virtual school technology and became actively involved in weekly eclass discussions. In one year, Michael was able to reach grade level or above in all his subjects. He still struggles with self-esteem but is much improved over the previous year spent in a traditional classroom. The personalized curriculum provided by the online school gave my children an opportunity to move through the curriculum at their own pace so I have decided to let them remain in online education at least through middle school.

Virtual School Parent of Student with Medical Problems

My daughter, Samantha, was enrolled in a traditional school for kindergarten and first grade but she missed more than half the year due to illness. Samantha continued into second grade but was under heavy medication and again missed many days of school. Third grade was her only unmedicated and uncompromised year of education but she continued to perform poorly. So I decided to place her in the virtual program provided by our school district. In this setting I was able to keep my finger on Samantha's academic pace every day. If she needed to rest she was able to do so and then continue her lessons later. Samantha has blossomed in fourth grade; in fact, she jumped into online learning without missing a beat and has performed beyond all of my expectations. Now I have a daughter who is relaxed, focused, and optimistic about all her work, which makes me a happy parent and learning coach.

Virtual School ESOL Family

When Valencia first entered my virtual school classroom her parents had difficulty communicating with me. Valencia's mother was from Uruguay and her father was from Italy. Neither spoke English fluently. Valencia was classified as an English Speaker of Other Languages (ESOL) when she entered kindergarten but was exited from the program in second grade. Upon entering third grade she had a good command of the English language. Valencia's parents owned a restaurant which meant that they had to work every night. This made it difficult for them to find time in the evening to help Valencia with her homework. So the decision was made to try the virtual school where they could work with Valencia during the day. Valencia's mother came to the virtual school eager to learn more English in order to help her daughter succeed. As the learning coach, Valencia's mother learned quickly the skills she needed to maneuver through the online instructions and create a good learning environment for her daughter. In fact, Valencia scored above average in the annual state assessments in math and reading. In the beginning, this family needed a great deal of direction but by the end of the first year, they had mastered the technology and were independent learners.

Virtual School Mother of ESE Student

I work from home taking care of my elderly father who is confined to bed. My son, Jamal, has been enrolled in Exceptional Student Education (ESE) due to speech/language and learning disabilities since he entered school. Jamal was retained twice in first grade due to low academic achievement and poor performance on district assessments. He has told me that he can't learn anything and I worry about his low self-esteem. I sought out the virtual school model for Jamal's third grade year as an intervention and an opportunity to be more involved in his education. After meeting with the virtual school personnel, Jamal was assigned remedial reading instruction from a certified reading teacher in addition to an online remedial reading program. He was also allowed to work at his own pace in a math series one year below his grade-level placement.

The online teacher worked closely with me to suggest instructional strategies I could use at home. We met in a face-to-face setting at least twice a month so Jamal could work with the reading specialist and associate with other students. I was also able to discuss Jamal's progress with his teacher. My goal was for Jamal to achieve two years' worth of growth in one year (reading and math). That didn't happen. Although Jamal's self image was much improved and he was happy to be learning at home, he did not make the academic progress I had expected.

At the end of the school year, Jamal's teacher advised that he needed a small group setting with a teacher certified to work with students who have learning disabilities. She suggested I seek out a school that offered this type of academic setting. However, we could not afford any of the private schools in the area. Then the virtual school guidance counselor worked with me to take advantage of a state scholarship offered to low-income families. After the paperwork was completed, Jamal was accepted into a school where he could have his needs met. The help and guidance I received from the virtual school helped me obtain the education I knew my son deserved.

Concluding Thoughts

In theory, everyone can participate in virtual schools and afterschool programs that emphasize the use of a variety of technologies. Assistive and adaptive technologies are available for the disabled to actively participate in these virtual schools and afterschool program offerings. As more and more students gain the necessary basic computer skills and acquire access to free or refurbished computers and the Internet, the potential for virtual schools and afterschool online programs will grow.

It is projected that online tutoring options will not only enhance their quantity and quality of offerings, but will develop highly innovative and more challenging opportunities for all levels of academic development and age groups as consumer demands for variety in online instruction increase. Similarly, as individuals and groups develop the necessary skills and utilize the free online tools for creating and maintaining online learning communities, more specialized websites will emerge as individuals seek out online support groups and share learning experiences, as well as personal successes and failures.

Chapter 4

Accommodations and Adaptations

Digital Access for All

World Perspectives on the "Haves" and "Have-nots"

The history of humans on our planet Earth has been one of struggles between the "haves" and the "have-nots." Archaeologists and cultural anthropologists have found evidence that tribes of Cro-Magnon humans, unlike tribes of Neanderthal humans, were able to hone their skills in creating tools that facilitated their successful hunting of animals for food. As the story goes, Cro-Magnon humans survived because of their ingenuity in creating effective tools and their adaptability in expanding their diets to include vegetation when meat was unavailable. Neanderthal humans did not survive because they relied solely on meat as their source of sustenance and were not as successful in creating the tools necessary for long-term survival.

Throughout Earth's history, civilizations, cultures, and countries have survived when they have created and used tools effectively and adapted their lifestyles to solve problems related to their survival. Examples of this range from the Romans who created aqueducts for accessing water, to the Native American tribes who created bows and arrows for hunting buffalo and deer as a source of food, clothing, and shelter. Even though, from today's global perspective, the "haves" and the "have-nots" are categorized as industrial nations and Third World countries, the goal is still the same: survival. For some humans, the basic necessities are still not equitably distributed; where survival means clean water to drink and sufficient food supplies. For other humans who have adapted their lifestyles so that water and food are more readily available, the issue of survival might be one of clothing and shelter for protection from the harsh elements and disasters caused by Mother Nature. Still, for other humans, who have adapted their lifestyles so that the basic necessities of life are readily available, survival means honing skills to create the appropriate tools to successfully complete "the hunt" and compete against all of the other "tribes" that populate the Earth. For most humans, the struggle for survival is related to inequities of distribution, whether that be the abundance or lack of natural resources, or events that lead to the inequitable distribution of goods, such as natural disasters, social and political uprisings, or economic collapse. Today, for some humans, honing skills for survival involves the use and application of technology, so that the "hunt" involves the effective and efficient use of technological skills to compete successfully against the "haves" as well as the "have-nots." If the technology is unavailable due to the inequitable distribution of goods, social or political uprisings or economic collapse, then the "tribe" cannot even compete in the "hunt" for digital solidarity.

The U.S. Perspective on the "Haves" and "Have-nots"

From its inception, the United States has had its own history of human struggles for survival, vying with Native Americans for natural resources, and world powers for economic, religious, and political freedom, as well as recognition. In competing as an industrial power against other "haves" around the world, the United States has developed its own unique system of "haves" and "have-nots," with individuals or groups found on the list of "Fortune 500 companies" and the "A-list," or belonging to a group labeled as "homeless" or "illiterate." Wood (2008) believed that, as a nation, we have "lost our commitment to equality—that for so long was one of the defining characteristics of American society" (p.30). Rios, Bath, Foster, Maaka, Michelli, and Urban (2009) questioned whether our nation has ever "had a full commitment to equality"(p.4), further asserting that national policies such as free, unrestrained capitalism, and global policies, such as free market reforms and war, have only exacerbated America's loss of commitment to equity and justice.

It is significant to note a distinction between equality, which provides the same options to everyone despite their needs, and equity, which provides individuals what they need to be successful from an academic, linguistic, cultural, social, or psychological perspective (Rios et al., 2009, p.5). Policy for the United States may continue to focus on being competitive with the rest of the world's "haves." Yet, such policy necessitates moving from a society mentality accepting of a digital divide that supports the concept of inequity towards one that embraces in both word and action the goal of digital solidarity. This will provide equity based on individual need, first within the United States, and then around the world.

A cursory review of the statistical data from the 2010 United States Census Briefs (Humes, Jones, & Ramirez, 2011) provided insight into the increasing racial and ethnic diversity of our nation. Noteworthy trends indicate that the non-Hispanic White alone population, although still proportionally the largest major racial and ethnic group in the United States, is growing at the slowest pace. From 2000 to 2010, it had been the Hispanic and Asian populations, supported by higher levels of immigration, which had experienced considerable growth. One significant finding in the U.S. Census data was that, in the last decade, more than 50 percent of the growth in the total population of the

United States was due to the increase in the Hispanic population. Another significant finding reported by the U.S. Census Bureau was that the Asian population experienced the fastest rate of growth among the major race groups, while the White population experienced the slowest rate of growth. Additionally, the Black or African-American population also experienced growth in the last decade, but at a slower rate than all other major racial groups, except Whites. Another trend to emerge from the latest U.S. Census focuses on persistent racial classification issues, particularly among the Hispanic population, which resulted in substantial proportions of that population being classified as "Some Other Race." (p.22). Also, another fast-growing population in the 2010 U.S. Census included people reporting origins in more than one race, particularly among the American Indian and Alaskan Native population as well as the Native Hawaiian and Other Pacific Islander population. According to the American Community Survey, conducted by the United States Census Bureau (2009), 11.2 million children between the ages of five and 17 spoke a language other than English at home. Of this number, eight million spoke Spanish at home. According to Howden and Meyer (2011), about 75 percent of Hispanics live in the southern or western United States and over 50 percent of the Hispanic population in the United States reside in California, Texas, and Florida.

What impact do these statistics have on our American public schools? Davis and Bowman (2011) reported that although the number of nursery school children in the United States in 2008 was not statistically different from the number of nursery school children ten years previously, the number of Hispanic nursery school children increased over the ten-year period from 13 to 18 percent. Among the 79.9 million students enrolled from kindergarten to grade 12 in the United States in 2008, 59 percent were non-Hispanic White, 18 percent were Hispanic, 15 percent were Black, 5 percent were Asian and 7 percent of the enrolled students were foreign-born. In addition to looking at statistics relative to ethnicity and race, another factor emerges as significant in reflecting U.S. societal changes and their impact on our American public school: poverty. According to the National Center for Education Statistics (2010), the number of high-poverty public schools is determined by the percentage (76–100 percent) of students eligible for free or reduced-price lunch. In 2008–2009, 6 percent White, 44 percent Black, 44.7 percent Hispanic, 16.5 percent Asian/Pacific Islander, and 30.8 percent American Indian/Alaskan Native students were enrolled in high-poverty public schools. The largest percentages (58.1 percent) of high-poverty schools were located in cities and schools in the South and West.

More significant, students from high-poverty schools scored lower than their low-poverty school counterparts on the National Assessment of Educational Progress (NAEP) reading, math, music, and art assessments. When analyzing the achievement of U.S. students across international assessments, it was found that seven countries outperformed the United States in reading in the 2006 Progress in International Reading Literacy Study (PIRLS). In mathematics,

U.S. 15-year-olds have been consistently placed at the bottom quarter of participating countries on the Program for International Student Assessment (PISA), which has been assessing 15-year-olds' performance in reading, math, and science literacy every three years since 2000. Among the 29 countries participating in the science test on PISA (2006), 15-year-olds in 23 other countries outranked their peers in the United States. These international studies include developed as well as developing countries (Provasnik, Gonzales, & Miller, 2009).

Digital Accommodations and Adaptations

Successful Projects

There are two significant means by which inequities have been addressed in the U.S.—through accommodation and by adaptation. Both require making changes to the existing status quo so that individuals or groups being denied access initially can become active participants. Accommodation and adaptation can also be used in a digital framework to broaden or enhance participation by those individuals or groups who previously had limited or no access. This may be interpreted as a small step, but for some individuals or groups experiencing a racial, socio-economic, gender, language, or disability inequity, it may be the "giant leap" towards digital solidarity.

In the past 20 years, there have been a number of successful projects providing accommodations and adaptations for special groups. Some are funded by the federal government, such as the Department of Commerce's Technology Opportunities Program (TOP), which advocated for widespread technology availability and innovative usage of digital network technologies in both the public and non-profit sectors; and some funded by private industry, such as Hewlett Packard's Digital Village Projects (Hewlett Packard News Release, 2004, June 29), which emphasized e-inclusion and community computing for those sectors of society previously denied digital inclusion or without equitable access to a range of technologies.

Some of the notable projects that have focused on providing digital access for special populations at the secondary and post-secondary education levels include: (a) Microsoft Corporation's grant to increase technology access and training for students at 11 African-American and Hispanic Universities across the nation (The Corporate Social Responsibility Newswire, 2000, January 12); (b) the Development Fund for Black Students in Science and Technology (DFBSST) that provides undergraduate scholarships to African-American students at historically Black colleges and universities who are majoring in science or technology; (c) the TOP-funded Holland Independent School Project in Texas that developed in a rural, low-socio-economic community an advanced communications and information network that linked the school with its large (77 percent) at-risk and profoundly disabled population of students with the local library and university libraries via the Internet (U.S. Department of Commerce, 1997); (d) the TOP-funded White Mountain Apache Project that provided Internet access to a geographically isolated Indian reservation with one of the largest poverty concentrations in the country, allowing students and teachers at the tribal school to reach greater educational resources (U.S. Department of Commerce, 1996); (e) the GCI-funded School Access Project (School Access, 2008, May 2) which ensured high-speed Internet access and an interactive, video distance learning network to Inuit students, including 29 percent English Language Learners, in the North Slope Borough School District in remote Barrow, Alaska; and (f) the U.S. Department of Education (DOE)-funded National Center for Accessible Media (NCAM) Projects which provided speech solutions for media centers by adapting an existing system (Talking MythTV) for blind and low-vision individuals (National Center for Accessible Media, 2009b) and is developing prototype models as captioning solutions for handheld media and mobile devices that will ultimately provide access for deaf, hard of hearing (National Center for Accessible Media, 2009a), including English as a Second Language (ESL) students (Knox & Anderson-Inman, 2001) with (Wahl & Duffield, 2005) or without disabilities (Curtin, 2005).

Unfortunately, as the federal deficit increases, the amount of government funding for similar types of project decreases. Therefore, the onus of responsibility is now being placed in the hands of private industry. Even though corporations like Microsoft with its national and international perspective and regional telecommunications companies like GCI in Alaska have taken the lead in addressing digital inequities among special populations, as more technologies are created and disseminated to the general population, it should be the mandate for those creators and disseminators to integrate appropriate accommodations and adaptations into their systems so that all sectors of U.S. society have equal access and can develop knowledge about usage. What better place for knowledge to be disseminated than in our public school system which reflects the diversity of our society?

It is evident that we have the potential in our country to provide appropriate accommodations and adaptations as existing technologies are distributed and new technologies are created; however, there is one sector in society that still has not participated equally in the "giant leap" towards digital solidarity—women. According to Schwartz (2012, May 30), "women have been flagrantly underrepresented in technology fields since the Internet first changed the way we interact with the world nearly two decades ago" with only 8 percent female leadership in new start-up technology companies and limited representation on boards of prominent Web 2.0 companies. One "glimmer of hope" is the Anita Borg Institute for Women and Technology (ABI) that provides a supportive community as well as the resources and financial support to recruit and sustain women in leadership roles in high-technology fields within the industrial, academic, and government sectors. By nurturing women in leadership roles in technology that reflect the diversity found in U.S. society, we create viable mentors for young girls in our elementary, middle and high schools to help them envision careers in technology. By supporting women to actively participate in making long-range plans and decisions that will impact the next generation of females deciding to enter fields in technology, we create the mechanism for providing equitable access into corporate America and various avenues that will ultimately lead to that "giant leap" into digital solidarity in the United States.

Technology and At-risk Students

At-risk students show substantial improvement when technology is introduced into their curriculum because educators are able to individualize and customize learning experiences to match learners' developmental needs. This type of personalized education accommodates the enormous diversity of today's students. It recognizes that students come from different socio-economic situations and cultural backgrounds, learn in different ways and at different speeds, and have different talents, problems, and aspirations (Wolk, 2010, April). Technology offers a variety of educational opportunities that match student diversity and can be a proponent in serving those students who are least well served by conventional schooling.

Specifically, online learning is being used as an option for students who have had academic setbacks and are using the virtual environment as a way to catch up and recover credits (O'Hanlon, 2009, February 1). School districts across the nation are looking to online programs as a credit recovery solution that allows students to retake courses previously failed while remaining active in their current set of courses. With the current national accountability practices pushing for high graduation rates, districts are using online programs as a way to help bring students into good academic standing, and bring back students whose poor academic performance is either driving them, or has driven them, to drop out of school. The use of video and the Internet as a means of delivering academic content helps more students comprehend subject matter originally not understood the first time around. Offering credit recovery online gives our most marginalized students (teen parents, working students, hospital homebound students, and those in the juvenile detention centers) a chance to graduate outside the traditional high school education system with its confining pace and timeline.

An example of how technology is enabling inclusion of at-risk students can be found in the STEP program at Plainview Elementary School in rural Chesterfield County in South Carolina and the story of a fourth-grade home-bound cancer student. He was provided a laptop and webcam as part of the school district's Student Technology and Education Proficiency Initiative (STEP). Prior to this initiative, the student's previous homebound learning experiences were isolated and had him working independently with little to no communication with his teachers or fellow students (Jones & Fox, 2009).

His only interaction with the school was hospital/homebound teachers visiting him briefly at home to review his work. By using the webcam he felt engaged in the class, with the ability to see his classmates and to be seen by them.

The STEP program has proven to be much more than a laptop program for the Chesterfield School District. It is a great example of a comprehensive approach to improving teaching and learning through the use of technology. The initial funding for the program came from Title II-D of the No Child Left Behind Act—Enhancing Education Through Technology (EETT) grant and provided sixth graders at two elementary and students at one high school with a laptop computer for use at school and home. Through an agreement with the local telephone company, students with limited economic means were provided free home internet installation and a reduced service fee of $5 per month. Included in the program was technology training for participating teachers to learn how to use digital tools such as document cameras, interactive whiteboards, and projectors. Through the assistance of a technology coach, teachers were able to reach a comfort level with the technology, enabling them to innovate and explore new avenues of teaching.

The technology coaches assisted teachers in changing their instructional delivery methods to include more project-based learning into the core subjects. School scores showed that 66 percent of students exceeded their expected scores in reading and 48 percent exceeded their normative growth expectation in math. The STEP program has also been given credit for improvement in student behavior, with the number of disciplinary incidents in the Chesterfield district going to 361 disciplinary incidents reported during the initial year of implementation, down from 823 incidents reported a year earlier.

Technology and English-language Learners

English-language Learners (ELL) have been identified as national origin minority students with limited English proficiency (LEP), many of whom struggle to learn in classrooms where English is the primary language (United States Department of Education, 2004). Projections show that by 2015, one in three American students will be an English-language learner (ELL). The number of students learning English as a second language has already nearly tripled to more than 9.9 million students in the last two decades. Roughly 70 percent of these students are Spanish speakers, but the group includes speakers of more than 400 languages (Smart, 2008). Rance-Roney (2008, October) asserted that the English-language learners, without the requisite experiences and opportunities to engage with technologies, may turn out to be the least empowered when it comes to gathering, analyzing, and synthesizing digitized information.

Meanwhile, as ELL needs outpace schools' human and financial resources, technology can be used to fill the gap. There are numerous advantages in using computer technologies and the Internet to assist in language education (NCREL, 2005). These advantages relate not only to language education but also in preparing students for today's information society. Christina Dukes of the National Center for Homeless Education at SERVE asserted that technology is a wonderful source of comprehensible input that offers additional demonstrations or concrete examples of concepts being taught in the classroom to students with different learning styles. "Multimedia CDs, digital tutorials, and the web provide a near endless source of sound, pictures, video, animation, and multimedia that can help situate learning within a meaningful context" (SEIR TEC, 2005, p.4). In addition, the computer is an excellent resource for giving students the chance to practice English skills without worrying about the response of other classmates or the teacher. As Butler-Pascoe (1997, p.21) explained, "The untiring, non-judgmental nature of the computer makes it an ideal tool to help second language learners feel sufficiently secure [in making] and [correcting] their own errors without embarrassment or anxiety."

Computer technologies and the Internet are powerful tools for language teaching because they enable student-centered learning while helping language learners learn by using various web technologies such as writing emails, participating in online discussions, and conducting online research through webquests and using basic word processing and presentation technologies (Wang, 2005, May; Rance-Roney, 2008, October). Zehr (2007, January) recommended the use of chat sessions for the middle and high school levels because they tend to draw out English learners who are hesitant to speak. English-language learners benefit from the reinforcement of vocabulary and concepts through pictures, graphics, and video. They also benefit from being able to use technology to express themselves (Brozek & Duckworth, n.d.). Meskill and Mossop (2000) found that within the classrooms they visited, ELL students, through the use of technology-supported instruction, were able to participate in classroom activities to the full extent of their intelligence and imagination. They noted that this is in contrast with the traditional classroom settings where the ELL students were unable to follow grade-level curriculum and participate in learning for many years after starting to learn English.

An example of how technology assists the teaching and learning of ELL students can be found at Cinnabar Elementary School, in Petaluma, California where students work amongst an array of computers, digital cameras, scanners, and printers (Smart, 2008). Technology assists students by providing one-on-one structured practice. There are computers in every classroom and the computer lab is used for multi-week projects. Specific software programs are used including Read Naturally, described as a multimedia reading program that assists students in developing fluency in English. A second software program, Rosetta Stone, associates images with English words and sentence structures in an effort to build students' vocabularies. The school's English language development teacher indicated that "software, online tools, and other technologies help students hone basic language skills they can later apply in authentic social settings" (para. 4). Educators at the school recommend the use of computer programs and other technologies because they say "they accelerate the acquisition of phonics, vocabulary, fluency, and reading-comprehension skills and other language building blocks" (para. 7).

A variety of software programs are used by the Laredo Independent School District, in Laredo, Texas. Scientific Learning's Reading Assistant is a guided oral reading program that works one-on-one with each individual student. It is a sophisticated speech recognition program that helps students with word pronunciation. Kurzweil 3000 scans and reads content in any text format and in multiple languages, and therefore offers accessibility to any grade level content. Lexia Reading program teaches phonics (the method of teaching beginning readers to connect the sounds of spoken language with letters or a group of letters) and phonemic awareness (the awareness of sounds where no print is used, no letters are introduced, and there is no correspondence between sound and symbol). Whereas My Reading Coach addresses articulation.

The drawback for using these programs is that their costs range from hundreds to thousands of dollars per license while granting a limited number of users or computers per license. Yet Laredo District administrators say that the results speak for themselves. By using a password, administrators can monitor the progress of any district student by accessing audio files of the student reading aloud. Teachers are able to email the audio files to parents, as well (Smart, 2008).

Technology Usage with Students with Disabilities

Assistive technology is technology used by individuals with disabilities in order to perform functions that might otherwise be difficult or impossible. It can include mobility devices such as walkers and wheelchairs, as well as hardware, software, and peripherals that assist people with disabilities in accessing computers or other information technologies (Access IT, 2011). For example, people with limited hand function may use a keyboard with large keys or a special mouse to operate a computer. People who are blind may use software that reads text on the screen in a computer-generated voice, whereas people with low vision may use software that enlarges screen content. Those who are deaf may use a text telephone (TTY), or people with speech impairments may use a device that speaks out loud as they enter text via a keyboard.

The tremendous variety of assistive technology that is currently available offers nearly all people access to information technology. However, an individual having proper assistive technology is no guarantee of having access. Information technology (IT) accessibility is dependent on accessible design. IT products must be designed and created in ways that allow all users to access them, including those who use assistive technologies.

Universal Design for Learning (UDL) takes advantage of the opportunity brought by rapidly evolving communication technologies to create flexible teaching methods and curriculum materials that can reach diverse learners and improve student access to the general education curriculum (Rose & Meyer,

2002). Universal Design is a philosophy for designing and delivering both products and services so that they are usable by people with the widest possible range of functional capabilities. As per Section 3(19) of the Assistive Technology Act, amended in 2004, these products and services should be directly accessible without requiring assistive technologies, as well as being interoperable with assistive technologies.

Drawing on knowledge of how the brain works and new technologies and media now available for teaching and learning, UDL is an approach to outlining a systematic educational framework for students with varying capabilities. CAST (2011) offered three primary principles that guide UDL: (a) to provide multiple means of representation, (b) to offer students multiple ways to express and demonstrate what they have learned, and (c) to provide multiple means of student engagement.

The rationale for why UDL is necessary stems from the fact that individuals demonstrate a huge variety of skills, needs, and interests in learning that are as varied and unique as our DNA or fingerprints (CAST, 2011). One central idea of UDL is that as new curricular materials and learning technologies are developed, they should be designed *from the beginning* to be flexible enough to accommodate the unique learning styles of a wide range of individuals, including children with disabilities. Some examples of UDL include: accessible webpages, electronic versions of textbooks and other curricular materials, captioned and/or narrated videos, word processors with word prediction, speaking spell checkers, talking dialog boxes, voice recognition, and picture menus. UDL asserts that building accessibility into new technologies and curricular materials in the development stages will help to ensure maximum inclusion of children with disabilities into the learning opportunities available to all children.

Snyder and Tan (2005, October) asserted that more than six million children with disabilities ages three to 21 are served in federally supported programs. Yet students with disabilities often experience inadequate access to and success in general education curriculum, specifically those that have an emphasis on learning from text (Kamil, 2003; Biancarosa & Snow, 2004). Since printed reading material can be problematic and challenging to students with disabilities, technology can assist by enabling a shift from printed text to electronic text which can be modified, enhanced, programmed, linked, searched, collapsed, and collaborative (Anderson-Inman & Reinking, 1998). In addition, text styles and font sizes can be altered by those with visual disabilities, computer-based text to speech readers can be utilized to read text aloud, electronic text can include videos and audio files, and electronic text can be structured in ways that scaffold the learning process (NCREL, 2005).

Seniors and Technology

According to the Pew Internet and American Life Project (Jones & Fox, 2009, January 28), "the biggest increase in technology use since 2005 can be found in the 70–75 year-old group. While just over one-fourth (26 percent) of 70–75 year-olds were online in 2005, 45 percent of that age group is currently online" (p.2). Seniors use the Internet for informational purposes, particularly to find answers to health questions. Also, they use the Internet for emailing, especially when the potential for grandchildren or relatives checking email daily is greater than in previous decades. Some members of Generation X have realized the benefits of using computers to stimulate brain functioning (Miller, 2009). Yet, even when the social and cognitive benefits of computing are presented to seniors, the homebound senior on a fixed income has to weigh the costs of buying and maintaining a computer and paying monthly fees for Internet access with the costs of food, housing, and medicine. So, for seniors, is technology a luxury or is it a means of helping them to "live better as they age"? (Miller, 2009, para. 3)

Since 1986, SeniorNet (http://www.seniornet.org) has been one organization committed to educating seniors about computers and the Internet. SeniorNet learning centers with their low-cost classes can be found in senior centers, community centers, public libraries, schools and colleges, clinics, and hospitals. More importantly, however, is SeniorNet's Underserved Initiatives which involve collaborating with funders, community groups, and other partners to provide training and online community support to seniors with disabilities and those in urban and rural underserved areas. For example, the Hope and Harmony for Humanity project funded by IBM in partnership with the Native American Chamber of Commerce and SeniorNet has provided technology access for low-income and remote Native American tribes across the U.S. Similarly, through collaborative efforts with the HRC Foundation and the UPS Foundation, funding has been made available for establishing SeniorNet learning centers in urban communities, such as Washington, D.C.; New Orleans, LA; Oakland, CA; and Corpus Christi, TX to provide free computer access to low-income seniors. These projects ultimately assist seniors in participating as active members of society, maintaining their independence, and contributing to their longevity (SeniorNet, 2012).

The Homeless: A Special Case

Another societal group that is often overlooked when discussing access to technology is the homeless. For members of this group, having a cell phone means having the opportunity to apply for a job, find housing, or get assistance when an emergency arises. For mothers with children that are homeless, having a cell phone provides instant communication with family and friends, the means to apply for a better paying job, establish residence so that children can be enrolled in school, and find childcare. Once on-going access to computers is achieved, usually at local libraries, local charities, or at work, members of this group have the capacity to search for jobs on the Internet and prepare résumés and cover letters as part of the job application process (Le Dantec, Farrell, Christensen, Bailey, Ellis, Kellogg, & Edwards, 2011).

For the homeless, who are constantly moving, it is critical that *mobile* technology be accessible as a means of resolving basic issues such as finding housing, but also as the basis for empowering homeless individuals in their successful pursuit of finding jobs, connecting with local agencies that can provide the necessary ongoing support, and establishing more permanent residence in a community. For Kristen, a homeless, diagnosed schizophrenic, college student it means staying in touch with people you meet online, providing safety, getting messages from "messengers of hope," and living a "virtual life" (McRae, 2010). Programs like Open Access Connections (Orrick, 2011), sponsored by the University of Minnesota, appear to be viable models for providing voice mail and cell phones to homeless individuals in need of vital services, such as housing, employment, health care, and safety resources in a localized area. The goal should be to develop a nationwide effort to research and create similar models that identify the specific technological needs of the homeless and provide solutions that address their transient lifestyles.

Case Studies of American Inequities

Racial Inequity

> Growing up as the child of a soldier was my background. We moved a lot. Every two years or so, I was in a new school, living in a new area, hoping to make new friends. The phrase "never met a stranger" applies to me, even today. In the early 1950s, Dad was stationed at Fort Riley, Kansas. I was not old enough to start school yet but our neighborhood in Manhattan, Kansas had children that were about my age and I made some friends there. Our next move would be to Temple, Texas while my father was serving at Ft. Hood, Texas. Mom did not like Army bases or "Army towns," and we would usually live some distance away from them. Whenever we went to the base for any kind of a party that involved my Dad's work, we were around African American families. By this time in history, the U.S. Army had been fully integrated and Black soldiers served alongside their White counterparts. It had not always been that way. For most of our nation's history, the Black soldiers were separated, but in 1947 that had all changed. As a result, by 1957 it was quite natural for me to be around African American children and interact with them. Even in Temple, Texas when I started school, I had Black classmates. I would realize later that was unusual. The Supreme Court order to desegregate school systems was still new, and for a school in a southern city to be integrated was not the norm.
>
> K. Sweet (personal communication, March 5, 2011)

Socio-economic Inequity

I am a middle-class African-American female. My sister and I were raised by both of our parents. My parents divorced, but our dad played an active role in our lives. The term used to describe this type of parenting is now called co-parenting. If my mother could not afford to buy us something that we wanted, we were unaware because we did not want for anything, but others are not as fortunate. Social class is a factor in educating students from multicultural backgrounds. The school where I work is a Title 1 school. The majority of the students get free or reduced lunch. Some teachers are not from the area or come from upper-middle-class families and do not understand all of the needs that the students that we serve may have. They do not know that some students only get to eat when they come to school, why these students do not have school supplies, why these students wear the same clothes, why the boys do not get a haircut, or why the child is sleeping in class. They sometimes think that the child is being defiant or disrespectful, but that is not always the case. Some students may not have food at home and that is why they are asking for everyone else's food at lunch. Some students have to take care of their brothers and sisters because their parents are working or their parents may be drug addicts. A large majority of our students are living in poverty.

S. K. Hill (personal communication, July 20, 2010)

Geographic Inequity

My experience of teaching on an Indian Reservation allowed me to work with a large group of students who had little personal experience outside of their traditional culture. This was interactive learning as we learned from each other. Through their history, values, behaviors, and perspective, I learned some of the traditional language which gave me insight to Lakota verbal and nonverbal communication (Marzano, 2003). This single group approach of multicultural education focused my own education in teaching on empirical research. My experience in learning about teaching came from a traditional tribal college. My philosophy of education is built on a strong foundation of understanding the perspectives of minorities and oppressed cultures, while I base instructional strategies on traditional values, learning styles, perceptions, and communication. I integrated instructional tools such as technology, engaged learning techniques, and encouraged students to build on their individual learning styles (Banks & McGee Banks, 2010). This was a valuable opportunity for me, as a teacher (Scott, 2002), to learn how to impact these students to embrace possibilities of working in a larger society as I integrated technology and exposure to a variety of other cultures similar and different from their own.

G. Foote (personal communication, July 6, 2010)

Gender Inequity

When I was younger, I was taught that there are certain things that girls and women can do, and the rest is for the boys and men. I was also taught that women stay home and keep up the house while the men and boys work and keep up the housework that deals with outdoors. But I am sorry to inform you that I was the rebellious type. I was what you would call a "tomboy." I felt that if a boy can do it, then I could do it. In today's society more women are taking the role of most men by working and becoming CEOs of major business, becoming lawyers, running for the presidency, etc. There is nothing that can hold us down. We are now coming into our own as potential leaders of this nation. I still have many conversations as to why I am pursuing a doctoral degree since I already have two degrees. Many of my family members and people that I work with constantly tell me that it is not necessary and that I have two children to take care of instead of worrying about continuing my education. Yes, I do have a good job that provides for my family, but I am not just an average woman. I am the type of woman that feels if it is out there, then I want it. I am a woman of goals and values, with the belief that failure is not an option. I am also teaching my daughter to become an independent, successful, African-American woman and, if she wants it, then strive and work hard to receive it. No dream is impossible no matter what gender you may be.

C. Landry (personal communication, July 6, 2010)

Language Inequity

Being of Hispanic descent is something that has defined me throughout my life. I was born in 1975 in Bogota, Colombia. Having moved to the United States at the age of seven, my cultural roots were not completely embedded in my being; however, my parents tried hard to maintain the values of our culture at the forefront of everything we did. At the time, most people of Latin descent in my community were Cuban. For some reason, I found deep shame in this and refused to speak in Spanish outside of my house. I am forever thankful to my parents who massaged those sentiments and let me come to terms with my internal conflict. However accommodating, my mother and father were absolutely adamant about my maintaining the language. My parents made an agreement with me: I did not have to speak Spanish publicly if I read an article from the newspaper in Spanish once a week and summarized it for my mom. This agreement lasted for two years until I was confident enough in my heritage to finally begin speaking in Spanish. Constant trips to visit my grandparents in Cali, Colombia, helped me develop a clear appreciation for the country in which I was born. Although not Hispanic by blood, purely by birthplace,

I still consider that my strong sense of family and tradition is acutely related to my Hispanic background.

M. Wagenberg (personal communication, March 8, 2011)

Disability Inequity

Currently, I work in a division of a school that is a clinical program for students diagnosed with learning disabilities (LD). Educating the school community on the importance of inclusion and how to interact appropriately with the population of students with learning disabilities continues to be a work in progress. Since the division's inception 13 years ago, there have been several professional development workshops that have included topics on inclusion and modifications and accomodations for students with learning differences. The level of acceptance and understanding of the staff who work directly with students with LDs has increased tremendously.

Another challenge is many of the parents of the typically developing students in the multi-age preschool inclusion class are not aware of the benefits of having a child be a member of this class setting. Unfortunately, at the beginning of each school year, many parents do not want their children in this class. A couple of parents have chosen to remove their children who are typically benefitting from the inclusion class because they were afraid the children with special needs would "rub off onto their children." A typical response from a parent is he or she does not want other parents to perceive his or her child has a learning problem, or the other children in the class will have a negative impact on his or her child.

M. Dolton (personal communication, March 8, 2011)

Concluding Thoughts

There are gross inequities in the United States, as evidenced in our societal interactions, educational access and performance, and economic stance. These inequities impact particularly the lives of individuals from lower-socio-economic backgrounds and/or racial, ethnic, or linguistic minority groups. The result is overall lower academic achievement when competing against other industrialized nations, an unprepared and non-competitive workforce, and diminished economic progress when comparing the U.S. on various global fronts. America still appears to have the "edge" technologically, but how long will that last? There have been some "glimmers of hope" in addressing digital inequities through government- and corporate-funded projects. But as government funding diminishes, the torch that lights the way to digital solidarity needs to be carried by the corporate sector in the United States. The American educational system, including public and private schools, has the potential to prepare future generations of Americans for global competitiveness, but serious inequities continue to persist across races, ethnicities, language groups, and social classes. In difficult economic times, the "haves" are struggling to maintain what they possess and the "have-nots" are struggling harder because their group is getting larger as the resources continue to decline. If the United States is to continue in its role as a World Power, there must be a change in the way goods and services are distributed; there must be a realization that digital solidarity will never be achieved as long as the concept of "divide" through race, ethnicity, language, socio-economic status, gender, geography, age, and ability continues to be the modus operandi.

Chapter 5

Technology Activities to Support Digital Solidarity

Developing a Plan of Action

Action Plan for Innovative, Technology-enhanced Programs and Activities

Developing a comprehensive plan for any endeavor is prudent. However, when it comes to technology, planning is a necessity. The action plan you develop for instructional programs must take into account a variety of factors. Your first guideline will probably be the budget, but a thorough knowledge of your stakeholders is also very important. It is essential that you meet the needs of your consumers and not offer them technologies they might find superfluous. Distribution of the equipment as well as the training to operate that technology needs to be considered too. Adequate training must be provided to acquaint each stakeholder with the software and hardware your program will offer. There also needs to be ongoing support for the consumers. Once they actually begin to use a new technology, people often have more questions than they do during training sessions. Finally, a plan to evaluate each step of the program needs to be in place before the technology reaches the consumers. This feedback will be valuable as you seek to replicate a successful program.

Planning

Planning for a technology-enhanced program should begin with a needs assessment conducted among all the stakeholders. This can be as simple as a survey set up on a free website such as Survey Monkey™ or Kwiksurveys.com. If you hold focus groups with interested consumers, you can record their reactions to your proposal. Communication with all your stakeholders prior to commencing planning sessions will allow everyone to voice their concerns and eventually produce better buy-in for your program. Make sure to ask consumers about their present use and understanding of technology. Also ask about the types of technology they would find most useful in their occupation or leisure activities. Dye (2011, March) observed, "Without a keen understanding of who's consuming the content, companies can overwhelm users with too much clutter and too little integration between features and functions" (p.18).

A key feature of your needs assessment should be to determine what is being done for marginalized people in your school, organization, or community. You need to identify what type of assistive or adaptive technology is available for disabled stakeholders. The Assistive Technology Industry Association (2012) defined assistive technology as "any item, piece of equipment, software or product system that is used to increase, maintain, or improve the functional capabilities of individuals with disabilities" (para. 2). Adaptive technology is sometimes specified as "a type of assistive technology that includes customized systems that help individuals move, communicate, and control their environments. Adaptive technologies are designed specifically for persons with disabilities and include augmentative and alternative communication devices, powered wheelchairs, and environmental control systems" (Family Center on Technology and Disability, 2012, Glossary). An inventory checklist should be developed to determine the types of technology available, how the technology is being used, and how it is being offered to those who need assistance. The sample survey, included as Appendix A, demonstrates this type of analysis.

Funding

Once you know the technology requirements of your community, it will be easier to raise the funds to meet those needs. Most grant applications require a needs assessment or a statement describing why your stakeholders want the equipment or personnel listed in your grant request. You should also prepare a detailed budget listing all end-user technology and hardware infrastructure spending for your project or program. If the grant you are seeking requires matching funds, then you will need to find that support before submitting your proposal. There are many organizations that list guidelines and links to agencies that offer technology grants. It is suggested that you check out the websites for the organizations listed in Table 5.1.

Table 5.1 Organizations Offering Grant Information

Organization	URL
International Association for K-12 Online Learning (iNACOL)	http://www.inacol.org/
United States Distance Learning Association (USDLA)	http://www.usdla.org/
Technology Grant News	http://www.technologygrantnews.com/
Government Benefits and Financial Aid	http://www.usa.gov/Citizen/Topics/Benefits.shtml
Microsoft Corporate Citizenship Tools	http://www.microsoft.com/about/corporatecitizenship/en-us/nonprofits/

Distribution

Deciding "who gets what" is essential to a smooth start-up for your technology program. All stakeholders need to be made aware of the distribution plan so they can be assured of receiving a benefit from the new technology. This will get everyone on the same page and eager to prepare for the beginning of the program. There will be some administrators or community leaders who will need to be trained on the new hardware before it is distributed to the general public, just as in schools where teachers learn how to use new technology before they can instruct their students. In these situations, some personnel will need to have their equipment and software before it is released to the general public. Make sure to have training for the personnel already set up upon delivery of the new equipment. Too often technology sits untouched because the proper training on its use was not ready at the time of delivery.

Training and Support

A training program is most often the first taste of the new technology that most people receive, so you will want to make each training session interesting and fun! Food is always a good incentive, but ice-breakers or other activities that bring people together will work well, too. Make sure that your trainers are knowledgeable in the new technology as well as acquainted with the type of people they will be training. Murray (2011, September 11) suggested that in order to reach all participants, "Let the type of training and the needs of your audience dictate the right vehicle for the training" (para. 4). Three major areas need to be addressed for implementing a successful training program: (a) hands-on access, (b) needs-directed criteria, and (c) technology support.

Hands-on access to the new technology must be provided during the training and implementation of the program. Each participant needs to be able to practice on the equipment he or she will use in the new technology program. Not only do consumers need to use the equipment during training, they must also be able to practice immediately following the training sessions so they do not forget what they have learned.

The training should also be needs directed where participants are prepared to use the new technology in their everyday schedule. This is where you will get buy-in from your stakeholders. If they feel that the new technology will make their job easier or add a new dimension to their work, then they will be more likely to implement the new program. Starr (2011, November 14) reported that the Oswego City School District created a successful technology training program using project-based learning activities. Teachers in this training were required to create projects that were used in their classrooms. Not only do they implement the program, but they also shared it online through a searchable database. Teachers reported that they "didn't get a chance to share with their colleagues; this allows them to share their talents and creativity with teachers throughout the district" (para. 21).

Finally, technology support should be active during the training sessions and ongoing throughout the program. No matter how well your trainers explain the new technology, there will still be questions and problems that will come up later. Every stakeholder must be able to contact support personnel for technology help when they encounter a problem. Therefore, setting up a support center staffed by knowledgeable personnel is extremely important. Too often technology goes unused because users were unable to get a question answered, hardware fixed, or software installed.

Evaluation

Evaluating your technology program should be an ongoing occurrence. The first evaluation will most likely occur when you seek financial support. Grant committees and corporate officers will make comments on your proposal. This initial evaluation will allow you to modify your request and resubmit the proposal, if necessary. The next evaluation will come during the training sessions. This feedback will help the trainers to modify or expand the information they present. As the technology is being distributed and the program implemented, make sure you offer a venue for comments and questions. Communication could be through a phone hotline, email correspondence, or online blog. At the conclusion of the project's first year, you will need to send out a formal evaluation. An evaluation format that stakeholders are comfortable with is vital. Make it available both online and in a paper format. Then allow stakeholders to choose their preferred format.

Sample Technology-enhanced Programs Including all Populations

There are many organizations that offer successful programs and activities to integrate technology into the mainstream of life. Some of these programs are directed towards a traditional classroom set-up with teacher training being paramount in their design, while other organizations seek to serve the general population outside of a school setting. The platforms used in these programs range from physical computer centers, where face-to-face technical support is readily available, to online courses that reach people around the world. These successful programs offer equitable access to all their clients through a variety of technology environments.

K–12 School Programs

Providing technology to every school and classroom, maintaining the infrastructure to support the integration of technology into the curriculum, and training teachers on how to effectively utilize the technology is extremely expensive and adds a substantial burden to any school system's budget. Recognizing the high rate by which technology becomes obsolete (Ringstaff & Kelley, 2002), it is prudent for school systems to build the cost of educational technology into their budgets on an ongoing and sustainable basis (The Education Alliance, 2005). ISTE (International Society for Technology in Education, 2008) recommended that all states have a dedicated funding stream for educational technology that is tied to a sustained, high-quality professional development as well as investment in hardware, software, and infrastructure. For those states that already have funding for this purpose, it must be sufficient to achieve targeted educational goals.

Florida represents an example of a state utilizing a community resource to supplement their local school district's technology budget. The Florida Legislature approved a law in 2006 "that allows sales and use tax dealers (retailers) who are entitled to a collection allowance (rebate) for calculating the sales tax they must transmit to the state, to instead, donate those funds to the *Educational Enhancement Trust Fund*. Those donated funds will go to the retailer's local school district to support technology" (Broward County Public Schools, 2013, para. 1). In Broward County Public Schools this legislation has been called "Send Your Sales Tax to School." Funds raised through this endeavor are used to purchase technology and train classroom teachers to use the new technology effectively.

Educational programs need to reach out to students who have a wealth of technology at their fingertips as well as those who are digitally disadvantaged. Forest Lake Elementary School in Columbia, South Carolina is a prime example of a school reaching out to all its students. One of the largest United States Army training centers is situated in Columbia, bringing students to Lake Forest from many different socio-economic, racial, and ethnic backgrounds.

> By integrating technology into the classroom, maintaining an affiliation with the National Aeronautics and Space Administration, and promoting project learning, Forest Lake accommodates the various learning styles of such a wide-ranging student body, developing strong literacy and strengthening students' science, technology, math, geography, and even engineering skills.
>
> (Best, 2012, para. 5).

Another technology program that has met with success is at the middle school level. For the past ten years every seventh- and eighth-grade student in the state of Maine has been given a laptop to use during the school year. Educators report that the laptops "level the playing field of access to technology and help students become technology-literate" (Washuk, 2011, March 20, p.2). Students and teachers alike say that the "laptops make learning and schoolwork more interesting" (p.2). Since the laptop program began in 2001, student's state test scores have risen in writing. In one school the number of ninth-grade students needing remedial math has been lowered by 50 percent. Teachers suggest that the reason for this improvement lies with the fact that math instruction at the middle school level uses laptops now instead of textbooks. Another area of improvement is science. Peter Robinson, a Maine educator, described how science projects were affected by the arrival of the laptops. In the past, students from affluent families would come in with professional-looking projects "compared to plain-looking reports from students whose parents did not have as much money. Having laptops means all students can do the same quality report, regardless of their parents' income, because they all have the same tools" (p.3).

Afterschool Programs

The traditional school day only reaches students for six to seven hours a day, ten months a year. That schedule does not come close to utilizing the vast technology resources of the school classroom. The After-School Corporation (TASC) believes that "expanded learning time schools, afterschool and summer programs offer the ideal time, places and conditions to equalize and advance technology-enabled learning" (Curry & Jackson-Smarr, 2012, para. 4). Research conducted by TASC suggests that schools and afterschool programs should form a partnership to design technology experiences that motivate students to learn wherever they are, not just in a classroom. For example, Thurgood Marshall Academy for Leadership and Social Change (TMALSC) is a middle school in Harlem that partnered with Abyssinian Development Corporation (ADC) to add three hours to the traditional learning day. Students spent the extra time viewing online tutorials while receiving face-to-face assistance from teachers and ADC personnel. This educational partnership with business allowed students to receive individualized instruction at their particular skill level. A further bonus was that students could access these tutorials online anytime. Parents and caregivers found this a help when working with their children at home.

Post-Secondary School Programs

Technology integration has also made a difference in education at the post-secondary level. Colleges and universities in the United States have embraced technology by providing their students with computer labs, Internet connectivity, email accounts, software downloads, 24/7 tech support, and online courses. Professors have been trained to use various web-conferencing programs and digital learning management platforms as part of their course instruction. Many students complete their entire degree online while others select a blended program of face-to-face courses together with their online studies.

Many people with disabilities now have an opportunity to access post-secondary courses using adaptive technology. Computers have been made fully accessible to those who are blind, deaf, or have other physical disabilities. Some of the adaptive technology equipment includes screen readers or speech synthesizers along with Braille printers, keyboards, and note takers. While some students have purchased their own assistive technology, many students find the devices cost prohibitive. So some colleges offer fully adapted computer labs and provide technology training for disabled students. The University of Oregon (2004) has created a Technology Access Program "to provide adaptive access to electronic technology that has become a fundamental element of student life" ("Adaptive Technology," para. 1). The university's program not only offers training for students but also provides training for professors. The instructors are taught how to prepare course materials for use with the assistive technology.

The Association on Higher Education and Disability (AHEAD) is an international organization that is working to meet the needs of people with disabilities at the post-secondary level (http://www.ahead.org/about). The AHEAD website has a special section devoted to parents and students. There is a question-and-answer section as well as a valuable list of resources for transitioning into college and beyond. Another website that provides free information on post-secondary education is the HEATH Resource Center (http://www.heath.gwu.edu/) managed by George Washington University and funded by the HSC Foundation. "The HEATH Resource Center gathers, develops and disseminates information in the form of resource papers, fact sheets, website directories, newsletters, and resource materials" ("About HEATH," para. 4).

Universities have also provided an outreach to their local community by setting up technology centers. The Holyoke Community College (HCC) opened the Thomas M. Gill III Community Technology Center on the first floor of the Holyoke Transportation Center in 2012. The Gill Technology Center contains a computer lab for adult education classes. Free or low-cost computer instruction is offered in English and Spanish. The University of Minnesota's Urban Research and Outreach-Engagement Center (UROC) established the Broadband Access Project (BAP) in 2009. The project was funded by a grant from the United States Department of Commerce with matching funds from the university and other community partners. The BAP established 11 computer centers throughout low-income neighborhoods in Minneapolis and St. Paul.

> The goal of the BAP is to help eliminate the digital divide by enhancing and expanding access to high-speed Internet (broadband) in underserved communities to expand access to information about employment, education, health, and community and economic development. The project will open doors, enhance lives, and create access and job opportunities through technology.
>
> (Urban Research and Outreach-Engagement
> Center, 2012, para. 2)

Community Programs

We have seen how schools provide technology programs as an outreach to their communities. There are also many professionals and social organizations within the community that reach out to disadvantaged populations. The Minnesota Justice Network is working to ensure adequate legal counsel is available to homeless veterans and people in rural areas. The network uses Interactive Television

(ITV) located in every courthouse in Minnesota to hold pro se clinics. Private attorneys make themselves available for consultation during these clinics without having to travel a great distance to give advice to the pro se litigants. The Minnesota Justice Network also uses Skype "to stretch across boundaries" as wireless hot spots can be easily accessed in a variety of settings outside of the courthouse (Sommarstrom, 2011, August).

Health professionals are using the social media and the Internet to connect with people who might not be able to afford routine preventive medical care. Text4baby is a free messaging service that supports expectant mothers by providing accurate, text-length health information and resources through text messages sent directly to their cell phones (http://text4baby.org/). The text messages are free and also available in Spanish. Another pioneer in the health information field is the Mayo Clinic. Its website has a wealth of accurate medical information about diseases, symptoms, drugs, medical procedures, first aid, and living a healthy lifestyle. Http://www.Mayo.com is written so the average person can easily understand the medical advice.

Many different social organizations are opening their own community technology centers to reach people caught in the low-end of the digital continuum. The Corinthian Baptist Church in Des Moines, Iowa, opened its new Community Technology Center in 2012. The center offers computer instruction, job training, General Educational Development (GED) classes, and testing. Target populations include senior citizens, unemployed, or underemployed adults and youth who need computer or Internet access. Julius Genachowski, chairman of the U.S. Federal Communications Commission (FCC), said that "connecting all Americans and teaching them digital skills is critical to reducing unemployment" (Gross, 2012, July 16, para. 6). In San Francisco, the Homeless Pre-Natal Program (HPP) sponsors a Community Technology Center (CTC). Patrons of the CTC can access computers while receiving counseling from trained professionals. A participant reported:

> When I first found out that HPP had a Community Technology Center, I was living in a shelter. I came in everyday looking for a job and housing, and the CTC truly became my second home until I got my apartment and my job.
>
> (Homeless Pre-Natal Program, 2010, "Success Stories")

National Technology Programs

The National Education Technology Plan 2010 (NETP), developed by the U.S. Department of Education, offers national long-range goals and recommendations to help school districts create an integrated approach to using technology in education. The NETP model suggests that educators bring "state-of-the-art-technology into learning to enable, motivate, and inspire all students, regardless of background, languages, or disabilities, to achieve. It leverages the power of technology to provide personalized learning and to enable continuous and lifelong learning" (United States Department of Education, Office of Educational Technology, 2010, para. 8).

In compliance with the NETP, states have developed their own technology integration models. Texas created the Long Range Plan for Technology, 2006–2020 to ensure that all Texans would be informed about the course for educational technology in their school districts. All pertinent features of a successful technology plan were in place including a needs study, timeline, educator preparation, instructional support, funding chart, and an infrastructure for technology. The Long Range Plan for Technology also promised digital tools and resources would be available 24/7 to students, parents, and educators (Texas Education Agency, 2006a). A special resource, the School Technology and Readiness (STAR) chart, was created for teachers and administrators as a tool for planning and self-assessment. The STAR chart assists teachers in "fulfilling the requirements in *No Child Left Behind, Title II, Part D* that all teachers should be technology literate and integrate technology into content areas across the curriculum" (Texas Education Agency, 2006b).

There are many other national initiatives seeking to improve digital solidarity. One such program is Connect2Compete (C2C), a nonprofit organization that is helping low-income Americans access technology. The C2C plan includes bringing high-speed broadband to low-income families across the United States. The United States Department of Commerce (2011) reported that broadband Internet adoption in families with an income of $25,000 or less was only 35 percent in rural areas and 45 percent in urban settings as compared with a national average of 68 percent (p.23). The C2C consortium began with a pilot program in six San Diego County, California school districts in 2012. Cox Communications and GoodPC were two of the local companies that partnered with C2C to make digital technologies available to the participants. Thirty-nine thousand families were offered high-speed Internet service and high-powered computers at discounted prices. To be eligible for the discounts, at least one student in each family needed to be enrolled in the National School Lunch Program, and for the broadband offering they could not have had service with Cox Communications during the previous 90 days, nor have overdue bills or unreturned equipment with Cox. With the success of this pilot, C2C is enlisting more companies across the country to expand their program. "Additionally, C2C will launch in the fall [2012] and promote via the 2013 ad campaign a finder tool as a one-stop search tool to locate nearby public computing centers or digital literacy providers" for low-income families in need of these services (Glover, 2012, July 18, para. 4).

Creating a Technology Plan of Your Own

Many agencies and websites offer guidelines for writing state, district, or local school technology plans. The United States Department of Education has a website with links to the technology plans from all 50 states (http://www2.ed.gov/programs/edtech/techstateplan.html). Most of the state departments of education also offer information and outlines that enable school districts to align their technology plans to state or national guidelines. The National Center for Technology Planning (NCTP) has an extensive list of links to educational technology plans from the national stage down to building-level examples. The NCTP website also offers many technology planning aids that will assist educators to implement technology plans (http://www.nctp.com/html/plan_state.cfm). E-Rate Central is a website that offers advice on completing a technology plan that will enable K–12 schools to qualify for a Universal Service discount (http://www.e-ratecentral.com/applicationTips/techPlan/). This website also provides technology plan outlines and sample plans from various educational agencies.

Private companies also provide white papers and online articles to assist organizations in developing their own technology plans. Microsoft recommends using a five-step process in creating a technology plan that will "reduce costs and increase efficiency" (Microsoft, 2012, para. 2). Techsoup.org (http://www.techsoup.org/learningcenter/techplan) is a website that provides an overview and examples of requests for proposals (RFP) for non-profit organizations. This website is full of valuable guidelines for efficiently using technology personnel, equipment, and software. Some non-profit organizations join together for planning and budgeting for technology. One such council is the Westchester Not-for-Profit Technology Council affiliated with Pace University in Westchester, NY (http://csis.pace.edu/wntc/resources/technology.htm). The Westchester Council hosts an electronic mailing list and a website with resources for technology planning.

Sample Technology-enhanced Activities for all Levels of Ability and Achievement

Educational Activities

Once you have a technology plan in place, the most important part of the process can begin: creating technology-enhanced activities to meet the needs of all your consumers. Even the most articulate plan will not enable your stakeholders to utilize the technology without appropriate activities. To wit, you will need to review a wide variety of technology-enhanced activities that have already proven to be successful. The Internet has an extensive offering of websites that will guide you in forming authentic activities. A good place to begin is the research and development website operated by SEDL, originally known as the Southeast Educational Development Laboratory (http://www.sedl.org/pubs/free.html). The SEDL was created as part of a network of ten regions funded through the Regional Technology in Education Consortia (RTEC) supported by a grant from the U.S. Department of Education. While the grant period for RTEC ended in 2005, many of the network members continue to provide an interactive website. Two such members are the Northwest Educational Technology Consortium (http://www.netc.org/focus/

technologies/) and the Southeast Initiatives Regional Technology in Education Consortium (http://www.seirtec.org/index.html). On all the active RTEC websites, you can find many free publications that can aid in establishing technology activities that are relevant to all your stakeholders. For instance, (a) *Planning into Practice: Integrating Technology into the Curriculum* (www.seirtec.org/plan/1Intro.pdf); (b) *Afterschool Toolkit* (http://www.sedl.org/afterschool/toolkits/); and (c) *Mosaic: An Integrated Approach to Mathematics, Science, Technology and Language* (http://www.sedl.org/pubs/mosaic/).

Including all stakeholders means beginning with the youngest learners, preschool children. Preschoolers do benefit from interactive media materials. Digital cameras have been used by three-year-olds in an Oregon preschool to photograph their toy building-block creations (http://spotlight.macfound.org/featured-stories/entry/learning-digital-media-and-creative-play-in-early-childhood/). Next, students dictated a narrative to their teacher describing their creations. The pictures and descriptions were then posted on their iPads. In Head Start centers in New York City, preschoolers learned basic skills using video and interactive computer games. Penuel, Pasnik, and Bates (2009) conducted an evaluative study in two of these Head Start centers and found that "Integrating digital content from public television video and online games into preschool literacy instruction can help low-income children develop early literacy skills to prepare them for kindergarten" (p.1). The study included training the preschool teachers how to integrate the video and games into their classroom instruction. Interactive games came from three Public Broadcasting Service's television shows: *Sesame Street, Between the Lions,* and *Super Why!*

Many publishers and practicing educators have provided electronic activities available through open access on the Internet. Scholastic offers engaging web activities for children in Kindergarten through twelfth grade (http://www.scholastic.com/teachers/student-activities). Edutopia hosts a wide-reaching variety of blogs on ways to integrate new technologies into the classroom (http://www.edutopia.org/blogs/beat/game-based-learning). The discussions range from game-based learning to integrating technology. There are many suggestions for activities to use in and out of the classroom. Laura McMullen presents ideas that will assist you in taking the first steps to introduce digital learning into a high school classroom (http://www.usnews.com/education/blogs/high-school-notes/2012/01/25/3-tips-on-integrating-technology-in-the-classroom). Hamilton's (2007) book, *It's Elementary! Integrating Technology in the Primary Grades,* includes methods for integrating technology with content knowledge. An extensive excerpt from the book has been made available on the International Society for Technology in Education (ISTE) website (www.iste.org/images/excerpts/ITSELE-excerpt.pdf).

Another curriculum concept that has been developed to meet the needs of all students is differentiated instruction. Willis and Mann (2000) suggest that "differentiated instruction is a teaching philosophy based on the premise that teachers should adapt instruction to student differences" (para. 3). Tech4D.I.

is a public wiki for sharing resources that combine technology and differentiated instruction (http://tech4di.wikispaces.com/). Here you can find technology tips and educational strategies to reach all learners including those with special needs. WestEd is another research and development agency that sponsors a website to help educators infuse technology into their instruction in order to support diverse learners. The WestEd website offers tips that allow teachers to use software and technology devices readily available in their classrooms (http://www.wested.org/cs/tdl/print/docs/tdl/home.htm).

Community Activities

Community members also have individual needs that can be met by technology activities. Many community centers offer special classes to introduce children, teenagers, and adults to the computer. The Community Development Technologies (CDTech) Center is a nonprofit organization that works to promote economic opportunities for low-income residents in Los Angeles, California. The CDTech has initiated a Digital Connectors program that meets three nights a week at the center to help disadvantaged young people become computer proficient. This program is supported by One Economy which partnered with the Broadband Opportunity Coalition to train over 2500 youth through Digital Connector programs throughout the United States. The City of Oakland, California (2012) has taken this concept one step farther by providing an Urban Electronics Technology course that "teaches students how to produce, store and use the clean energy of the future" (*Hacking—The OPR Way*, para. 2). Students are supplied with all the materials to build a wind turbine. Then students learn how to use a solar panel with a PEM fuel cell and a hydrogen storage system to keep the turbine operating efficiently.

The growing senior population in the United States will require more assistance as they age. This will necessitate communities to ensure that seniors have access to technology. Status Solutions has produced a self-service program called Communication and Access to Information Everywhere (CATIE) for members of senior living communities. CATIE "functions as an intercom, message center, electronic bulletin board and concierge to help seniors stay connected to the world around them for a better quality of life" (Status Solutions, 2012, para. 2). The Assisted Living Federation of America has recognized CATIE as part of the Alfa 2012 Best of the Best Awards to Watch.

The Consumer Electronics Association Foundation (CEA Foundation) is another organization that has a "mission to link seniors and people with disabilities with technology to enhance their lives" (Consumer Electronics Association Foundation, 2012, para. 1). The SelfHelp Community Services in Flushing, New York received a grant from the CEA Foundation to create a virtual senior center. Participating seniors will be able to use video technology in their homes to create an interactive experience with people at traditional senior centers. Homebound seniors will also be able to access community services through this program.

Concluding Thoughts

Planning for technology integration is just the first step to ensure that the underserved populations in your organization or community will benefit from your project. A continuing process of advertisement, training, support, and enhancement will be necessary to enable all the stakeholders to master the technology. Make sure that the equipment is kept in good working order and software is up-to-date. There needs to be technical support readily available whenever the technology is in use so the learner's progress is not impeded by hardware problems. Initial excitement for the technology integration will some-times fade as skills are practiced but no new challenges are offered. Contests, prizes, and technology fairs will allow the new technology users to display their achievements at all levels of proficiency.

There are many government grants and private endowments available to fund technology programs today. However, those who need the assistance the most are often not prepared to complete the lengthy forms associated with applying for the grants. This is where we need more organizations to help underserved populations receive funding. To that end, Table 5.2 lists a few websites that will assist a novice writer in completing grant applications.

Regardless of the type of funding source for your technology integration, you will be asked to account for the money allotted to the program. It is a good practice to record the benchmark progress of your program through text, photos, and video. The Internet is a perfect tool for logging progress and reporting the success of your program. You can even encourage the stakeholders to contribute information regarding the program to a blog or wiki set up on the website.

Once your integration program has been fully implemented and the stake-holders are comfortable with the technology, look for the next step in bringing

Table 5.2 Grant-writing Resources

Organization and URL	Article
Step by Step Fundraising http://www.stepbystepfundraising.com/ 20-free-grant-writing-resources-non-profits/	20 Free Grant Writing Resources for Non-Profits
National Association of Social Workers http://www.naswdc.org/pressroom/events/ ssw_grants/chavkin.asp	Beginner's Guide to Grant Writing
Rural Assistance Center http://www.raconline.org/topics/funding/ grantwriting.php	Grantwriting
Character Counts http://charactercounts.org/getstarted/ funding/grantwriting-links.html	Grant-writing Resources

the "have-nots" into the digital age of the 21st century. If you opened a computer lab, look for an opportunity to reach out to those who cannot come to the lab. Seek out ways to offer computers with Internet access to shut-ins or homemakers with small children. If you have provided laptop computers to high school students, investigate extending that program down to younger students. The possibilities are endless, as are the needs of the underserved in our country. "Technology can be a means to access content on any topic, a tool for thinking and creating, a connection to peers and experts, and a window into other cultures" (International Society for Technology Education, 2012, p.6). We need to make sure that every person in America has the opportunity to grasp the brass ring of technology.

Chapter 6

Taking Educational Technology Innovations to Scale

The primary goal for digital solidarity within the educational arena is to identify and replicate innovative technology programs and models that have demonstrated the ability to motivate all students towards academic excellence and global competitiveness. A part of the current challenge for the digital solidarity movement is to understand what is involved in taking pilot projects that are effective in one area and bring them to scale so that they reach and positively affect more people. We therefore need to have a clear understanding of what is meant by such terms as *scalability*, *scaling up*, and *going to scale*.

Diamond (2007) separated *scalability* into two levels, the first being *scaling up* and the second being *going to scale*. While she defined *scaling up* to mean the ability for an innovation to be adopted and replicated in other venues such as schools, *going to scale* referred to the ability of an innovation to sustain itself over time and for those participating in the reform effort to ultimately assume its ownership. Scaling up refers to the expansion of a program, practice, or product. It can be viewed as the replication of a successful educational reform in more classrooms, schools, and districts—more numbers, and the inclusion of more teachers and students. This definition offers scaling up as simply a marketing problem needing strategies and incentives to persuade local decision-makers and teachers to adopt a particular reform and scale up its use (Diamond & Pisapia, 2008).

Going to scale presents an alternative view of scalability; one that implies full utilization of the reform in a jurisdiction (a nation, state, region, or school district) such that the reform becomes routine and embedded in the fabric of the organization. The result is to achieve reform in such a large number of schools and classrooms that the norms of the profession are altered, and the reformed practice becomes the new standard.

Through an extensive literature review that examined numerous education reforms, Diamond identified a list of 39 attributes within five broad categories, along with seven contextual factors that are pertinent in bringing a technology innovation to scale. The five categories include: (a) the design of the innovation, (b) time, (c) communication channels, (d) effectiveness, and (e) leadership capabilities. These attributes were categorized as either a level 1 (scaling up) attribute or level 2 (going to scale) attribute. Her research concluded that the level 1 attributes were necessary but not sufficient in successfully bringing a technology innovation to scale. Technology innovations that are able to *go to scale* need to also include those attributes identified as level 2. You can find her attribute checklist in Appendix B. Some of the theoretical frameworks from which these attributes emerged are discussed below. An understanding of these frameworks and their attributes assist in successfully implementing and sustaining educational technology initiatives that help to support digital solidarity efforts.

Scaling Up

Diffusion of Innovations Theory explains the process by which an innovation is adopted by members of a certain community. It offers a powerful paradigm to conceptualize the development, acceptance, and successful implementation of technology innovations. Everett Rogers, the most widely cited author in the area of General Diffusion Theory, was identified as the researcher who had done the most to synthesize the major findings and compelling theories related to diffusion (Surry, 1997). Rogers' (1995) Innovation Decision Process is a process through which an individual (or decision-making unit) passes from first *knowledge* of an innovation to being *persuaded* to form an attitude toward the innovation, to making a *decision* regarding its adoption or rejection, where upon adoption the innovation moves into the *implementation* phase, eventually leading to *confirmation* of this decision.

Ely (1999), a widely cited researcher working on the implementation of instructional technology innovations, studied successful implementation of innovations to determine the nature of their success. He concluded that implementation, the phase after adoption and before confirmation in Rogers' model, was an essential and often overlooked part of the innovation process. Surry and Ely (2001) suggested that *implementation* should naturally lead into *institutionalization*; and proposed that "the ultimate criterion for a successful innovation is that it is routinely used in settings for which it was designed. At that point, it becomes integral to the organization or the social system and is no longer considered to be an innovation" (p.190). Surry and Ely's diffusion model assumed that an innovation will pass through adoption, diffusion, implementation, and institutionalization before it can be widely accepted, and in effect, *go to scale*. Their model is depicted in Figure 6.1.

Duflo (2003, May) suggested, "*Scaling up* is possible only if a case can be made that programs that have been successful on a small scale would work in

Figure 6.1 **Surry and Ely's Diffusion Model**

other contexts" (p.1). Others framed scaling up in terms of *"geographic proximity,* defining scale in terms of an increase in the number of schools involved in a reform effort to achieve a critical mass in a bounded area such as a school district" (Bodilly, 1998). Most research on the topic of scaling up external reforms has involved quantitative analyses that focus on the increased number of teachers, schools, or districts involved in implementing a reform initiative. Over 20 years ago, Rand Education stated that the process of scaling up "was often expressed as a *replication model* characterized by a one-way flow of information and mandates from external providers or district to schools and teachers" (2004, p.2). Success was determined by the level of fidelity of implementation at multiple sites; while "failure was attributed to teachers not supporting the effort" (p.2).

This definition corresponds with other one-dimensional conceptions of scaling up that merely involve the replication of the reform in greater numbers of schools or define it as a process of mutual adaptation where schools adapt reform models to fit the needs of their local context. McDonald, Keesler, Kauffman, and Schnieder (2006) offered an algorithm for scale: Scale = number of students x time x impact; claiming that interventions that do not affect a larger number of students and teachers are merely local interventions with promising results.

The research of Bodilly, Glennan, Galegher, and Kerr (2004) consisted of descriptive analyses of scaling up processes conducted by leaders and external provider organizations. The authors offered a historical perspective on the changing nature of scaling up reforms. The authors also referred to the process of scaling up that prevailed in education from the 1960s through the 1970s as the *replication model.* With its basis in management science precepts about organizational change, this model consisted of an external provider who would "respond to a felt need for change or a performance failure in schooling by developing an idea or sets of ideas for curriculum, instruction, and associated training for teachers intended to improve teaching practices and eventually student performance" (p.11). New ideas would be tested, with either a set of teachers or a specific school designated as a *demonstration site,* where the set of ideas would become refined and perfected. The program may or may not be evaluated to assess its abilities to improve student achievement, at which time it would then be "assumed that the interventions could be adopted with great fidelity at multiple sites in the same way that had worked at the demonstration site" (p.11). In this context, scale meant quantity—an increased number of teachers, schools, classrooms, or districts adopting the reform.

The research of Bodilly et al. (2004) focused on "how the providers created interventions and built and sustained organizations and networks that assisted educators, schools, and school districts in implementing the improved practices more systematically than in the past" (p.4). Their inquiries were directed towards the process of how these reforms spread from their demonstration sites to reach more students, more teachers, and more schools. The researchers offered several contextual factors to explain why educational interventions were unable to take hold. One factor involved the difficulty in changing the practice of teachers who were embedded in a system of rules and regulations that did not support new practices. In addition, both the hierarchical mandates and the market forces that work in the private sector do not operate well on schools. Bodilly et al. affirmed that public schools are "governed by political processes and were administered by entrenched bureaucracies characterized as a system of fragmented centralization prone to seeking legitimacy by remaining the same, not by innovating" (p.13).

The essays of Bodilly et al. (2004) offered a list of critical factors in determining the success or failure of a reform implementation that affect its ability to go to scale. These factors related to the intervention itself, school conditions, the level of assistance provided to implement the reform, and the alignment of policy and infrastructure support. Specifically, they included characteristics of the intervention that affect implementation including comprehensiveness, ambitiousness, and elaboration. Additionally, there are school factors that affect implementation, including teacher buy-in and participation, as well as principal support and leadership. Specific support required for implementation and sustainability also appear in the form of technical assistance, training, and resources. These are all critical factors that influence the success or failure of educational efforts directed towards digital solidarity.

Going to Scale

Coburn's (2003) analysis of scale confirmed the development of a growing body of research work addressing the theoretical challenges involved in creating a meaningful definition of scale that provides evidence for its multidimensional nature. She argued for identifying scaling up as a complex endeavor, one to be characterized and analyzed across its multiple layers. According to Coburn, scaling up involved issues of spreading the reform to multiple teachers, schools, and districts while "sustaining change in a multilevel system characterized by multiple and shifting priorities" (2003, p.3). Coburn's four levels of scale include **depth, spread, sustainability**, and **shift in reform ownership**.

The dimension of depth pertains to the nature of change in classroom practice, including indicators such as changes in teachers' beliefs, norms of interaction, and underlying pedagogical principles. As such, the "central purpose of taking a reform to scale is to improve teaching and learning for a large number of students" (Coburn, 2003, p.4). An innovation has been adequately adopted at the classroom level when clear evidence exists of changes in the way instruction unfolds. "More specifically, to be 'at scale,' reforms must effect deep and consequential change in classroom practice" (p.4).

A second important component relating to the construct of depth involves classroom *norms of social interaction*. Coburn defined these as "teacher and student roles in the classroom, patterns of teacher and student talk, and the manner in which teachers and students treat one another" (2003, p.5). Many of the recent external reform efforts attempted to disrupt and alter traditional student–teacher roles, and specifically target this aspect of classroom life for change. Reform efforts such as ATLAS that were rooted in the constructivist approach to teaching and learning, Success for All with its emphasis on collaborative learning that alters the student–student dynamic in a classroom, and the Coalition of Essential Schools with its attempt to change the environment for learning in schools and classrooms, all sought to reshape the nature and the quality of teacher–student and student–student relationships (Diamond, 2007). This disruption and altering of traditional learning relationships can also be found in the steady growth of the virtual school movement. Virtual schooling is capable of reaching a more diverse audience, has individualized the learning process and enabled students to take a more responsible role in their own learning while allowing teachers to facilitate the process. In order to reach the most marginalized of our students, the atypical roles of teacher and student will need to be revised to offer a more inclusive learning environment that meets the needs of a variety of learners.

The second construct in Coburn's theory involves the key component of the traditional definition of scale: spread. Spread involves the reform getting to greater numbers of classrooms and schools. In addition to the spread of activity structures, materials, and classroom organization, successful reforms must also include "the spread of underlying beliefs, norms, and principles to additional classrooms and schools" (Coburn, 2003, p.7). Spread should not be thought solely in terms of expanding the reform innovation outward to more schools and classrooms but should also pertain to the spread of "reform related norms and pedagogical principles within a classroom, school, and district" (p.7). Spread of a reform initiative *within* can be identified when teachers "draw on pedagogical principles and norms of interaction in areas of the classroom beyond those subjects, time of day, or particular activities targeted by the reform" (p.7). As new educational reforms that support digital solidarity are incorporated in additional school settings, reformers must clearly identify the beliefs, norms, and principles governing the reform effort so that they can firmly take root. This will help to sustain the reform over time.

Sustainability, Coburn's third component, might be the central challenge in bringing reform initiatives to scale because the dimension seeks to determine whether or not, as well as how, schools sustain reforms after the external partner or funding dissipates. Coburn found "the distribution and adoption of an innovation are only significant if its use can be sustained in original and even subsequent schools" (p.6). She concluded that the notion of going to scale only had meaning when considered over a period of time, yet found that few studies looked at school reform that went past the initial implementation period. Her research suggested that most studies merely focus on the first few years of implementing a new external reform, thereby failing to capture sustainability. Dede, Honan, and Peters (2005) defined sustainability to mean that "an effort can continue without special or external resources . . . that the effort can continue without the involvement of the researcher and developers who were involved in the initial classroom implementation" (p.53). Rand Education (2004) described sustainability as the "policy and infrastructure systems in place to support continued, deep improvement in classroom practice over time" (p.2). McDonald (2005) cited three interrelated aspects of the sustainability challenge as: financial, human, and intellectual. These too are the challenges that plague sustainability efforts for both current and future educational reforms supporting digital solidarity.

The concept of shift in reform ownership is the ultimate goal for any innovation. Here the ownership is transferred to multiple constituencies within a school or school district. It occurs when there is a move from external reform controlled by a reformer, to internal control with the knowledge and authority held by schools, teachers, and administrators who are capable of sustaining, spreading, and deepening the reform principles themselves. Depth of reform-centered knowledge among leaders at various levels of the system, as well as at the classroom and school levels, is imperative for the successful transfer of any reform's ownership and authority.

This last characteristic for a successful scale-up effort has only recently been articulated in the research conducted on effective education reform initiatives. Reformers and researchers are now distinguishing between "reform ownership" as ensuring teacher and school "buy-in," with a more relevant definition of a shift in knowledge of and authority for the reform. The former relates to the reforms' "initial adoption and implementation rather than long-term sustainability and growth" (Coburn, 2003, p.7). Rand Education (2004) described shift in reform ownership to mean a "transfer of knowledge and authority to sustain the reform to the site, allowing continuous improvement and further scale-up" (p.2).

Research showed (Corcoran, n.d.; Coburn, 2003; Lynch, 2004; McDonald et al., 2006) that the ability to shift the authority and ownership for a reform from external to internal control rests on the ability to develop the capacity to provide reform-related professional development or other structures for ongoing teacher and administration learning. Such ongoing activities to spread and deepen reform require a funding stream, and creative thinking about reallocating existing budgets or securing additional grant dollars to support the reform over time. Essential to the successful transfer of ownership and authority of any reform is the ability to transfer reform-centered knowledge among leaders at various levels of the system as well as at the classroom and school levels. While both knowledge and authority shift from an external reform organization to the local school and district personnel, so too shifts the control of deciding which aspects of the reform remain emphasized, and which become adopted. This can have a direct impact on those reforms that place a high priority on reform fidelity.

The contention is that without a shift in reform ownership, adopters remain reliant on developers to sustain the core practices of the school. This relationship cannot be sustained over the long haul. Coburn (2003) predicted that "shift in reform ownership may be a central element in sustaining and spreading reform in the face of shifting priorities, changes in funding, and challenges to policy coherence" (p.8). Coburn offered some preliminary indicators that suggest the viability for a shift in reform ownership at the school and district levels. These include structures and mechanisms for ongoing teaching and learning about the reform, established strategies to provide continued funding for reform activities, a high degree to which districts take responsibility for the continued spread of the reform, and the use of reform-centered ideas or structures in school's or district's decision-making. Development of internal capacity for a reform is critical if we are to expect digital solidarity programs to thrive over time.

Alignment of Theoretical Frameworks on Scale

Rogers' notion of going to scale was confirmation; Surry and Ely's model ended at the stage of institutionalization. Coburn (2003), however, noted that scale, in the traditional sense, had been restricted to one dimension that involved solely or predominantly the expansion of the given reform effort to a greater number of schools. She rejected this singular approach, theorizing that the notion of going to scale was a far more complex endeavor that should be seen as a multidimensional problem. She pressed for a definition of scale that includes the challenges of implementing reform and sustaining change in multilevel systems characterized by shifting priorities. Diamond (2007) offered Figure 6.2 aligning Coburn's conception of scale which includes the four interrelated dimensions of depth, spread, sustainability, and shift in reform ownership with the scale theories of Rogers, and Surry and Ely.

Diamond's (2007) depiction showed how Coburn extended Rogers' Diffusion Theory by indicating that going to scale cannot be attained by an innovation that has only gone through the first two stages of depth (adoption) and spread (diffusion). Instead, innovations attempting to go to scale must develop attributes that allow for sustainability (implementation) and shift in reform ownership (institutionalization). Rogers' final stage of confirmation implied that there was either a reaffirming or a rejection of the decision to adopt the innovation, but confirmation does not define the mechanisms needed to enable the innovation to continue once said confirmation had taken place. In this regard, Coburn's stage of sustainability identifies the human, technological, and financial resources necessary to perpetuate the innovation. A shift in reform ownership is needed to enable the control of the reform to be held by internal constituents. Only when these four interrelated constructs have proved viable and effective should it be concluded that an innovation has gone to scale. The attribute checklist (Appendix B) can be used as a guide in the development

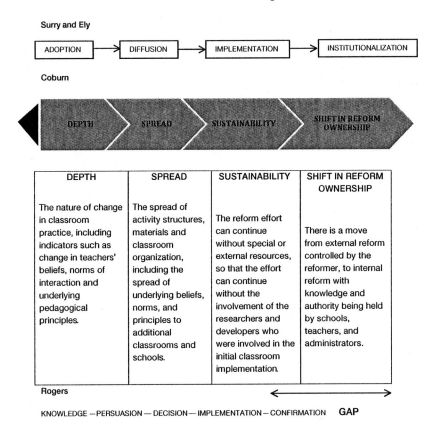

Figure 6.2 Alignment of Surry and Ely's Diffusion Model, Coburn's Four Levels of Scale, and Rogers' Diffusion Theory

of technology implementation plans. Assuring the success of level 2 attributes will enhance the chances for success of the technology program.

Leave No Child Behind—The Federal Government's Role in Education 2002–2012

History of the Mandate

Lynch (2004) found it "strange that students' role in scale-up is not emphasized, nor is the importance of timely assessments (even though Coburn's research focused on a comprehensive school reform effort)" (p.11). Coburn's omission in mentioning the importance of positive student outcomes and their effect on the likelihood of an intervention going to scale was puzzling, especially within the current educational climate. The ability to demonstrate an intervention's impact on student achievement seems absolutely necessary for its spread and sustainability. Engelmann and Engelmann (2004) confirmed, "The only possible evidence that a reform model is successful, therefore, is student performance" (p.108).

So it is prudent for us to take a look at the primary statute governing the federal government's role in education—the law that is known as "No Child Left Behind (NCLB) Act of 2001" (2002), to determine whether or not this education reform has been successful in going to scale, and its role in bringing digital equity to all schools in the nation. The law was first passed during the Johnson administration as the Elementary and Secondary Education Act (ESEA) and was rebranded after its overhaul in 2001 by President George W. Bush. So it has had ample time, over a decade, to demonstrate success for its goals and objectives. Its focus has been on the use of standardized tests scores in schools, particularly those serving minority students. Tests were administered annually to demonstrate that a growing population of the students was proficient on state exams. It has been praised for making schools more accountable for the education of poor and minority students.

The law dictated that every state would identify standards for both reading and math and set as its goal that all students would be proficient in those standards by 2014. Students in grades 3 through 8 would be tested annually and the results would be made public. By the 2005–2006 school year, states were required to begin testing students in grades 3–8 annually in reading and mathematics. By 2007–2008 they had to test students in science at least once in elementary, middle, and high school. The tests had to be aligned with state academic standards. A sample of fourth and eighth graders in each state also had to participate in the National Assessment of Educational Progress (NAEP) testing program (also known as the "Nation's Report Card") in reading and math every other year to provide a point of comparison for state test results. Schools were required to break down their data by race, gender, and socio-economic status, which meant that they could not use average scores to hide their failing students behind the more accomplished kids (Johnson, 2012, January). Reports were issued detailing whether or not schools have made "adequate yearly progress" (AYP) towards that goal (based on a formula spelled out in the law) for both student populations as a whole and for certain demographic groups. Scores for minority, disabled, and English-language learners were broken out separately. Schools that did not make AYP faced a variety of sanctions, some as minor as providing tutoring for underperforming students to as serious as being shut down by the state. Specifically, for an underperforming school receiving federal Title 1 funding, failure to make AYP for two years in a row meant that it was provided technical assistance and students were given a choice of other public schools to attend; for three years in a row it needed to offer supplemental educational services including private tutoring; for continued "failure" it was subject to outside corrective measures including possible governance changes.

Starting in the 2002–2003 school year, states were required to furnish annual report cards showing information pertaining to student achievement, data broken down by subgroup, and information on the performance of school districts. Individual school districts needed to provide similar information showing school-by-school data. By the end of the 2005–2006 school year, every teacher in a core content area working in a public school had to be deemed "highly qualified" in each subject taught. This meant that teachers had to be certified and demonstrate proficiency in his or her subject area. For those teachers working in schools funded by federal Title 1 dollars, they needed to be "highly qualified" by the 2002–2003 school year. All Title 1 schools had to have their parapro-fessionals complete at least two years of college, obtain an associate's degree or higher, or pass an evaluation to demonstrate knowledge and teaching ability by the end of the 2005–2006 school year.

NCLB created a new competitive grant program called Reading First, funded at $1.02 billion in 2004. This was designed to help states and districts set up "scientific, research-based" reading programs for children in grades K–3. Priority was given to high-poverty areas. A smaller early-reading program sought to help states prepare three- to five-year-olds in disadvantaged areas to read. This program was later cut drastically by Congress due to budget constraints. The NCLB Act was expected to better target resources to school districts with high concentrations of poor children through alterations to the Title 1 funding formula. The law included provisions that gave states some flexibility in how they spent some portions of their federal allotments.

The Mandate's Evaluation

But as the proficiency date rapidly approaches, the decade old law has been derided for its "obsessive focus on test results, which has led to some notorious cheating scandals" (N.Y. Times, 2012, July, para. 3). Neill (2010) chastised the legislation based on its obsessive testing requirements stating that the United States significantly stands alone among nations in testing in so many grades. "Top-ranked Finland barely tests at all, while Singapore tests in a few grades" (para. 2). This represents the range amongst nations with better results than the United States on international exams, graduation rates, and college entry and completion.

Also found unjust was the law's system of rating schools which labeled so many of them as failing that it "rendered the judgment meaningless" (N.Y. Times, 2012, July, para. 3). In 2007 the law expired; Congress failed to rewrite it thereby missing the deadline for refreshing the law. Through the use of executive powers, the Obama administration made sweeping changes to the law in March 2010 and offered states some relief from its toughest parts. The administration allowed states to request waivers to free them from the "central provisions of the law, raising the question of whether the decade-old federal program has been essentially nullified" (N.Y. Times, 2012, July, para. 6). In July 2012, 32 states and the District of Columbia received waivers from the NCLB law. Eight of the 32 NCLB waivers granted are conditional because those states have not completely satisfied the administration's requirements and parts of their plans are still under review.

Schools and districts now must set targets for preparing students for colleges and careers. In addition, there still are accountability measures, but these will look to "reward high-performing schools and single out low-performing schools for 'rigorous and comprehensive interventions' and to develop and implement plans for improving educational outcomes for poor and minority students and other underperforming groups" (*N.Y. Times*, 2012, July, para. 7). Evaluation of teachers and schools is still attached to student achievement and standardized tests, which is a departure from the original law.

A report from The Center on Education Policy shows more than 43,000 schools—or 48 percent—did not make "adequate yearly progress" in 2011 (Associated Press, 2011). The failure rates ranged from a low of 11 percent in Wisconsin to a high of 89 percent in Florida. The report found that states' scores varied wildly. In Georgia, 27 percent of schools did not meet targets, compared with 81 percent in Massachusetts and 16 percent in Kansas. One reason for this is that some states give harder tests, while others have high numbers of immigrant and low-income children. In addition, the law required states to raise the bar each year for how many children must pass the test, but allowed states to set their own annual benchmarks. Some states put off the largest increase specifically to avoid sanctions. These numbers provided evidence that the NCLB law is "'too crude a measure' to accurately depict what is happening in schools" (Associated Press, 2011). Ladner and Lips (2009) identified an unintended consequence resulting from the penalties placed on schools failing to demonstrate progress on state exams. The penalties incentivized the states to lower testing standards to avoid federal sanctions. Research showed that NCLB was the cause for curriculum narrowing, intense teaching to the test, and worsening school climate (Neill, 2010).

Ladner and Lips (2009) concurred, that NCLB, like previous federal reform interventions, failed to yield meaningful improvements in students' learning. While the National Assessment of Educational Progress (NAEP) suggested that American students have made modest advances in fourth- and eighth-grade math, particularly minorities, not so in reading. The rate of progress on the NAEP has declined since the law was implemented, indicating that scores on state tests are greatly inflated (Neill, 2010). Downey (2010, May) detailed that the results were mixed with improvements concentrated in the earlier grades, most notably in grade 4 NAEP math scores. These improvements were mostly among Hispanic and low-income students. Downey cautioned on the interpretation of the success of the education reform, stating that "the impact NCLB has had on student achievement since its implementation in 2002 has always been difficult to gauge" (para. 11). This is due to the fact that there is no comparison group since the law applied to all public school students, and it was impossible to determine which of countless factors contributed to student achievement.

Ladner and Lips (2009) proposed that NCLB gave the federal government the power to regulate policies previously determined by governors, state legislators, and local leaders. These expanded regulations "significantly increased the resources that must be allocated by state and local governments simply to comply with federal requirements" (p.3). Ladner and Lips (2009) stated that since the passage of NCLB, the federal government's budget for the Department of Education has funded programs that were either ineffective or unnecessary.

Johnson's (2012, January) research posited that the one undisputed success of No Child Left Behind was its focus on student achievement. The major change that NCLB brought to education was its intense focus on students' reading and math proficiency within different subgroups. She believed that this will endure into the next chapter of education policy. Her research also identified some clear failures: (a) the law's teacher effectiveness and school choice provisions are ineffective in making real change as the achievement gap between well-off white children and poorer minorities still exists, although all students are performing better than they did 20 years ago, and (b) the law did not achieve its ultimate goal, accountability. But it did push states and school boards to rethink how they assess and run their education systems. Ravitch (2012, July) in her education blog identified a statistical rationale for the faulty measurement and evaluation piece of NCLB. Included in the blog was a letter from Harry Frank, an author of textbooks about measurement and evaluation. In that letter, Frank identified the flaw to be that the Act did not follow the first principle relating to workplace performance evaluation. That is, no assessment can be used at the same time for both counseling and for administrative decisions (retention, increment, tenure, promotion). It assumes that the same tests may be used both to evaluate the teacher and to counsel the teacher. "All this does is promote cheating and teaching to the exam" (para. 7).

Neill (2010, para. 5) concluded that Congress's inability to admit to the ineffectiveness of NCLB stems from a "de facto alliance among corporate groups . . . a growing list of high-tech and hedge-fund billionaires, a few large foundations (Gates, Broad and Walton among them), Duncan's Education Department, and major national media" who have invested millions of dollars to promote their educational ideas. The result is that the very groups of students the law was designed to protect and support (poor, of color, speaking English as a second language, the disabled) are not getting a good enough education and are victims of these policies.

Perhaps the issue is one of complexity. Other educational options besides NCLB exist but they have been "under-financed, not supported by the most visible and wealthy sectors in society" (Neill, 2010, para. 11). These solutions cost more because they deal with overcoming poverty and segregation that "are still the most significant factors in student outcomes" (para. 12). Testing is much less expensive and is an easier option in comparison to more complex and politically difficult factors.

How No Child Left Behind Addressed the Digital Divide

The federal government's hallmark mandate, the No Child Left Behind Act, should have provided support for the nation's digital solidarity movement as it earmarked all marginalized students in the K–12 arena for attention and academic improvement. Yet according to most, it was ineffective and failed to demonstrate academic success that should have closed the achievement gap between whites and other minorities. Some support the notion that it has even widened the gap with its focus on remediation and teaching to the test, rather than creating a teaching and learning process that develops the kinds of skills that are needed to exist in a 21st-century world and benefit from the techno-logical advances that are being made within it.

The Henry J. Kaiser Family Foundation Issue Brief (2004) outlined the various types of technology access issues inherent in the implementation of No Child Left Behind as federal educational policy. First, there were basic access issues dealing with students' abilities to get to use a wired computer somewhere, at some time. Second, there was the quality of access issue referring to the gap between high-speed access enabling the use of graphics and rapid downloads/uploads and dial-up access with its much slower connectivity. Third, there was the issue of technological literacy and the degree to which students know what they are doing while being online, the types of software applications they know how to use while online, and their ability to learn and utilize new software applications. Last, there was the issue of access to useful and relevant content which would include "information and software they need to do their homework, protect their health, or find a job" (p.1).

During the years of the NCLB policy implementation, Congress questioned the role of the federal government in closing the digital divide. While recognizing the need to connect schools and libraries for low-income, rural and urban areas underserved by the private sector, Congress objected to the perceived "top-down" or "big government" approach of the federal government. Many believed that too big an involvement could "stifle innovation in the telecommunications sector" (The Henry J. Kaiser Family Foundation Issue Brief, 2004, p.6). The NCLB Act of 2001, while not explicitly designed to address the digital divide, included "substantial resources that could be used to improve children's access to technology" (p.7). The NCLB Act "created and absorbed a range of programs with potential relevance to the digital divide" (p.8). The Bush administration tried to eliminate duplication and inefficiency among educational programs, "including those focused on bringing technology into the schools" (p.8). The Enhancing Education through Technology (EETT) block grant program addressed the digital divide most directly. Its primary goal was to "improve student academic achievement through the use of technology in school" (p.8). It also included the mandate to make every student technologically literate by the end of the eighth grade.

But the first decade of the new millennium saw the end of the technology boom and an economic downturn which had disastrous effects on many digital divide programs being implemented in collaboration between the government and the telecommunication and private sectors. Additionally, the country saw (a) an economy that moved from surplus to deficit, (b) philanthropic and other types of equipment donations dry up, (c) foundation endowments disappear and with it the reduction of support from the non-profit sector regarding advocacy and programs, and (d) the laying off of workers while sending technology jobs overseas. "These changes, combined with improved rates of Internet access and dropping computer and connection prices, lowered the pressure to close what was left of the digital divide" (The Henry J. Kaiser Family Foundation Issue Brief, 2004, p.6). As pressure mounted on state budgets, there was a shift of federal dollars from technology programs to meet other education priorities.

Will the Common Core State Standards Support Digital Solidarity?

The Common Core State Standards Initiative began in 2009 as a collaborative effort between most of the U.S. states and territories, the National Governors Association, and the Council of Chief State School Officers. For the first time state governments, rather than the federal government, have developed common standards to improve the content of instruction in Mathematics and English Language Arts. The common standards identify the most essential skills and knowledge that students need to know at each grade level. Currently 46 states and the District of Columbia have adopted the Common Core State Standards (CCSS) which affect instructional materials, curricula, professional development, and assessment. What this means is "every public school student in the United States will be exposed to roughly the same content, especially in grades 1–8" (Schmidt & Burroughs, 2012, p.54). This suggests that the CCSS have the potential to ensure greater *equality* in the instructional material that students will be taught in school.

Roscorla (2010) indicated that although the CCSS have a focus on both Mathematics and English Language Arts, they also emphasize technology to learn the skills and knowledge in both of these content areas. Technology is integrated into the academics instead of being taught separately. The CCSS include basic technology skills such as keyboarding, but also require students to use technology in the learning process to help them understand the content. Anchoring the K–12 CCSS are the College and Career Readiness Standards, which call for students to learn skills through technology and multimedia. The belief is that students who are college and career ready in mathematics, reading, writing, speaking, listening, and language are able to use technology and digital media strategically and capably.

Although the CCSS do not cover everything that students need to know about technology, the technologies used enhance the instructional practices within the content areas. The writers of the CCSS have approached technology as a tool, and not as a set of skills in and of itself. Students can be using technology tools to help solve math problems, to access relevant information, or to promote literacy and communication skills. In all instances, technology is part of the learning solution. Some technology literacy skills that students should be able to demonstrate when they are college and career ready include: producing and publishing documents, interacting and collaborating, communicating using web tools, and evaluating information presented in different media formats. The Partnership for 21st Century Skills has for over a decade advocated for standards that address the core academic knowledge and the complex thinking skills that are necessary to be successful in college, life, and career in the 21st century. The Partnership promotes the use of the CCSS and "has published a P21 Common Core Toolkit" showing how both the Common Core and the partnership's frameworks are aligned and support each other (Loveless, 2012, p.62). The Partnership's framework of skills include: life and career skills; information, media, and technology skills; and the 4Cs (critical thinking, communication, collaboration, and creativity).

The two standards documents for Mathematics and English Language Arts address technology skills very differently (Skills for 21st Century, 2010). The Mathematics Standards document says under Standards for Mathematical Practice: *5. Use appropriate tools strategically.* It goes on to say that mathematically proficient students consider the available tools when solving a mathematical problem. These might include: pencil and paper, concrete models, a ruler, a protractor, a calculator, a spreadsheet, a computer algebra system, a statistical package, or dynamic geometry software. Students should be able to use technology when making mathematical models, and that these models help them to visualize the results of assumptions while exploring consequences and comparing predictions with data. The Mathematics Standards suggest when a student is proficient in mathematics they should be able to identify relevant external mathematical resources such as digital content on a website, and use that information to solve problems. In addition, they should be able to use technological tools to explore and deepen their understanding of mathematical concepts.

The English Language Arts (ELA) Standards document has more to say regarding technology and in several different sections. Research and media skills are blended into the Standards as a whole rather than treated in a separate section. To be ready for college, workforce training, and life in a technical society, the ELA Standards expect students to be able to use higher-level thinking skills while conducting research and analyzing print and non-print texts in both old and new media. Within the Language Arts vision statement it claims that "Students who are College and Career Ready in Reading, Writing, Speaking, Listening, and Language use technology and digital media strategically and capably" (Skills for 21st Century, 2010). In three of the four College and Career Readiness (CCR) anchor standards for Reading, Writing, Speaking, and Listening, there are standards for which technology skills are embedded, such as:

- Reading:
  7. Integrate and evaluate content presented in diverse media and formats, including visually and quantitatively, as well as in words.
- Writing:
  6. Use technology, including the Internet, to produce and publish writing and to interact and collaborate with others.
  8. Gather relevant information from multiple print and digital sources, assess the credibility and accuracy of each source, and integrate the information while avoiding plagiarism.
- Speaking & Listening:
  2. Integrate and evaluate information presented in diverse media and formats, including visually, quantitatively, and orally.
  5. Make strategic use of digital media and visual displays of data to express information and enhance understanding of presentations.

Concluding Thoughts

Educational technology can facilitate communication, engagement, interaction, and understanding. This works best when technology in education creates a balance between technological advancement and academic goals. This balance is not very easily achieved because of issues such as budget limitations, teacher and student performance standards, and state and federal mandates. The educational arena has been putting all of its hopes on standards for more than two decades, and "about half of our high school graduates are no better prepared for college or work than they were 20 years ago, when standards and testing became the nations' school improvement strategy" (Wolk, 2012). Although the CCSS are seen as being much better than the state standards they are replacing, some find it difficult to believe that the results of their implementation will be any different from those we have currently.

Wolk (2012) identified some glaring reasons why not much hope is held for the successful implementation of the CCSS. Tied to such a failure would be the continued inability for marginalized students to be exposed to and learn from educational technologies used in the delivery of the standards. For one, our teachers have not been trained to teach the way the new standards require, nor have they been trained to successfully integrate the technologies that are embedded within the standards. Second, math and science are critical shortage content areas and states would be hard pressed to replace those teachers who are retiring or leaving education for other jobs. Third, there would need to be a commitment of a substantial amount of financial resources, which most states do not have, to provide things such as: up-to-date science labs, renovated school buildings, and adequate learning materials. Most importantly, we have to commit financial resources to eradicating the "glaring and persistent discrimination that condemns millions of low-income, minority, and immigrant students to a poor and mediocre education that does not prepare them to meet the new common standards" (Wolk, 2012). It is unreasonable to assume just because the CCSS are better and more rigorous than those previous, that these students will be capable of meeting them.

Loveless (2012) predicted that the Common Core initiative "will have little to no effect on student achievement. Moreover, on the basis of current research, high-quality professional development and 'excellent' curricular materials are also unlikely to boost the Common Core standards' slim chances of success" (p.63). Brooks and Dietz (2012) warned that the increased standardization that is inherent in the CCSS threatens to repeat those instructional methods regarded as best practices during the No Child Left Behind era. These practices, particularly in high-poverty environments, had the effect of "narrowing, if not entirely eliminating opportunities for students to develop the skills and dispositions associated with 21st-century learning. Curiosity, exploration, perseverance, critical and creative thinking, and complex problem solving are being pushed aside and replaced with test preparation curriculums" (Loveless, 2012, p.66).

Although there is more evidence of technology usage embedded within the CCSS, giving all students access to such technology, training all teachers to use such technology effectively, and ensuring that the technology will be used to support 21st-century skills remains problematic. These concerns do not bode well for the Common Core State Standards helping to boost digital solidarity for the underserved.

Chapter 7

Epilogue

What Remains as Barriers for Selected Populations

Case Study

My aunt Sadie is a senior citizen, 88 years of age, and living on a fixed income. When she was growing up, she never had access to computers in schools. She first encountered using computers in her fifties when she was a state employee. The on-the-job computer training that she received was minimal, presented informally, and specifically focused on how to retrieve limited data from a database.

Since retirement, Sadie has moved to Central Florida from the Northeast. She is living in an unincorporated area of her city, so, in a way, she is geographically isolated from access to some city services. Hoping to gain better access to community services and information, she purchased an inexpensive laptop computer and pursued connecting with the Internet. She contacted her local phone company and was told that she would be sent a "kit" with the necessary equipment (modem) for Internet connectivity. Also, she was told if she were unable to connect the modem to her computer that technical assistance would be provided. When she received the "kit," she was unable to follow the technical instructions for connecting the modem to her computer to access the Internet. A second call to her local phone company was made for technical assistance. Sadie was frustrated since the online technical assistance did not provide her with the hands-on support that she needed. After making a third call to the local phone company, a technician was sent to her home. The individual connected Sadie to the Internet, but failed to provide any explanation of the connectivity process other than "hit this button." She tried to follow the minimal instructions, but after a month, she was no longer able to access the Internet. When she contacted the local phone company to explain her problem, she was told that when the technician visited her home, she signed a form that indicated she was "satisfied" with the service, so if she needed additional technical support, there would be another service charge. Since she was unable to access the Internet and was not willing to pay another service charge, she requested removal of Internet services from the local phone company. She was told that she had agreed to pay for the "free" modem with a contract and therefore would be charged on her phone bill for the Internet service for the remaining ten months.

Still determined to secure Internet access on her computer, Sadie visited a local computer store to seek information from their technicians regarding options for Internet connections, other than the phone company's DSL (Digital Subscriber Line). She brought her laptop with her and was told that there was a problem with her laptop's memory which was probably the reason for not being able to connect to the Internet. After sending the laptop back to the factory for repair, she was assured by the local computer store's technician that she would be able to secure Internet connectivity by contacting (by phone) a low-cost Internet access company. However, the connection would entail uploading a disk into her laptop computer. She called the company and, after providing her geographical location, was told that she did not have access to high-speed Internet services because she was in an unincorporated section of the city; therefore she would have to locate a copy of the disk for low-speed Internet access at a local department store. Sadie secured the disk and took it with her laptop back to the local computer store. The technician installed the disk but told her that to assure that she had Internet access she would have to pay for a technician to visit her house. Again, Sadie was frustrated, called customer service and requested cancellation of Internet access.

Another option for Sadie was contacting her local cable company. Since she already had cable TV, all she wanted was to pay the additional monthly fee for Internet access. She was told by the customer service representative that she would be required to "bundle" her services and that there was no option of adding only Internet access fees to her monthly cable bill. After more than a year of trying to secure Internet access, Sadie was extremely frustrated, with her fixed income providing limited options. Finally, she decided to "bite the bullet" and go with the "bundle only" option provided by the cable company. The technician came to her home and set her up for Internet access and showed her "which button to press." That was the extent of her training. However, thanks to a home care provider who comes to visit, Sadie has had exposure to the repetitive training that she needs on the laptop. Thanks to the one-on-one, hands-on training, Sadie now is able to get to Google to secure medical information from the Mayo clinic. Recently, she learned how to click on the link for email. Her email messages continue to be prefaced by the statement "I hope that you are getting this e-mail message," but Sadie is learning and her persistence has paid off, but at a cost.

Access to High-speed Internet

Crawford (2012a) equated Americans' Internet access today with the way privately owned electric companies offered electricity to them in the 1880s. Back then electricity was made available to cities and the homes of the rich, with everyone else receiving it either intermittently or not at all. By the mid-1920s, there were 15 holding companies that controlled 85 percent of the nation's electricity distribution. At that time, the Federal Trade Commission determined that consumers were routinely gouged by the power trusts, resulting in thousands of communities forming their own electrical utilities to provide their own power. Electricity is now a regulated public utility. Perhaps it is time for access to the Internet to be a regulated public utility as well.

The Internet is "the world's basic, general-purpose, two-way communication medium" (Crawford, 2012a, para. 33). In order to benefit from all that it is capable of providing, Americans need reliable, high-speed access to it. But in America we have believed in the "power and benevolence of the free market" (para. 33) from which no competition amongst and no regulation of our Internet providers has resulted. Today there are "two enormous monopoly submarkets— one for wireless and one for wired transmission [and each is] dominated by two or three large companies" (Crawford, 2012b, para. 10). Comcast is the wired giant and is the "country's largest cable operator, its largest residential high-speed Internet access company, its third-largest phone company, the owner of many cable content properties . . . and the manager of a robust video-on-demand platform" (para. 11). In 2009, Comcast had almost 16 million subscribers for its high-speed Internet access, with Time Warner (the second-largest cable provider) having about nine million. AT&T and Verizon are the wireless giants but are "too slow to compete with the cable industry's offerings" (para. 12). Each of the large cable companies across the nation "dominates its own region and can raise prices without fear of being undercut" (para. 17). This does not need to be, as other developed countries have oversight that ensures its citizens cheap connection rates to fiber optic networks (Crawford, 2012b).

Today, cable and telephone companies are attempting to hold onto their telecommunications dynasties by taking legal action against requests made by communities for local municipal, community-owned fiber optic networks. Communities are requesting fiber optics because they generally deliver faster and cheaper Internet services than those offered by the private carriers. In essence, Americans are paying more for Internet usage and are receiving slower service as a result of the strangle-hold these telecommunications companies have on the market. In fact "the U.S. is rapidly losing the global race for high-speed connectivity, as fewer than 8 percent of households have fiber service. And almost 30 percent of the country still isn't connected to the Internet at all" (Crawford, 2012a, para. 20).

Fiber connections are expensive—approximately $1,200 to $2,000 a house-hold (Crawford, 2012a). It can take up to three years for customers to offset the initial investment with savings made from its use. But the difference is that fiber optics can last for decades and provide significantly faster service. When citizens of Lafayette, Louisiana asked for speedier Internet access through a fiber-to-the-home service in 2004, the new network called LUS Fiber was met with push-back from the local telephone and cable companies. The telephone and cable companies sued the city, tried to pass laws that would stop the network, and forced the town to hold a referendum regarding the project. In 2007, after five lawsuits, the Louisiana Supreme Court ruled in favor of LUS Fiber and voted to allow the fiber optic network. Approximately $110.4 million in bonds were issued for the LUS Fiber project (LUS Fiber, 2012).

In computer networking, a **kilobit** normally represents 1000 bits of data. A **megabit** represents 1000 kilobits and a **gigabit** represents 1000 megabits (equal to one million kilobits) (Mitchell, 2013). This information is important when comparing the national broadband plans of the United States with other countries, for it delivers additional evidence that Americans are paying more for inferior broadband access. The FCC's National Broadband Plan 2010 stated that the appropriate speed for American households by 2020 should be 4 megabits per second (Mbps) for downloads and 1 Mbps for uploads. They believe that these speeds allow end users to send and receive emails, download webpages and use simple videoconferencing (Crawford, 2012a). Other countries, such as South Korea, China, Japan, and the Netherlands plan for far more extensive capabilities. South Korea's plan was to install 1 gigabit (Gb) per second of symmetric fiber data access in every home by 2012, with Hong Kong, Japan, and the Netherlands offering similar access. South Korea has more than half of its households connected to fiber lines. This is in comparison to the U.S. of about 7 percent of households having fiber access, and that access costing six times as much as what it costs in Hong Kong (Crawford, 2012b, para 18). In Australia, the plan is to have 93 percent of homes and businesses connected to fiber and the United Kingdom plans to offer a 300 Mbps fiber-to-the-home service on a wholesale basis.

Crawford (2012a) insists that the FCC's 4 Mbps Internet access goal is shortsighted and "allows the digital divide to survive" (para. 27). She recommends giving Americans access to 1 Gb of reasonably priced symmetric fiber-to-the-home networks. This gives Americans connection speeds hundreds of time faster than what they currently have. What this means in practice is that "movies could be downloaded in 12 seconds, video conferencing would become routine, and every household could see 3D and Super HD images. Americans could be connected instantly to their co-workers, their families, their teachers and their health care monitors" (para. 30). To accomplish this, the recommendation is for the U.S. to move to a utility model where all Americans receive fiber optic Internet access at reasonable prices.

Using Technology Seamlessly in the Classroom by all Teachers

Lytle (2012) suggested that teachers in the United States are not trained well enough to integrate technology into the classroom effectively. He argued that it is not the technology itself that will be responsible for preparing students for jobs in the future, but rather the teachers who use the technology. With the first microcomputers becoming available in our schools in the 1980s, our nation's teachers have had over 30 years to learn how to effectively integrate technology into classroom curricula in ways that enrich teaching and learning. As a nation, we need to determine why this has become such an arduous task to accomplish. We now have generations of students who have grown up "wired" and active participants in a digital world, who are unwilling to attend school where they are confronted with the traditional lecture model that is not conducive to student engagement. In addition, as we have detailed in this book, there are marginalized students arriving at our schools' doorsteps daily that do not have the digital access or the digital skills to use such access. It is imperative that our nation's teachers take on the role of teaching with technology in order to guide students in developing the much needed digital literacy skills.

Spencer (2012) identified 11 reasons why teachers do not use technology in the classroom. These reasons help to identify some root causes and perhaps can shed light on what educators can do to change current teaching models. They include:

- Fear—fear of not having the right skills to implement technology-enriched lessons along with fear of giving up control of the classroom
- Low Self-Efficacy—teachers who have not grown up with technology lack a belief in their own ability to create and implement technology-integrated lessons
- Era of Testing—even when teachers know that technology integration helps to improve student achievement, there is a disconnect between teaching with technology and high-stakes assessments that are made up of multiple-choice questions
- Consumerism—teachers may use computers only for entertainment and social interaction and are ill equipped to use them for educational purposes
- Lack of Leadership—principals are concerned with other facets of their school and do not care to manage the liabilities that come from ongoing technology use; e.g., cyber-bullying, Internet safety, technology theft
- Inconsistent Paradigms—teachers who are able to run multiple centers and groups within a classroom using traditional teaching devices, such as chart paper, worry about how students will behave when having groups of students work on computers
- Personal Experience—teachers are more comfortable delivering instructional strategies that align with what they did when they were growing up and have little experience using new media in their free time or through professional development; e.g., blogs and wikis
- Pride—many teachers are unwilling to admit that their non-technology approach might be wrong or that maybe implementing technology in the classroom could offer positive results

- Using Technology is Optional—leadership needs to make technology use a priority and not a personal choice by mandating its use in the classroom
- Lack of Technology—recent budget cuts have made it difficult to replace outdated equipment with new equipment that can run the latest software. Bring your own devices (BYOD) programs could prove helpful here
- Lack of Research—more solid research needs to be conducted that demonstrates the positive correlation between teacher training, technology integration into the curriculum, and student achievement to convince educators to use technology routinely.

Our suggestion to improve the use of technology in American classrooms is to give teachers the opportunity to see good technology integration in practice. Identifying those educators in a school building who can act as mentors to others is one way to get started. Enabling teachers to visit each other's classrooms and participate in these lessons is important. Another tool that depicts teachers incorporating technology in action is the Technology Integration Matrix (TIM) which can be found at http://fcit.usf.edu/matrix. The TIM provides a framework for defining and evaluating technology integration while setting a clear vision for effective teaching with technology. It gives teachers and administrators a common language for setting goals as they relate to technology integration, while helping to target professional development resources effectively.

The matrix has on one axis five interdependent characteristics of meaningful learning environments: active, constructive, goal directed, authentic, and collaborative (Johanssen, Howland, Moore, & Marra, 2003). On its other axis it has five levels of technology integration: entry, adoption, adaptation, infusion, and transformation. Through videos of teachers in classrooms, the TIM illustrates how teachers can use technology to enhance learning in K–12 students. Each cell in the matrix has a video (or several videos) which illustrates the integration of technology in classrooms where only a few computers are available and/or in classrooms where every student has access to a laptop computer. The TIM is designed to assist schools and districts in the state of Florida in evaluating the level of technology integration in classrooms and to provide teachers with models of how technology can be integrated into instruction in meaningful ways. The intent was for the TIM to be used in the context of comprehensive technology planning and for the Enhancing Education through Technology (EETT) program's accountability.

Sustainability in Educational Technologies

In the United States, there is sufficient evidence of innovative technology-based programs in education that serve as unique examples in supporting the digital solidarity movement. In designing, selecting, and using the various technologies available currently and planning for emerging technologies, one important issue emerges if we want to secure a better world for the future—sustainability. Sustainability means the ability to be maintained; the capacity for endurance. In the education sector, the question is whether or not technology can be sustainable if it is viewed as something separate from the curriculum, if it's not part of the discussion on educational reform, or if funding is available only if the school district's standardized test scores warrant it (Poggione, 2012). Even though a case can be argued that the integration of technologies in our schools promotes meaningful, engaged learning, allows students to work on authentic, challenging problems, and fosters the development of higher-order thinking skills, obstacles to maintaining and sustaining existing technologies and providing forums for new technologies still exist. In order to implement technology correctly and bring technology-enriched programs to scale, we have made the point that long-range plans must be developed at the local, state, and national levels to ensure sustained funding for ongoing educator training, easily accessible technical support, and the necessary equipment maintenance and upgrades. Numerous funding sources have been identified from various federal governmental agencies (Department of Education, Department of Labor, etc.) to private companies and foundations (Bill and Melinda Gates Foundation, Annenberg Foundation, Hewlett-Packard, etc.) to non-profit groups (KidTech, Computer Clubhouse, etc.) that fund the access of technologies to underrepresented groups as a model for supporting digital solidarity in the United States. But, does this model that has been created ensure the ongoing flow of funds for technology in schools and communities beyond tomorrow? Have educators and policy-makers been trained in planning for the best use of limited financial resources in creating short-term and long-term technology plans?

In addition to accessing and maintaining funding resources, the sustainability of innovational technologies in schools demands ever-present and always-available support, i.e., troubleshooters who can alleviate the educator's frustration when the current technology fails to work and the new technology elicits fear. Providing incentives that encourage participation in technologies training by educators, such as university credit and administrative recognition, is a key element in developing sustainability, as is community support of school funding, increases for technology purchases, and stakeholders' (local policy-makers, parents, administrators, teachers, students) verbal support of innovative technologies (Center for Implementing Technology in Education, n.d.).

The ever-changing pace of technologies in education presents the dilemma of promising opportunities and, at the same time, burgeoning challenges (Education Week, 2011, September 1). In the United States, learners from preschoolers to senior citizens *can* benefit from greater access to multimedia content and global information, increases in online course offerings that were previously unavailable, the expanding function of social networks as tools for professional development, and the widespread availability of devices to access the Internet. However, the rapid and dynamic pace of digital innovations mandates upgrading infrastructures and training. In order to "keep up" some schools need to "catch up." The speed with which innovative technologies emerge and are disseminated to a "hungering public" leaves little opportunity to determine which technologies are the most educationally effective.

How can digital solidarity be successfully addressed in the United States when the quality of educational technologies has not been systematically researched? To ensure a vision for sustainability of educational technologies in schools, there must be ongoing professional development that is relevant and engaging; there must be ongoing research of the quality and educational effectiveness of technologies before distribution to schools and society; and there must be research of the multiple ways of funding technologies.

How to Be a Good Digital Citizen

Themes of Digital Citizenship

Digital citizenship (sometimes referred to as digital wellness or digital ethics) is a topic that is currently being discussed not only here in the United States but around the world. It refers to how technology users should act when they are online and relates to the norms of appropriate and responsible behavior with regard to technology use. It also relates to developing the digital skills that enable people to use technology safely, critically, and proactively to contribute to society. Its efforts are to create an online world that is both responsible and respectful, enabling users to make the most out of technology, social networking, and online educational resources. Many states are requiring that their districts' technology plans include a component to educate pupils and teachers on the appropriate and ethical use of information technology in the classroom. Current concerns being raised by technology leaders, school administrators, teachers, students, and parents revolve around whether or not, and how, digital citizenship is being taught in our classrooms. Additionally, we need to determine if educators are receiving the appropriate preparation necessary to teach it.

Ribble (2013) identified nine themes pertaining to digital citizenship. The first involves *digital access* and the full electronic participation of all in society. He claimed that "digital exclusion of any kind does not enhance the growth of users in an electronic society" (para. 2). The second theme relates to *digital commerce* and the electronic buying and selling of goods. Technology users need to recognize the risks involved when a large share of the market economy is being conducted over the Internet. While there are widespread legal and legitimate purchases occurring, there are recent accounts of goods and services which conflict with laws and morals of some countries such as "illegal downloading, pornography, and gambling" (para. 3). Learning how to be an effective consumer in the new digital economy is important.

Digital communication, or the electronic exchange of information, is a significant change in how we communicate with each other today compared with in the past. The 21st century has seen communication options explode and enable people to stay in constant contact with each other. People can communicate and collaborate with people from anywhere at any time. Now we need to train consumers to learn how to use the different communication options effectively and appropriately.

A pivotal theme identified by Ribble is *digital literacy*. He suggested "a renewed focus must be made on what technologies must be taught as well as how it should be used" (para. 5). These technologies include web conferencing, video-conferencing, online sharing spaces such as online courses and just-in-time learning, blogs and wikis, virtual worlds, and social media sites. Digital citizenship involves helping people develop a high degree of information literacy skills. This must include *digital etiquette* training that details electronic standards of conduct and procedure. Rather than banning technology from use when improperly utilized, deliver training for consumers to develop the appropriate communication techniques for a digital environment. Digital etiquette involves more than just the creation of policies and procedures, and includes training on the rationale for them as well as the benefits derived from their use.

Digital law pertains to the responsibility for one's electronic actions and deeds while being online. Unethical use conducted online can be found in the form of theft that causes damage to people's work, identity, or online property. "Hacking into others' information, downloading illegal music, plagiarizing, creating destructive worms, viruses or creating Trojan Horses, sending spam, or stealing anyone's identity or property is unethical" (para. 7) and users of the Internet need to understand that they are subject to the full extent of the law if caught carrying out any of these malicious activities.

Users of the Internet have certain *digital rights and responsibilities* extended to them. Some of these rights include the right to privacy and free speech. But along with these rights come digital responsibilities. One of these responsibilities is for users to "help define how the technology is to be used in an appropriate manner" (para. 8) and promote that usage in their daily online activities. *Digital health and wellness* includes the physical and psychological well-being that one should feel when participating in a digital world. With the extended exposure to computers and the tasks associated with them, "eye safety, repetitive stress syndrome, and sound ergonomic practices are issues that need to be addressed" (para. 9).

Digital security or self-protection pertains to the electronic precautions one should take to guarantee safety online. This involves making sure to use virus protection on computers, provide backups of data, and use surge protectors for all equipment. A digital citizen must learn how to protect their "information from outside forces that might cause disruption or harm" (para. 10). Ribble (2013) suggested teaching digital citizenship through the concept of REPs (Respect, Educate, and Protect). Each REP contains three topics that should be taught beginning in Kindergarten: (1) Respect yourself/Respect others—Etiquette, Access, Law; (2) Educate yourself/Connect with others—Communication, Literacy, Commerce; (3) Protect yourself/Protect others—Rights and Responsibilities, Safety and Security, Health and Welfare.

Social Media Guidelines

Free speech protects individuals who want to participate in social media, but the laws and the courts have ruled that schools can discipline students and staff if their speech, including online postings, disrupts school operations. Social media guidelines need to be created that allow employees to participate in online social activities within an atmosphere of trust and individual accountability. One should always keep in mind that information produced by the district/university staff and students is a reflection on the entire school district/university and should be subject to the district's/university's Acceptable Use Policy, State Statutes, and Educator Code of Ethics.

By accessing, creating, or contributing to any blogs, wikis or other social media, staff and students should mutually agree to abide by specific guidelines. Table 7.1 contains some general guidelines and best practices for staff, students, and parents that have been adapted from those provided by Montgomery (2010) at http://socialmediaguidelines.pbworks.com.

While there are many conversations going on regarding the importance of teaching digital citizenship to students and teachers in this information society, not many educators are sure what that really looks like. In addition, educators need to be able to identify available tools for teaching it, while determining how this too can fit into an already overcrowded curriculum. One approach that has been having success and can be replicated involves collaboration between educators and developers on a gaming project known as MinecraftEdu, which aims to teach digital citizenship in the classroom. Through virtual interactions with others in the class, "the game exposes students to a wide variety of concepts such as ethics, privacy, research and safety" (Lutz, 2012, para. 3). Educators then use the in-game experiences to lead students in discussions pertaining to how to protect oneself in a virtual environment as well as taking responsibility for one's actions. Using technology to teach digital citizenship is a novel approach that young students enjoy. Using games such as this at the elementary and middle school grades is a great way to prepare them to be digitally prepared for high school. Prepackaged materials for teachers to use assist in the design and delivery of digital citizenship lessons.

Advocacy for Digital Solidarity in Education

A remaining barrier in the United States to the realization of digital solidarity in education stems from the inability to accurately articulate the current state of the digital disparity for those most marginalized. In the past, advocates for

Table 7.1 Social Media Guidelines for Educators, Students, and Parents

General Guidelines	Explanation
Be yourself	Always be transparent about who you are and who you represent.
Know you are always "on"	You represent your school district and you must assume that your social media usage is visible to students, parents, and stakeholders. Keep in mind that while we all have the occasional frustration, social media are not the best venues in which to air them.
Be respectful	Make no remarks that are off topic or offensive. Demonstrate respect for others' points of view. Never pick fights.
Think ahead	Be smart about protecting yourself, your privacy, and confidential information. What you publish is widely accessible and will be around for a long time so consider the content carefully.
The Internet is not anonymous, nor does it forget	Everything written on the Web can be traced back to its author one way or another and very easily. Information is backed up often and repeatedly, and posts in one forum are usually replicated in others through trackbacks and reposts or references.
Avoid hazardous materials	Do not post or link to any materials that are defamatory, harassing, or indecent.
Maintain confidentiality	Do not post any confidential or proprietary information in regards to the school district, its staff, students, or stakeholders. This also means that the personal information of the employees and other individuals associated with the services that the school district delivers to students and staff should not be shared or disclosed through social media.

Faculty and Staff Guidelines	Explanation
Employees are personally responsible for the content they publish online	Be mindful that what you publish will be public for a long time and subject to your state's Public Records law.
Establish that your views are your own	When making posts be sure that the information is representative of your views and opinions and not necessarily the views and opinions of your school district. Include disclaimers within your personal blogs that the views are your own and do not reflect those of your employer.
No student information	When contributing online do not post confidential student information. No last names, school names, addresses, or phone numbers should appear on blogs or wikis.

Table 7.1 continued

Faculty and Staff Guidelines	Explanation
Moderate content contributed by students	Classroom blogs, wikis, and podcasts do not require a disclaimer, but teachers are encouraged to moderate content distributed by students.
Copyright and fair use guidelines	Respect copyright and fair use guidelines, and teach your students to do likewise. Do not plagiarize and give credit where it is due.
There are no "private conversations"	By posting your comments, having online conversations, etc. on social media sites you are broadcasting to the world. Be aware that even with the strictest privacy settings what you "say" online should be within the bounds of professional discretion.
Posting photographs and videos	Before posting photographs and videos permission should be sought from the subject where possible. This is especially the case where photographs of professional colleagues are concerned.

Student Guidelines	Explanation
Leaving a digital footprint	Be aware of what you post online. Social media venues including wikis, blogs, photo and video sharing sites are very public. What you contribute leaves a digital footprint for all to see. Do not post anything you wouldn't want friends, enemies, parents, teachers, or future employers to see.
Follow the school's code of conduct	It is acceptable to disagree with someone else's opinions; however, do it in a respectful way. Make sure your criticism is constructive and not hurtful. What is inappropriate in the classroom is inappropriate online.
Be safe online	Never give out personal information, including, but not limited to, last names, phone numbers, addresses, exact birthdates, and pictures. Do not share your password with anyone besides your teacher and parents.
Do your own work!	Do not use other people's intellectual property without their permission. It is a violation of copyright law to copy and paste others' thoughts. When paraphrasing another's idea(s), be sure to cite your source with the URL. Be aware that pictures might also be protected under copyright laws. Verify you have permission to use the image or whether it is under Creative Commons' attribution.
Write well	Blog and wiki posts should be well written. Follow writing conventions including proper grammar, capitalization, and punctuation.
Inappropriate material	If you run across inappropriate material that makes you feel uncomfortable, or is not respectful, tell your teacher or parent about it.

Parent Guidelines	Explanation
A child's involvement in using social media	Parents should expect communication from teachers prior to their child's involvement in any project using online social media applications.
Release forms	Parents will need to sign a release form for students when teachers set up social media activities for classroom use.
Parents' use of social media	Parents will not attempt to destroy or harm any information online. Parents will not use classroom social media sites for any illegal activity, including violation of data privacy laws. Parents should not distribute any information that might be deemed personal about other students participating in the social media project. Parents are encouraged to read and/or participate in social media projects, when appropriate.

closing the digital divide discussed issues of inadequate access to information, knowledge, and communication networks; but those issues are no longer as prevalent as they once were. Computer prices, Internet access and its monthly cost have been dramatically reduced. Through newer mobile technologies and Wi-Fi hotspots, access is no longer as big an issue as it had once been.

Digital inclusion was about empowering people, organizations, and businesses to apply information technology in ways that result in greater participation in our growing knowledge-based society. The need for relevant, consumable content that would develop 21st-century digital skills became a key objective. Digital inclusion involved stimulating demand and active participation from all people. Those who knew how to use the most current technologies were able to derive the educational, social, and economic benefits from that use. The implication for those who remained excluded was digital illiteracy. Advocates for digital inclusion worked diligently to bring the individuals on the outside into the conversation.

Promoters of digital solidarity seek to obtain an inclusive and sustainable information society through access to information and communications technologies (ICT) and advanced services, such as education and health care, that these technologies can provide. In this process, we (educators, policy-makers, politicians, and the media) need to make sure that we incorporate the term "digital solidarity" to accurately reflect our current national needs as it relates to ensuring that all people regardless of race, nationality, gender, ability, or disability participate fully in the digital world.

Community Technology Survey

1. Please identify your place in the community. (*Check all that apply.*)

a. Parent of a preschool and/or elementary student	
b. Parent of a middle and/or high school student	
c. Elementary teacher	
d. Middle or high school teacher	
e. School administrator	
f. Elementary student	
g. Middle or high school student	
h. Concerned citizen (age 19–30)	
i. Concerned citizen (age 31–50)	
j. Concerned citizen (age 51–64)	
k. Concerned senior citizen (age 65 +)	
l. Physically disabled (any age)	

2. Please indicate which of the following devices (in working condition) you currently own or are available in your home. *(Check all that apply.)*

a. Land-line phone	
b. Cell phone (without Internet access)	
c. Smartphone (with camera and Internet access)	
d. Television (without Internet access)	
e. Television (with Internet access)	
f. Desktop computer (PC or Mac)	
g. Laptop computer (PC or Mac)	
h. Printer (without copying or scanning capabilities)	
i. Printer, Copier, and Scanner	
j. FAX machine	
k. Dial-up modem to access Internet	
l. DSL or other high-speed Internet service	

3.   Are you physically disabled?

No _____

If you answered "no" please proceed to question 4.

Yes _____

If you answered "yes" please answer the question below.

Please indicate which of the following assistive or adaptive devices (in working condition) you currently own or are available in your home. Also indicate which devices you need.
(Check all that apply.)

	Devices I own or are available in my home	Devices I do not have but need
a. **Alternative Input Devices**: Alternative and adaptive keyboards, alternative and ergonomic mouse/pointing systems, head-operated pointing devices, Eyeglaze pointing devices, mouth/tongue pointing devices, Morse code input devices, brain-actuated pointing devices, switches, touch screens, voice input systems, speech-to-text software, voice recognition/command software, dictation software, on-screen keyboards, cursor enlargement software, ergonomic computer-based equipment, etc.★		
b. **Alternative Output Devices**: Includes computer-based output devices. Includes Braille display/output devices, Braille embosser/printer, screen reading software, screen magnification/enlargement software, large print monitor, etc.★		
c. **Accessible Software**: Includes software applications adapted for children and adults with disabilities, operating system accessibility options, accessible web browsers, etc.★		

★ *Categories supplied by RehabTool.com*

4. Do you agree or disagree with each of the following statements about the technology hardware available in the local school system. *(Circle one number on each line.)*

	Strongly Agree	Agree	Disagree	Strongly Disagree	Do Not Know
a. School computers are used by more than 90% of all *elementary* students every day.	4	3	2	1	0
b. School computers are used by more than 90% of all *middle school* students every day.	4	3	2	1	0
c. School computers are used by more than 90% of all *high school* students every day.	4	3	2	1	0
d. iPods and/or iPads are used in at least 80% of classrooms in the school district.	4	3	2	1	0
e. Laptops or computers with presentation hardware are used in at least 80% of classrooms in the district.	4	3	2	1	0
f. Videoconference equipment is readily available in every school for teachers and administrators to use for meetings or virtual field trips.	4	3	2	1	0
g. Personal handheld devices (e.g. iPod, iPads, iPhones) *are currently* permitted in classrooms if they are used for educational purposes.	4	3	2	1	0
h. Personal handheld devices (e.g. iPod, iPads, iPhones) *should be* permitted in classrooms if they are used for educational purposes.	4	3	2	1	0
i. All *elementary* students should be provided with a personal laptop computer for use during the school year.	4	3	2	1	0
j. All *middle school* students should be provided with a personal laptop computer for use during the school year.	4	3	2	1	0

	Strongly Agree	Agree	Disagree	Strongly Disagree	Do Not Know
k. All *high school* students should be provided with a personal laptop computer for use during the school year.	4	3	2	1	0

5.   Do you agree or disagree with each of the following statements about the technology software available in the *local school system*. *(Circle one number on each line.)*

	Strongly Agree	Agree	Disagree	Strongly Disagree	Do Not Know
a. At least 80% of all *elementary* students receive help in basic skills through technology software programs twice a week.	4	3	2	1	0
b. At least 80% of all *middle school* students receive help in basic skills through technology software programs twice a week.	4	3	2	1	0
c. At least 80% of all *high school* students receive help in basic skills through technology software programs twice a week.	4	3	2	1	0

6. Do you agree or disagree with each of the following statements about the technology available in *local libraries and community centers*. *(Circle one number on each line.)*

	Strongly Agree	Agree	Disagree	Strongly Disagree	Do Not Know
a. Computers are readily available to the public in the library or community centers.	4	3	2	1	0
b. Computers are easy to use with clear instructions available in these locations.	4	3	2	1	0
c. Computers are in constant use and it is difficult to find an available machine in these locations.	4	3	2	1	0
d. Free printers are available in the library and/or community center.	4	3	2	1	0
e. Computer classes are scheduled for people of all ages to learn how to operate current technology.	4	3	2	1	0
f. eBooks (i.e. Nook, Kindle) are available for checkout at the local library.	4	3	2	1	0
g. The library offers digital copies of many books for download on your own eBook.	4	3	2	1	0

Source: Nelson-Weaver, 2012.

Attributes Enabling a Technology Innovation to Go to Scale

Category	Attribute	Scale Level*
The Design Itself	1 The technology innovation is easy to use and is not complex.	1
	2 The technology innovation demonstrates high levels of instructor–learner, peer-to-peer interaction, and academic advisement.	1
	3 The technology innovation offers students a motivating curriculum that is important and relevant.	1
	4 The technology innovation offers quality curriculum aligning to national/state standards.	1
	5 The technology innovation demonstrates improvement in teaching and learning.	1
	6 The technology innovation is compatible with existing practices, values, political context, and policy climate such that there is a perception that it legitimately belongs.	1
	7 The technology innovation allows learners to decide whether to adopt or implement its design.	1
	8 The technology innovation demonstrates a relative advantage and is perceived to be a better idea than ideas it supersedes.	1

* 1 = *Scaling Up* 2 = *Going to Scale*

Communi-cation Channels	9 The communication channels exist to disseminate information about the technology innovation.	1
	10 The communication channels enable shared ownership and shared decision-making and communication among all parties involved in the planning and process (parents, students, teachers, and community members).	2
	11 The communication channels identify resources to support and sustain the technology innovation.	2
	12 The communication channels identify potential adopters who could benefit from the technology innovation.	1
	13 The communication channels offer the implementers of the technology innovation information about what users want and are willing to accept regarding its implementation and how it should be done.	1
	14 The communication channels inform policy-makers outside the existing network about the technology innovation.	2
	15 The communication channels create networks with other adopters of the technology innovation.	1
Time	16 Time is given for teachers and students to acquire and practice knowledge and skills.	1
	17 Time is given to test (trialability) the technology innovation for a while prior to adoption.	1
	18 The rate of adoption of the technology innovation is determined by the number of members within the organization adopting the reform within a given time-frame (how fast did it diffuse?).	1

Time	19 The stability and routine of the technology innovation are demonstrated (or not demonstrated) over time (critical mass achieved).	2
	20 The number of years the technology innovation has functioned.	2
Effective-ness	21 The technology innovation has measurable goals and benchmarks for student achievement.	1
	22 The technology innovation conducts both formative and summative evaluations.	1
	23 The technology innovation offers observable results in the academic achievement of students, or demonstrates evidence that it will improve the academic achievement of students.	2
	24 The technology innovation develops quality measures and accreditation standards.	1
	25 The technology innovation finds, grows, and hones a local expertise capable of its implementation.	2
	26 The technology innovation offers equitable access to all courseware, hardware, and software enabling digital inclusion.	2
Leadership Capabili-ties	27 The technology innovation's leadership staff manages the interrelated financial, human, and intellectual resources needed to maximize the benefits and build the infrastructure of the organization.	1
	28 The technology innovation's leadership staff commits to and demonstrates evidence of endorsement and continued support for the project.	2

Leadership Capabilities	29 The technology innovation's leadership staff minimizes the constraints from external factors (legal mandates, community pressures) and internal factors (union contracts, followers' expectations, unwritten rules) that can limit what the organization accomplishes.	2
	30 The technology innovation's leadership staff promotes change and a new normative order by challenging the mental models of all members of the organization.	2
	31 The technology innovation's leadership staff uses knowledge of best practices as the basis for action by focusing on what needs to be done and what is right and wrong.	2
	32 The technology innovation's leadership staff is allowed to stay the course of the reform effort.	2
	33 The technology innovation's leadership staff places a high priority on individual and organization learning through continuous professional development opportunities.	2
	34 The technology innovation's leadership staff constructs and communicates a compelling shared vision, values, and priorities.	2
	35 The technology innovation's leadership staff creates a process that strategically places the organization into its competitive environment.	2
	36 The technology innovation's leadership staff motivates people to work through rewards and punishments.	2
	37 The technology innovation's leadership staff displays self-determination to reaching organizational goals.	1

Leadership Capabili- ties	38 The technology innovation's leadership staff establishes formal plans, policies, routines, and priorities to maintain reliable performance and task accomplishments.	1
	39 The technology innovation's leadership staff monitors and emphasizes the organizational priorities and operational standards by enforcing organizational rules to ensure success.	1
Contextual Factors	40 The technology innovation addresses a well-understood need and the educational reform is locally driven.	N/A
	41 The technology innovation has adequate technology infrastructure to support the program.	
	42 The population which the technology innovation serves.	
	43 The participants' experiences with technology.	
	44 The location of the technology innovation: urban, suburban, rural, metropolitan.	
	45 The type of organization that is responsible for student learning: state-sponsored, district-wide, consortium, cooperative, public, private.	
	46 Student profile using the technology innovation: minority, advantaged, at-risk, special education, gifted, motivated, incarcerated, expelled, hospital/homebound, etc.	

Source: Diamond, 2007.

Glossary

acceleration for the gifted Going above and beyond grade-level studies.

app A mobile application (or mobile app) is a software application designed to run on smartphones, tablet computers, and other mobile devices.

augmented reality (AR) "A simple combination of real and virtual (computer-generated) worlds" (Maxwell, 2010, p.2).

Common Core State Standards (CCSS) Common standards to improve the content of instruction in mathematics and language arts developed by a collaborative effort between most of the U.S. states and territories, the National Governors Association, and the Council of Chief State School Officers.

depth Pertains to the nature of change in classroom practice, including indicators such as changes in teachers' beliefs, norms of interaction, and underlying pedagogical principles.

differentiated instruction "A teaching philosophy based on the premise that teachers should adapt instruction to student differences" (Willis & Mann, 2000, para. 3).

digital citizenship Refers to how technology users should act when they are online and relates to the norms of appropriate and responsible behavior with regard to technology use.

digital divide This concept focused mostly on broadband infrastructure investment offering access to the Internet for the underserved.

digital inclusion "Activities and initiatives aimed at stimulating demand and generating relevant content, which increases the overall broadband market and generates more benefits to society" (Muente-Kunigami, 2011).

digital literacy Describes the skills, expectations, and perspectives involved in living in a technological society. It includes the ability to locate, organize, utilize, understand and analyze information, evaluate, and create content using information technologies and the Internet.

digital solidarity A movement enabling the engagement and mobilization of individuals from *diverse cultural* and *linguistic backgrounds*, as well as *economic strata* to be active participants on the technology playing field (Voicu, 2004).

ELD (English Language Development) A program that includes strategies for improving students' English skills.

ELL (English Language Learners) Students whose native language is not English.

enrichment for the gifted Going more in depth into on-grade-level studies.

ESL (English as a Second Language) Refers to students who are learning English in a country where English is the dominant or official language.

excluded people Women, minorities, the elderly, disabled and economically disadvantaged individuals.

flipped classroom The core idea in this method is to flip the common instructional approach through the use of teacher-created videos and interactive lessons. Instruction that once occurred in class is accessed at home in advance of class. Class then becomes the place to work through the problems, and work in collaboration with other students and the teacher.

gamification Relates to the use of game design techniques, game thinking, and game mechanics to enhance non-game contexts (Wikipedia, 2012b).

Generation X (Gen Xers) Individuals born between 1965 and 1979.

Generation Y Individuals born from 1980 past 1999 to include The Millennials.

gigabit 1000 megabits (equal to one million kilobits) represented as 1 Gbps used to measure very fast connections like high-speed Ethernet.

going to scale The ability of an innovation to sustain itself over time and for those participating in the reform effort to ultimately assume its ownership.

ICT (Information and Communication Technologies) include the Internet, the World Wide Web (WWW), online services, digital content, email, other Internet-related services, computer networks and devices, cell phones, and other applicable services or technologies either currently in use or to be implemented in the future.

iGeneration A generation of learners born in the 1990s and beyond where the "i" refers to the types of digital technologies used by these learners (iPhone, iPod, Wii, iTunes).

Intranet A computer network used for sharing information and services *within* an organization as opposed to the Internet which allows for the sharing of information and services *between* organizations.

kilobit 1000 bits of data represented as 1Kbps used to measure slower network connections such as modem links.

Massively Open Online Courses (MOOCs) These are online courses that institutions are offering totally free of charge.

megabit 1000 kilobits of data represented as 1 Mbps used to measure faster links such as WiFi wireless.

Millennials, The The title given to the group of individuals born after 2000.

Moodle An open source learning management system (LMS) or Virtual Learning Environment (VLE) that provides documents, graded assignments, quizzes, discussion forums, and other basic online features and functionalities to students.

norms of social interaction "Teacher and student roles in the classroom, patterns of teacher and student talk, and the manner in which teachers and students treat one another" (Coburn, 2003, p.5).

online community A site on the Internet where learners meet virtually for the purpose of sharing information and communicating with others of similar interests and/or collaborating on projects.

Open Source Movement A "broad-reaching movement of individuals who support the use of open source licenses for some or all software" (Wikipedia, 2012a).

scaling up The ability for an innovation to be adopted and replicated in other venues such as schools.

shift in reform ownership A "transfer of knowledge and authority to sustain the reform to the site, allowing continuous improvement and further scale-up" (Rand Education, 2004, p.2).

spread Involves a reform getting to greater numbers of classrooms and schools.

sustainability "An effort can continue without special or external resources . . . that the effort can continue without the involvement of the researcher and developers who were involved in the initial classroom implementation" (Dede, Honan, & Peters, 2005, p.53).

underserved populations Women, minorities, the elderly, disabled, and economically disadvantaged individuals.

viral marketing The wide-spread dissemination of information across the Internet.

virtual schools "Educational organizations that offer K–12 courses through Internet or Web-based methods" (Clark, 2001, p.1).

virtual simulations 3D multi-user environments utilized in education to immerse children in educational tasks.

virtualization "Uses digital technology to provide virtual training for students to help them master any number of fields within which they might find future employment" (Center for Digital Education, 2012, p.10).

Web 1.0 The first stage of the World Wide Web released to the public in 1993 that merely linked webpages with hyperlinks.

Web 2.0 This term has been used to describe a more social web where users have the ability to contribute content and interact with other web users.

Web 3.0 A semantic web that changes the web into a language that can be read and categorized by the system rather than by humans, where search engines understand who you are, what you have been doing, and where you would like to go next. It will also include personalization that contextualizes the web based on the people using it; intelligent searches that extract meaning from the way people interact with the web; a portable personal web that offers everything, everywhere, all the time; and behavioral advertising where contextual advertising becomes more engaging and online purchase behavior turns users into brand advocates (Nations, n.d.).

wireless network An infrastructure for communication that allows an electronic device to exchange data wirelessly where no cables are needed to connect from one point to another over a computer network.

References

Access IT. (2011). *What is assistive technology?* Retrieved from http://www.washington. edu/accessit/articles?109/.

Afterschool Alliance. (2004). *Afterschool alert issue brief #1.* Retrieved from http://www. afterschoolalliance.org/issue_briefs/issue_needs_1.pdf.

Afterschool Alliance. (20z07). *Afterschool alert issue brief #4.* Retrieved from http://www. afterschoolalliance.org/issue_briefs/issue_rural_4.pdf.

Afterschool Alliance. (2011). *STEM learning in afterschool: An analysis of impact and outcomes.* Retrieved from http://www.afterschoolalliance.org/STEM-Afterschool-Outcomes. pdf.

Aldrich, C. (2009). *Learning online with games, simulations, and virtual worlds: Strategies for online instruction.* San Diego: Pfeiffer.

Allen, E. I., & Seaman, J. (2007). Online nation: Five years of growth in online learning. *Sloan Consortium.* Retrieved from http://sloanconsortium.org/publications/survey/ pdf/online_nation.pdf.

Anderson, P. (2007). What is Web 2.0? Ideas, technologies and implications for education. *JISC Technology and Standards Watch.* Retrieved from http://www.jisc.ac.uk/ media/documents/techwatch/tsw0701b.pdf.

Anderson-Inman, L., & Reinking, D. (1998). Learning from text in a technological society. In C. Hynd, S. Stahl, B. Britton, M. Carr, & S. Glynn (Eds.), *Learning from text across conceptual domains in secondary schools* (pp. 165–191). Mahwah, NJ: Lawrence Erlbaum Associates Inc.

Apple Computer, Inc. (2002). *The impact of technology on student achievement.* Retrieved from http://gayleberthiaume.com/FGO/AppleEduResearch.pdf.

Apple Computer, Inc. (2005). *Research: What it says about 1 to 1 learning.* Retrieved from www.ubiqcomputing.org/Apple_1-1_Research.pdf.

Apple, Inc. (2011). *Apple in education.* Retrieved from http://www.apple.com/ education/ipodtouch-iphone/#accessibility.

Assistive Technology Industry Association. (2012). *What is assistive technology?* Retrieved from http://www.atia.org/i4a/pages/index.cfm?pageid=3859.

Associated Press. (2011). *Report: Half of U.S. schools fail federal standards.* Retrieved from http://www.usatoday.com/news/education/story/2011-12-15/schools-federal-standards/5149126/1.

Associated Press. (2013). Leading education group recommends college credit for free online courses offered by Coursera. *Washington Post.* Retrieved from http://www. washingtonpost.com/business/technology/leading-education-group-recommends-college-credit-for-free-online-courses-offered-by-coursera/2013/02/07/c7847a54-70e5-11e2-b3f3-b263d708ca37_story.html.

Atkisson, M. (2011). *Comparing MOOCs, MIT's OpenCourseWare, and Stanford's Massive AI Course.* Retrieved from http://woknowing.wordpress.com/2011/08/28/comparing-moocs-mits-opencourseware-and-stanfords-massive-ai-course/.

Baiasu, K. (2011). Social media: A force for political change in Egypt. *The New Middle East Blog.* Retrieved from http://new-middle-east.blogspot.com/2011/04/social-media-force-for-political-change.html.

Banks, J. A., & McGee Banks, C. A. (2010). *Multicultural education: Issues and perspectives* (7th ed.). New York: John Wiley & Sons.

Barber, D. A. (2012, January). 5 K-12 ed. tech trends for 2012. *T.H.E. Journal.* Retrieved from http://thejournal.com/Articles/2012/01/10/5-K-12-Ed-Tech-for-2012.aspx?Page=1.

Barseghian, T. (2012, January). New startup launches high-tech math program. *Mind/Shift.* Retrieved from http://blogs.kqed.org/mindshift/2012/01/new-startup-launches-high-tech-math-program/.

Becker, H. J. (2000). Who's wired and who's not: Children's access to and use of computer technology. *Future of Children, 10*(2), 44–75. Los Altos, CA: The David and Lucile Packard Foundation. Retrieved from http://www.crito.uci.edu/tlc/FINDINGS/WhosWiredWhosNot.pdf.

Becta. (2006). *Making a difference with technology for learning: Evidence for school leaders.* Retrieved from https://wmrict.wikispaces.com/file/view/BECTA_making_difference_school_leaders.PDF.

Bedi, J. E. (1999). *Innovative lives: Exploring the history of women inventors.* Retrieved fromhttp://invention.smithsonian.org/centerpieces/ilives/womeninventors.html.

Best, M. (2012). Educators innovate through technology integration. *Edutopia.* Retrieved from http://www.edutopia.org/forest-lake-nasa-technology-integration.

Biancarosa, C., & Snow, C. E. (2004). *Reading next—A vision for action and research in middle and high school literacy: A report to Carnegie Corporation of New York* (2nd ed.).Washington, DC: Alliance for Excellent Education.

Bodilly, S. (1998). Lessons from New American Schools; scale-up phase: Prospects for bringing designs to multiple schools. *Rand Corporation.* Retrieved from http://www.rand.org/publications/MR/MR942.

Bodilly, S., Glennan, T. K., Galegher, J. R., & Kerr, K. A. (2004). *Expanding the reach of education reforms: Perspectives from leaders in the scale-up of educational interventions.* Santa Monica, CA: RAND Corporation. Retrieved from http://www.sreb.org/programs/hstw/publications/special/MG248ch12.pdf.

Bradley, W. (2005). *An insider's perspective on the Sakai Project: Reality and promise for sustainable economics and innovation.* Retrieved from http://hdl.handle.net/1885/47025.

Bronston, B. (2009, November 22). At-risk Hispanic students get a hand up in after-school program at Bonnabel. *The Times-Picayune.* Retrieved from http://www.nola.com/education/index.ssf/2009/11/at-risk_hispanic_students_get.html.

Brooks, J. G., & Dietz, M. (2012). The dangers and opportunities of the Common Core. *Educational Leadership, 70*(4), 64–67.

Brooks, S., Donovan, P., & Rumble, C. (2005). Developing nations, the digital divide and research databases. *Serials Review, 31*(4), 270–278.

Broward County Public Schools. (2013). *Send your sales tax to schools.* Retrieved from http://www.broward.k12.fl.us/becon/syst/.

Brozek, E., & Duckworth, D. (n.d.). Supporting English language learners. *Educators Voice, 4*, 10–15. Retrieved from http://www.nysut.org/files/edvoiceIV_ch2.pdf.

Butler-Pascoe, M. (1997). Technology and second language learners: The promise and the challenge ahead. *American Language Review, 1*(3), 20–22.

Carvajal, A., Mayorga, O., & Douthwaite, B. (2008). Forming a community of practice to strengthen the capacities of learning and knowledge sharing centres in Latin America and the Caribbean: A Dgroup case study. *Knowledge Management for Development Journal, 4*(1), 71–81.

CAST. (2011). *Universal Design for Learning Guidelines version 2.0*. Wakefield, MA: Author.

Cavanaugh, C. (2004). *Development and management of virtual schools*. Hershey, PA: Information Science Publishing.

Cavanaugh, C., Gillan, K. J., Kromrey, J., Hess, M., & Blomeyer, R. (2004). *The effects of distance education on K-12 student outcomes: A meta-analysis*. Naperville, IL: Learning Point Associates. Retrieved from http://www.ncrel.org/tech/distance/k12distance.pdf.

Center for Digital Education. (2012). *Full STEAM ahead: Sparking student interest in these high-need fields*. Retrieved from http://images.erepublic.com/documents/CDE12+SPQ4-V.pdf.

Center for Implementing Technology in Education (CITE). (n.d.). *Technology implementation in schools: Key factors to consider*. Retrieved from http://www.cited.org/index.aspx?page_id=187.

Chapman, C., Radmondt, L., & Smiley, G. (2005). Strong community, deep learning: Exploring the link. *Innovations in Education and Teaching International, 42*(3), 217–230.

Cisco (2006). *School district's wireless initiative helps raise computer literacy*. Retrieved from http://www.cisco.com/web/strategy/docs/education/BrowardSchools_Wireless.pdf.

City of Oakland, California. (2012). *Hacking—the OPR way*. Retrieved from http://www2.oaklandnet.com/Government/o/opr/index.htm.

Clark, T. (2001). *Virtual schools: Trends and issues, a study of virtual schools in the United States*. Macomb, IL: Distance Learning Resource Network, Western Illinois University. Retrieved from http://www.wested.org/online_pubs/virtualschools.pdf.

Cobb, S. (2004). *Timeline for distance education technology*. Retrieved from http://www.scobb.com/UALR/timeline.pdf.

Coburn, C. E. (2003). Rethinking scale: Moving beyond numbers to deep and lasting change. *Educational Researcher, 32*(6), 3–12.

Cole, C., Ray, K., & Zanetis, J. (2004). *Videoconferencing for K-12 classrooms: A program development guide*. Eugene, OR: ISTE Publications.

Consumer Electronics Association Foundation. (2012). *CEA launches foundation in support of seniors and people with disabilities*. Retrieved from http://www.ce.org/News/News-Releases/Press-Releases/2012-Press-Releases/20120627-CEA-Foundation-Announcement.aspx.

Corcoran, T. (n.d.). Scaling up best practices in education: Building a more responsible profession. In Roundtable discussion 4, *For our schools, for our children: Excellence and opportunity* (pp. 5–15). The James MacGregor Burns Academy of Leadership, University of Maryland. Retrieved from http://www.academy.umd.edu/publications/leadership_publicpolicy/Education/Educ-FINAL.pdf.

Cormier, D., & Siemens, G. (2010). Through the open door: Open courses as research, learning, and engagement. *Educause Review, 45*(4), 30–39.

Cornu, B. (2007). New media and open and distance learning: New challenges for education in a knowledge society. *Informatics in Education, 6*(1), 43–52.

Council of the Great City Schools. (2012, March). *Memphis district launches STEM Virtual High School, 21*(2). Retrieved from http://www.cgcs.org/cms/lib/DC00001581/Centricity/Domain/4/March2012.pdf.

Coupland, D. (1991). *Generation X: Tales for an accelerated culture.* New York: St. Martin's Griffin.

Crandall, M., & Fisher, K. (2009). *Digital inclusion: Measuring the impact of information and community technology.* Medford, NJ: Information Today, Inc.

Crawford, S. (2012a). U.S. Internet users pay more for slower service. *Bloomberg View.* Retrieved from http://www.bloomberg.com/news/2012-12-27/u-s-internet-users-pay-more-for-slower-service.html.

Crawford, S. (2012b). Merger made Comcast strong, U.S. Web users weak. *Bloomberg View.* Retrieved from http://www.bloomberg.com/news/2012-12-25/merger-made-comcast-strong-u-s-web-users-weak.html.

Cummins, J., Brown, K., & Sayers, D. (2006). *Literacy, technology, and diversity: Teaching for success in changing times.* Boston: Pearson.

Curry, J., & Jackson-Smarr, R. (2012). *Where the kids are: Digital learning in class and beyond.* Retrieved from http://www.expandedschools.org/sites/default/files/digital_learning_beyond_class.pdf.

Curtin, E. (2005). Teaching practices for ESL students. *Multicultural Education.* Retrieved from http://www.accessmylibrary.com/article-1G1-130276337/teaching-practices-esl-students.html.

Davis, J. W., & Bowman, K. (2011). *School enrollment in the United States: 2008, population statistics.* Washington, D.C.: United States Census Bureau.

Dede, C., Honan, J., & Peters, C. (2005). *Scaling up success: Lessons from technology based educational improvement.* San Francisco, CA: Jossey-Bass.

Diamond, D. (2007). Attributes that enable a virtual high school to go to scale. *ProQuest Dissertations and Theses, 297.* Retrieved from http://search.proquest.com.ezproxylocal.library.nova.edu/docview/304847921?accountid=6579 (304847921).

Diamond, D., & Pisapia, J. (2008). *The role of leadership in scaling up virtual high school programs.* Retrieved from www.usdla.org/mini_websites/old/White_Pape_Submission.doc.

Dickard, N., & Schneider, D. (2011). The digital divide: Where we are? A status report on the digital divide. *Edutopia.* Retrieved from http://www.edutopia.org/digital-divide-where-we-are-today.

DiRaimo, D., & Wolverton, M. (2006). Integrating learning communities and distance education: Possibility or pipedream? *Innovative Higher Education, 31*(2), 99–113.

DO-IT Center, University of Washington. (2013). *DO-IT projects, programs, and resources.* Retrieved from http://www.uw.edu/doit.

Downey, M. (2010, May). *Major review of No Child Left Behind: Kids moved in math, but in little else* [Get Schooled Blog]. Retrieved from http://blog.ajc.com/get-schooled-blog/2010/05/19/major-review-of-no-child-left-behind-kids-moved-ahead-in-math-but-in-little-else.

Duflo, E. (2003, May). Scaling up and evaluation. Paper prepared for the ABCDE in Bangalore. Retrieved from http://siteresources.worldbank.org/INTBANGALORE2003/Resources/Duflo.pdf.

Dye, J. (2011, March). Mapping out a mobile strategy. *EContent, 34*(2), 16–20. Retrieved from http://www.econtentmag.com/default.aspx.

Education Week. (2011, September 1). *Technology in education.* Retrieved from http://www.edweek.org/ew/issues/technology-in-education/.

Ely, D. P. (1999). New perspectives on the implementation of educational technology innovations. Paper delivered at the Association for Educational Communications and Technology Conference, Houston, TX.

Engelmann, S. E., & Engelmann, K. E. (2004). Impediments to scaling up effective comprehensive school reform models. In RAND, *Expanding the reach of education reforms: Perspectives for leaders in the scale-up of educational interventions* (pp.107–133). Santa Monica, CA: RAND Corporation.

eSchool News (2005a, July). Mich. laptop program shows early success. *Staff and wire service reports.* Retrieved from http://www.eschoolnews.com/2005/07/11/mich-laptop-program-shows-early-success.

eSchool News (2005b, September). Study: Web use nearly ubiquitous for today's teens. *Staff and wire service reports.* p.17. Retrieved from http://www.eschoolnews.com/2005/07/11/study-web-use-nearly-ubiquitous-for-todays-teens.

Family Center on Technology and Disability. (2012). *Glossary.* Retrieved from http://www.fctd.info/.

Foss, J. (2002). The "digital divide" goes to school. *Children's Advocate*, December, p.5.

Gagne, R. (1987). *Instructional technology foundations.* Hillsdale, NJ: Lawrence Erlbaum Assoc.

Garrison, D. R. (1985). Three generations of technological innovation in distance education. *Distance Education, 6*(2), 235–241.

Getting, B. (2007). Basic definitions: Web 1.0, Web 2.0, Web 3.0. *Practical ecommerce: Insights for online merchants.* Retrieved from http://www.practicalecommerce.com/articles/464-Basic-Definitions-Web-1-0-Web-2-0-Web-3-0.

Ginsburg, F. (2006). Rethinking documentary in the digital age. *Cinema Journal, 46*(1), 128–133.

Global Cities Dialogue (2011). *City of Brussels on foursquare.* Retrieved from http://www.globalcitiesdialogue.com/.

Glover, M. (2012, July 18). *FCC chairman and labor secretary announce digital literacy coalition* [Blog post]. Retrieved from http://techwire.net/fcc-chairman-and-labor-secretary-announce-american-job-centers-to-join-national-digital-literacy-coalition-connect2compete/.

Goodwin, B. (2011, February). One to one laptop programs are no silver bullet. *Educational Leadership, 68*(5), 78–79.

Greenberg, A. (2004). *Navigating the sea of research on videoconferencing-based distance education.* Retrieved from http://www.wainhouse.com/files/papers/wr-navseadistedu.pdf.

Gross, G. (2012, July 16). *Broadband program adds more digital literacy training* [Blog post]. Retrieved from http://www.pcworld.com/businesscenter/article/259332/broadband_program_adds_more_digital_literacy_training.html.

Guillet, L., Diouf, A., & Haenen, I. (2009). *Towards responsible digital solidarity: A study on digital solidarity initiatives in France, the Netherlands and Senegal.* Retrieved from http://ewasteguide.info/files/Guillet_2009_Enda-WASTE.pdf.

Gulek, J. C., & Demirtas, H. (2005). Learning with technology: The impact of laptop use on student achievement. *Journal of Technology, Learning, and Assessment, 3*(2), 1–38.

Hamilton, B. (2007). *It's elementary! Integrating technology in the primary grades*. Eugene, OR: International Society for Technology in Education.

Harris, J. (2001, May). Teachers as telecollaborative project designers: A curriculum-based approach. *Contemporary Issues in Technology and Teacher Education* [Online serial]. *1*(3). Retrieved from http://www.citejournal.org/vol1/iss3/seminal/article1.htm.

Hart, J. (2011). *Tools for building online learning communities*. Retrieved from Centre for Learning and Performance Technologies at http://c41pt.co.uk/.

Hewlett-Packard News Release. (2004, June 29). *HP technology program advances education and economic development in East Baltimore*. Hewlett-Packard.

Homeless Pre-Natal Program. (2010). Success stories: *Community technology center*. Retrieved from http://www.homelessprenatal.org/success/tech.

Hood, L. (2011, August). Smartphones are bridging the digital divide. *Wall Street Journal*. Retrieved from http://online.wsj.com/article/SB1000142405311190332790457652 6732908837822.html.

Hord, S. (1997). *Professional learning communities: Communities of continuous inquiry and improvement*. Austin, TX: Southwest Educational Development Laboratory.

Howden, L. M., & Meyer, J. A. (2011). *Age and sex composition: 2010, 2010 census briefs*. Washington, D.C.: United States Census Bureau.

Hu, W. (2007, May 4). Seeing no progress, some schools drop laptops. *The New York Times*, 1. Retrieved from http://www.nytimes.com/2007/05/04/education/04 laptop.html.

Humes, K. R., Jones, N. A., & Ramirez, R. R. (2011). *Overview of race and Hispanic origin: 2010, 2010 census briefs*. Washington, D.C.: United States Census Bureau.

Ibrahim, Y. (2011). *Digital inclusion for all*. Asia Pacific Regional Forum on Digital Inclusion for All, Suntec Convention Centre, Singapore. Retrieved from http://www.egov.gov.sg/media-room/speeches/2011/digital-inclusion-for-all.

Intel Computer Clubhouse Network. (2013). *Welcome to the Intel Computer Clubhouse Network!* Retrieved from http://www.computerclubhouse.org/.

International Association for K-12 Online Learning (iNACOL). (2010). *A national primer on K-12 online learning*. Retrieved from http://www.inacol.org/research/docs/iNCL_NationalPrimerv22010-web.pdf.

International Society for Technology in Education (ISTE) Policy Brief. (2008). *Technology and student achievement—The indelible link*. Retrieved from http://www. k12hsn.org/files/research/Technology/ISTE_policy_brief_student_achievement.pdf.

International Society for Technology in Education (ISTE). (2012). *Maximizing the impact: The pivotal role of technology in a 21st century education system*. Retrieved from www.p21. org/storage/documents/p21setdaistepaper.pdf.

Jackson N. (2011). Internet essentials: Comcast joins effort to bridge digital divide. *The Atlantic*. Retrieved from http://www.theatlantic.com/technology/archive/2011/08/internet-essentials-comcast-joins-effort-to-bridge-digital-divide/243290/.

Jerald, C. (2009). Defining a 21st century education. *The Center for Public Education*. Retrieved from http://www.centerforpubliceducation.org/Learn-About/21st-Century/Defining-a-21st-Century-Education-Full-Report-PDF.pdf.

Johanssen, D. H., Howland, J., Moore, J., & Marra, R. M. (2003). *Learning to solve problems with technology: A constructivist perspective* (2nd ed.). Columbus, OH: Merrill/Prentice-Hall.

Johnson, C. M. (2001). A survey of current research on online communities of practice. *Internet and Higher Education, 4*, 45–60. Retrieved from http://www.sciencedirect.com/science/article/pii/S1096751601000471.

Johnson, F. (2012, January). *The legacy of No Child Left Behind* [Education Experts Blog]. Retrieved from http://education.nationaljournal.com/2012/01/the-legacy-or-no-child-left-be.php.

Johnson, L., Smith, R., Willis, H., Levine, A., & Haywood, K. (2011). *The 2011 horizon report.* Austin, Texas: The New Media Consortium. Available at http://net.educause.edu/ir/library/pdf/HR2011.pdf.

Johnstone, S. (2005). Open educational resources serve the world. *Educause Quarterly, 28*(3). Retrieved from http://www.educause.edu/apps/eq/eqm05/eqm0533.asp?bhep=1.

Jones, S., & Fox, S. (2009, January 28). Generations online in 2009. *Pew Internet and American Life Project.* Retrieved from http://pewresearch.org/pubs/1093/generations-online.

Judge, S., Puckett, K., & Cabuk, B. (2004). Digital equity: New findings from the early childhood longitudinal study. *Journal of Research on Technology in Education, 36,* 383–396.

Kahn, T. (1999). *A new model of education: Designing virtual communities for creativity and learning.* Retrieved from http://www.edutopia.org/designing-virtual-communities-creativity-and-learning.

Kamil, M. L. (2003). *Adolescents and literacy: Reading for the 21st century.* Washington, DC: Alliance for Excellent Education.

Kaya, T. (2010). Enrollment in online courses increases at the highest rate ever. *The Chronicle of Higher Education.* Retrieved from http://chronicle.com/blogs/wired campus/enrollment-in-online-courses-increases-at-the-highest-rate-ever/28204.

King, R. (2009). Digital Workforce Initiative transforms gulf coast job prospects. Retrieved from http://www.policyinnovations.org/ideas/innovations/data/000094.

Knox, C., & Anderson-Inman, L. (2001). Migrant ESL high school students succeed using networked laptops. *Learning and Leading with Technology, 28*(5), 18–21, 52–53.

Koch, M., Gorges, T., & Penuel, W. R. (2012, Fall). Build IT: Scaling and sustaining an afterschool computer science program for girls. *Afterschool Matters.* Retrieved from http://www.niost.org/pdf/afterschoolmatters/asm_2012_16_fall/ASM_2012_16_fall_7.pdf.

LA's BEST. (2012). *31/2beats. The heart of our program.* Retrieved from http://www.lasbest.org/what/programs.

Ladner, M., & Lips, D. (2009). *How "No Child Left Behind" threatens Florida's successful education reforms.* Retrieved from http://www.heritage.org/research/reports/2009/01/how-no-child-left-behind-threatens-floridas-successful-education-reforms.

Le Dantec, C., Farrell, R. Christensen, J., Bailey, M., Ellis, J., Kellogg, W., & Edwards, W. (2011). *Publics in practice: Ubiquitous computing at a shelter for homeless mothers.* Retrieved from http://ledantec.net/wp-content/uploads/2011/01/ledantec-1142-paper.pdf.

Lemagie, S. (2010, November). 1 student, 1 laptop proves costly. *Minneapolis Star-Tribune.* Retrieved from http://www.startribune.com/local/109779099.html.

Lenhart, A., Ling, R., Campbell, S., & Purcell, K. (2010). *Teens and mobile phones.* Retrieved from Pew Research Center's Internet and American Life Project at http://www.pewinternet.org/Reports/2010/Teens-and-Mobile-Phones.aspx.

Lenhart, A., Rainie, L., & Lewis, O. (2001). *Teenage life online: The rise of the instant-message generation and the Internet's impact on friendships and family relationships.* Washington, DC: Pew Internet & American Life Project.

Levine, A. (2009). *The School of One: The school of tomorrow*. Retrieved from http://www.huffingtonpost.com/arthur-e-levine/the-school-of-one-the-sch_b_288695.html.

Light, D., Reitzes, T., & Cerrone, M. (2009). *Evaluation of the School of One summer pilot: An experiment in individualized instruction*. New York: Center for Children and Technology Education Development Center, Inc. Retrieved from http://school ofone.org/resources/edc_2009_eval.pdf.

Loveless, T. (2012). The common core initiative: What are the chances of success? *Educational Leadership, 70*(4), 60–63.

Lowther, D. L., Ross, S. M., Strahl, J. D., Inan, F. A., & Pollard, D. (2005). *Freedom to learn program: Michigan 2004–2005 evaluation report*. Prepared for the Michigan Department of Education and Ferris State University. Memphis, TN: Center for Research in Education Policy. Retrieved from http://www.ftlwireless.org.

Lowther, D. L., Strahl, J. D., Inan, F. A., & Bates, J. (2007). *Freedom to learn program Michigan 2005–2006 evaluation report*. Prepared for Freedom to Learn and the One-to-One Institute. Memphis, TN: The University of Memphis, Center for Research in Educational Policy.

LUS Fiber. (2012). *About LUS fiber: Historical timeline*. Retrieved from http://www.lusfiber.com/index.php/about-lus-fiber/historical-timeline.

Lutz, Z. (2012). Educators battle eternal September by teaching digital citizenship with MinecraftEdu. *Engadget*. Retrieved from http://www.engadget.com/2012/11/20/educators-teach-digital-citizenship-with-minecraftedu/.

Lynch, S. (2004). ISO metaphor and theory scale-up research: Eagles in the Anacostia and activity systems. A paper presented to The Graduate school of Education and Human Development at the George Washington University, Washington, D.C. Retrieved from http://www.gwu.edu/~scale-up/coburn_march_21_04.pdf.

Lytle, R. (2012). Teacher training needed to meet technology needs in classrooms. *U.S. News*. Retrieved from http://www.usnews.com/education/high-schools/articles/2012/09/20/teacher-training-needed-to-meet-technology-needs-in-classrooms.

Madelin, A. (2008). Action for digital solidarity. *Connect World*. Retrieved from http://www.connect-world.com/index.php/magazine/emea/item/1767-action-for-digital-solidarity.

Maeroff, G. (2003). *A classroom of one*. New York, NY: Palgrave MacMillan.

Malamed, C. (2011). Learning technology trends to watch in 2011. *The eLearning Coach*. Retrieved from http://theelearningcoach.com/elearning2-0/2011-learning-technology-trends/.

Martin, M. (2005). Seeing is believing: The role of videoconferencing in distance learning. *British Journal of Educational Technology, 36*(3), 397–405.

Marzano, R. (2003). *What works in schools*. Alexander, VA: Association for Supervision and Curriculum Development.

Mathews, D. (1999). The origins of distance education and its use in the United States. *T.H.E. Journal, 27*(2), 54–61.

Maxwell, K. (2010). *Augmented reality*. Retrieved from http://www.macmillan dictionary.com/buzzword/entries/augmented-reality.html.

McDonald, J. P. (2005). *Scaling up the big picture*. From a study funded by an anonymous foundation. Retrieved from http://www.nyu.edu/iesp/publications/Scaling_up_the_big_picture.pdf.

McDonald, S. K., Keesler, V. A., Kauffman, N. J., & Schnieder, B. (2006). Scaling up exemplary interventions. *Educational Researcher, 35*(3), 15–24.

McRae, K. (2010). *Homelessness 2.0: How technology helps the homeless.* Retrieved from http://www.techvibes.com/blog/homelessness-20-how-technology-helps-the-homeless.

Means, B., & Penuel, W. R. (2005). Research to support scaling up technology-based educational innovations. In C. Dede, J. P. Honan, & L. C. Peters (Eds.), *Scaling up success: Lessons from technology-based educational improvement* (pp.176–197). San Francisco: Jossey-Bass.

Medina, J. (2009). Laptop? Check. Student playlist? Check. Classroom of the future? Check. *New York Times.* Retrieved from http://nytimes.com/2009/07/22education/22school.html.

Meskill, C., & Mossop, J. (2000). Technologies use with ESL learners in New York State: Preliminary report. *Journal of Educational Computing Research, 22*(3), 265–284.

MGS Consulting. (2008). *Community access to technology program: Evaluation report—Year 3.* Seattle, WA: Bill & Melinda Gates Foundation.

Microsoft. (2012). *Developing an accessible technology plan.* Retrieved from http://www.microsoft.com/enable/business/plan.aspx.

Milholland, C. (2011). Low-income households get free Internet access. *KPBS.* Retrieved from http://www.kpbs.org/news/2011/jul/26/low-income-households-get-free-internet-access/.

Miller, M. (2009). *Surfing the web may be good for aging brains.* Retrieved from http://retirementrevised.com/health/surfing-the-web-may-be-good-for-aging-brains.

Millington, R. (n.d.) *Richard Millington's online community manifesto.* Retrieved from http://richchallenge.typepad.com/files/communitybuildingmanifesto-1.pdf.

Mitchell, B. (2012). Kilobit—megabit—gigabit. *About.com Guide.* Retrieved from http://compnetworking.about.com/od/basicnetworkingconcepts/g/bldef_kilobit.htm.

Mohan. (2012). Closing the digital divide: The 2012 STEM Summit. *Citizen Schools New Jersey.* Retrieved from http://www.citizenschools.org/newjersey/news/closing-the-digital-divide-the-2012-stem-summit/.

Montgomery, K. (2010). Social media guidelines for schools. *PBWorks.* Retrieved from http://socialmediaguidelines.pbworks.com/w/page/17050879/FrontPage.

Moore, M. G. (2003). *From Chautauqua to the virtual university: A century of distance education in the United States.* Columbus, OH: Center on Education and Training for Employment. Retrieved from http://www.eric.ed.gov/PDFS/ED482357.pdf.

Moore, M. G., & Kearsley, G. (1996). *Distance education: A systems view.* Belmont, CA: Wadsworth Publishing Company.

Muente-Kunigami, A. (2011). *Digital inclusion: Beyond access to broadband.* Retrieved from http://blogs.worldbank.org/ic4d/digital-inclusion-beyond-access-to-broadband.

Murray, K. (2011, September 11). Five tips for planning training sessions that actually work [Blog post]. Retrieved from http://www.techrepublic.com/blog/five-apps/five-tips-for-planning-training-sessions-that-actually-work/1016.

Nagel, D. (2009, April). Study ties student achievement to technology integration. *T.H.E. Journal.* Retrieved from http://thejournal.com/articles/2009/04/02/study-ties-student-achievement-to-technology-integration.aspx.

Nagel, D. (2010). 5 trends in education technology leadership. *T.H.E. Journal.* Retrieved from http://thejournal.com/articles/2010/04/23/5-trends-in-education-technology-leadership.aspx.

Nagel, D. (2011). K-12 to see double-digit growth in e-learning through 2015. *T.H.E. Journal*. Retrieved from http://thejournal.com/articles/2011/07/21/k-12-to-see-double-digit-growth-in-e-learning-through-2015.aspx.

Nasseh, B. (1997). *A brief history of distance education*. Retrieved from http://www.seniornet.org/edu/art/history.html.

National Broadband Plan. (n.d.). *Connecting America: Executive summary*. Retrieved from http://www.broadband.gov/plan/executive-summary/.

National Center for Accessible Media. (2009a). *Speech solutions for next-generation media centers*. Retrieved from http://ncam.wgbh.org/invent_build/analog/speech-solutons-for-next-generation-media-centers.

National Center for Accessible Media. (2009b).*Captioning solutions for handheld media and mobile devices*. Retrieved from http://ncam.wgbh.org/invent_build/web_multi media/mobile-devices.

National Center for Education Statistics. (2010). *High-poverty public schools*. Retrieved from http://nces.ed.gov/programs/coe/analysis/2010-section1a.asp.

National Center for Learning Disabilities. (2012). *Types of LD*. Retrieved from http://www.ncld.org/types-learning-disabilities.

National Center for Technology Innovation and Center for Implementing Technology in Education. (2006). *Boosting inclusion in after school activities with AT and supplemental services*. Retrieved from http://www.ldonline.org/article/9924/.

National Economic Council, the Council of Economic Advisors, and the Office of Science and Technology Policy. (2011). *A strategy for American innovation: Securing our economic growth and prosperity*. Retrieved from http://www.whitehouse.gov/sites/default/files/uploads/InnovationStrategy.pdf.

Nations, D. (n.d.). *What is Web 3.0?* Retrieved from http://webtrends.about.com/od/web20/a/what-is-web-30.htm.

(NCREL) North Central Regional Educational Laboratory. (2005). *Critical issue: Using technology to improve student achievement*. Retrieved from http://www.ncrel.org/sdrs/areas/issues/methods/technlgy/te800.htm#factor.

Neill, M. (2010). Why won't Congress admit NCLB failed? *The Answer Sheet*. Retrieved from http://voices.washingtonpost.com/answer-sheet/guest-bloggers/why-wont-congress-admit-nclb-f.html.

Nelson-Weaver, E. (2012). Community technology survey. [Survey]. Unpublished instrument.

Newman, B. (2012, June). Don't write off ALA's work on digital literacy and the FCC before reading this. *Librarian by Day*. Retrieved from http://librarianbyday.net/2012/06/12/dont-write-off-alas-work-on-digital-literacy-and-the-fcc-before-reading-this/.

Nielsen Wire. (2010, October 14). *U.S. teen mobile report: Calling yesterday, texting today, using apps tomorrow* [Blog post]. Retrieved from Nielsenwire at http://blog.nielsen.com/nielsenwire/online_mobile/u-s-teen-mobile-report-calling-yesterday-texting-today-using-apps-tomorrow.

No Child Left Behind Act of 2001. (2002). Retrieved from http://www2.ed.gov/policy/elsec/leg/esea02/107-110.pdf.

North Central Regional Educational Laboratory. (2005). *Critical issue: Using technology to improve student achievement*. Retrieved from http://www.ncrel.org/sdrs/areas/issues/methods/technlgy/te800.htm#factor.

N.Y. Times. (2012, July). No Child Left Behind Act. *Times Topics.* Retrieved from http://topics.nytimes.com/top/reference/timestopics/subjects/n/no_child_left_behind_act/index.html.

O' Hanlon, C. (2009, February 1). Credit recovery software: The new summer school. *T.H.E. Journal.* Retrieved from http://thejournal.com/articles/2009/02/01/credit-recovery-software-the-new-summer-school.aspx.

Ohler, J. (2009). Orchestrating the media collage. *Educational Leadership, 66*(6), 8–13.

Olgren, C., & Parker, L. (1983*). Teleconferencing technology and applications.* Dedham, MA: Artech House Inc.

Online Education Database. (2007). *How the open source movement has changed education: 10 success stories.* Retrieved from http://oedb.org/library/features/how-the-open-source-movement-has-changed-education-10-success-stories.

Orrick, R. (2011). *Envisioning an Internet center for homeless individuals: One group's quest to reduce the digital divide.* Retrieved from http://openaccessconnections.org/wp-content/uploads/2011/06/Envisioning-an-Internet-Center-for-Homeless-Individuals.pdf.

Pandolfo, N. (2012, January). As some schools plunge into technology, poor schools are left behind. *The Hechinger Report.* Retrieved from http://hechingerreport.org/content/as-some-schools-plunge-into-technology-poor-schools-are-left-behind_7463.

Penuel, R., Pasnik, S., & Bates, L. (2009). *Preschool teachers can use a media rich curriculum to prepare low income children for school success: Results of a randomized controlled trial (Summative Evaluation of the Ready to Learn Initiative).* Retrieved from http://www.cct.edc.org/rtl/pdf/RTLEvalReport.pdf.

Peterson, E. (2012). Tools and resources. *Partnership for 21st century skills.* Retrieved from http://www.p21.org/tools-and-resources/p21blog/1061-erik-peterson-blog.

Picciano, G., & Seaman, J. (2009). *K–12 online learning: A 2008 follow-up of the survey of U.S. school district administrators.* Retrieved from http://www.sloan-c.org/publications/survey/pdf/k-12_online_learning_2008.pdf.

Poggione, P. (2012). *Is technology sustainable?* Retrieved from http://www.digitalapes.org/2012/03/25/edtech-sustainability/.

Pozo-Olano, J. (2007). *New report shows how e-rate is connecting communities and schools to 21st century academic and employment opportunities.* Retrieved from http://www.edlinc.org/pdf/10-yearAnniversaryReportReleaseandStatements.pdf.

Prensky, M. (2007). Simulation nation: The promise of virtual learning sctivities. *Edutopia.* Retrieved from http://www.edutopia.org/computer-simulations-virtual-learning.

PRLog. (2012, October 2). *Women in technology honored for driving innovation.* Retrieved from http://www.prlog.org/11989143-women-in-technology-honored-for-driving-innovation.html.

Provasnik, S., Gonzales, P., & Miller, D. (2009). U.S. performance across international assessments of student achievement: Special supplement to the condition of education 2009. Retrieved from http://nces.ed.gov/pubsearch/pubsinfo.asp?pubid=2009083.

Rance-Roney, J. (2008, October). Technology in the English language learner classroom. *National Writing Project (NWP).* Retrieved from http://www.nwp.org/cs/public/print/resource/2728.

Rand Education. (2004*). Expanding the reach of education reforms: What have we learned about scaling up educational interventions?* Santa Monica, CA: Rand Education Research Brief. Retrieved from http://www.rand.org/ppubs/reserach_briefs/RB9078/index1.html.

Ravitch, D. (2012, July). *Why NCLB and Race to the Top fail* [Blog post]. Retrieved from http://dianeravitch.net/2012/07/17/3136.

Reckles, D. (2007). Lessons in wireless for K-12 schools. *Aruba Networks*. Retrieved from http://www.arubanetworks.com/pdf/technology/whitepapers/wp_k12.pdf.

Research and Policy Support Group. (2010). *School of One evaluation—2010 spring after school and short term in-school pilot programs*. New York City Department of Education. Retrieved from http://schoolofone.org/resources/so1_final_report_2010.pdf.

Rhodes, M. (2009, February 23). *Examples of online communities in the retail industry.* Retrieved from http://www.freshnetworks.com/blog/2009/02/examples-of-online-communities-in-the-retail-industry/.

Rhodes, M. (2009, March 24). *Examples of online communities in the telecoms industry.* Retrieved from http://www.freshnetworks.com/blog/2009/03/examples-of-online-communities-in-the-telecoms-industry/.

Rhodes, M. (2009, April 8). *Examples of online communities in healthcare.* Retrieved from http://www.freshnetworks.com/blog/2009/04/examples-of-online-communities-in-healthcare/.

Ribble, M. (2013). Nine themes of digital citizenship. *Digital Citizenship: Using technology appropriately.* Retrieved from http://digitalcitizenship.net/Nine_Elements.html.

Rideout, V. J., Foehr, U. G., & Roberts, D. F. (2010). *Generation M2: Media in the lives of 8- to 18-year-olds.* Retrieved from Kaiser Family Foundation at www.kff.org/entmedia/upload/8010.pdf.

Riel, M. (1993). *Learning circles: Virtual communities for elementary and secondary schools.* Retrieved from http://lrs.ed.uiuc.edu/Guidelines/Riel-93.html.

Ringstaff, C., & Kelley, L. (2002). *The learning return on our educational technology investment.* San Francisco, CA: WestEd. Retrieved from http://www.wested.org/online_pubs/learning_return.pdf.

Rios, F., Bath, D., Foster, A., Maaka, M., Michelli, N., & Urban, E. (2009). *Inequities in public education.* Seattle, WA: Institute for Educational Inquiry.

Roblyer, M. D. (2006). *Integrating educational technology into teaching* (4th ed.). Upper Saddle River, NJ: Pearson Education, Merrill.

Rogers, E. M. (1995). *Diffusion of Innovations* (4th ed.). New York: Free Press.

Roscorla, T. (2010). Technology permeates Common Core Standards. *Center for Digital Education.* Retrieved from http://www.centerdigitaled.com/policy/Technology-Permeates-Common-Core-Standards.html.

Roscorla, T. (2012). Massively open online courses are "here to stay." *Center for Digital Education.* Retrieved from http://www.centerdigitaled.com/policy/MOOCs-Here-to-Stay.html.

Rose, D. H., & Meyer, A. (2002). *Teaching every student in the digital age: Universal design for learning.* Alexandria, VA: ASCD.

Rose, M. (2010). Reform: To what end? *Educational Leadership, 67*(7), 6–11. Retrieved from http://www.ascd.org/publications/educational-leadership/apr10/vol67/num07/Reform@-To-What-End%C2%A2.aspx.

Rosen, L. (2011). Teaching the iGeneration. *Best of Educational Leadership, 68*, 10–15. Retrieved from http://www.ascd.org/publications/educational-leadership/feb11/vol68/num05/Teaching-the-iGeneration.aspx.

Rovai, A. P. (2002). Development of an instrument to measure classroom community. *The Internet and Higher Education, 5*, 197–211.

Sanders, K. (2013). Bus becomes mobile learning center for underprivileged kids. *NBC Nightly News*. Retrieved from http://dailynightly.nbcnews.com/_news/2013/01/28/16741739-bus-becomes-mobile-learning-center-for-underprivileged-kids.

Schaffhauser, D. (2009, June/July). Scale: Growing innovative programs isn't about adding more users. *T.H.E. Journal, 36*(6), 31–36.

Schaffhauser, D. (2009/August). The VOD Couple. *T.H.E. Journal, 36*(7), 19–23.

Scherer, M. (2010). A time for audacity. *Educational Leadership, 67*(7), 5.

Schmidt, W. H., & Burroughs, N. A. (2012). How the Common Core boosts quality and equality. *Educational Leadership, 70*(4), 54–58.

Schofield, J. W., & Davidson, A. L. (2000). Achieving equality of student Internet access within schools. In A. H. Eagly, R. M. Baron, & V. L. Hamilton (Eds.), *The social psychology of group identity and social conflict: Theory, application, and practice* (pp. 97–109). Washington, D.C.: APA Books.

School Access. (2008, May 2). *GCI school access partners with North Slope Borough school district*. Retrieved from http://www.schoolaccess.net/news_2008_02_05.html.

Schrum, L. (2002). Oh, what wonders you will see: Distance learning past, present, and future. *Learning and Leading with Technology, 30*(3), 6–9.

Schwartz, C. (2012, May 30). Women in technology: Four reasons why females will rule the future. *Huffington Post online*. Retrieved from http://www.huffington post.com/2012/05/30/women-in-technology-kara-swisher_n_1519806.html.

Scott, M. (2002). Journey toward sensitivity: An examination of multicultural literature. *Montessori Life, 14*(4), 26–29. Retrieved from http://www. wilsonweb.com.

SEIR TEC (Southeast Initiatives Regional Technology in Education Consortium). (2005). *English language learners and technology, 7*(1), Retrieved from http://www. seirtec.org/publications/newswire/vol7.1.pdf.

SeniorNet. (2012). *Underserved initiatives*. Retrieved from http://seniornet.org/index. php?option=com_content&task=view&id=68&Itemid=115.

Shapley, K., Sheehan, D., Sturges, K., Caranikas-Walker, F., Huntsberger, B., & Maloney, C. (2009). *Evaluation of the Texas Technology Immersion Pilot: Final outcomes for a four-year study (2004–05 to 2007–08)*. Austin, Texas: Center for Educational Research.

Shaughnessy, P. (2009). Reaching millennials through innovation in teaching. *Perspectives on Issues in Higher Education, 12*, 4–15. Retrieved from http://div10perspectives. asha.org/cgi/content/abstract/12/1/4.

Silvernail, D. L., & Gritter, A. K. (2007). *Maine's middle school laptop program: Creating better writers*. Portland, ME: Center for Education Policy, Applied Research, and Evaluation, University of Southern Maine.

Singh, P., & Pan, W. (2004). Online education: Lessons for administrators and instructors. *College Student Journal, 38*(2), 302–308.

Skills for 21st Century. (2010). *New Common Core Standards—Where's the Tech?* Retrieved from http://skillsfor21stcentury.wordpress.com/2010/06/04/new-common-core-standards-wheres-the-tech.

Smart, M. (2008). Edutopia. The word and the world: Technology aids English-language learners. *Edutopia*. Retrieved from http://www.edutopia.org/technology-software-english-language-learners.

Smith, A. (2011). *Pew Internet report on smartphones*. Washington, DC: Pew Research Center. Retrieved from http://www.pewinternet.org/~/media/Files/Reports/2011/PIP_Smartphones.pdf.

Smith, C. (n.d.). *Digital divide defined (Hint: It's not about access.)*. Retrieved from http://www.digitaldivide.org/digital-divide/digital-divide-defined/digital-divide-defined/.

Snyder, T. D., & Tan, A. G. (2005, October). *Digest of education statistics, 2004*. U.S. Department of Education. Washington, DC: National Center for Education Statistics.

Sommarstrom, S. (2011, August). Minnesota Justice Foundation Pro Se Clinics. *Using technology and social media to assist underserved populations*. Panel conducted at the meeting of the American Bar Association.

Spencer, J. (2012). 11 reasons teachers aren't using technology. *EdThink*. Retrieved from http://www.educationrethink.com/2012/07/11-reasons-teachers-arent-using.html.

Starr, D. (1998). Virtual education: Current practices and future directions. *Internet and Higher Education, 1*(2), 157–165.

Starr, L. (2011, November 14). Technology training programs that work. *Education World.com*. Retrieved from http://www.educationworld.com/a_tech/tech165.shtml.

Status Solutions. (2012). *Press*. Retrieved from http://www.statussolutions.com/news-events/press/story/52/status-solutions-catie-self-service-technology-recognized-by-the-assisted-living-federation-of-america.

STEM Education Caucus. (n.d.). *Why was the STEM Education Caucus created?* Retrieved from http://stemedcaucus2.org/.

Stephey, M. J. (2008). Gen-X: The ignored generation? *Time Entertainment*. Retrieved from http://www.time.com/time/arts/article/0,8599,1731528,00.html.

Strangman, N., & Hall, T. (2003). *Virtual reality/computer simulations*. Wakefield, MA: National Center on Accessing the General Curriculum. Retrieved from http://aim.cast.org/learn/historyarchive/backgroundpapers/virtual_simulations.

Sumner, J. (2000). Serving the system: A critical history of distance education. *Open Learning, 15*(3), 267–285.

Surry, D. W. (1997). Diffusion theory and instructional technology. Paper presented at the Annual Conference of the Association for Educational Communications and Technology (AECT), Albuquerque, New Mexico. Retrieved from http://www2.gsu.edu/~wwwitr/docs/diffusion.

Surry, D. W., & Ely, D. P. (2001). Adoption, diffusion, implementation, and institutionalization of educational innovations. In R. Reiser & J. V. Dempsey (Eds.), *Trends & Issues in Instructional Design and Technology* (pp.183–193). Upper Saddle River, NJ: Prentice-Hall. Retrieved from http://www.southalabama.edu/coe/bset/surry/papers/adoption/chap.htm.

Tackett, L., & Cator, K. (2011). *The promise of communities of practice*. Retrieved from http://www.ed.gov/oii-news/promise-communities-practice.

Tapscott, D. (1999). *Growing up digital: The rise of the Net Generation*. New York: McGraw-Hill.

Taylor, I. (2009). Online learning gaining credibility. *Richmond Times-Dispatch*. Retrieved from http://www2.timesdispatch.com/business/2009/jun/28/iris28_20090627-184803-ar-38924/.

Taylor, V., & Rudy, C. (n.d.). *Using educational technology to increase student achievement in a standards based environment*. Retrieved from http://www.icte.org/T99_Library/T99_48.pdf.

Texas Education Agency. (2006a). *Long range plan for technology, 2006–2020*. Retrieved from http://www.tea.state.tx.us/index2.aspx?id=5082.

Texas Education Agency. (2006b). *School technology and readiness chart*. Retrieved from http://starchart.epsilen.com/docs/TxTSC.pdf.

The Children's Aid Society. (n.d.). *Dunlevy Milbank Center, Club Tech Center for Excellence*. Retrieved from http://www.childrensaidsociety.org/dunlevy-milbank-center/club-tech-center-excellence.

The Corporate Social Responsibility Newswire. (2000, January 12). *Microsoft grants increase technology access, training for students at African-American and Hispanic universities across the nation*. Retrieved from http://www.csrwire.com/press_releases/25077-Microsoft-Grants-Increase-Technology-Access-Training-for-Students-At-African-American-and-Hispanic-Universities-Across-the-Nation.

The Education Alliance. (2005). Closing the achievement gap. *Integrating technology into the K-12 classroom: Implications for public policy*. Retrieved from http://www.educationalliance.org/files/Integrating-Technology.pdf.

The Henry J. Kaiser Family Foundation Issue Brief. (2004). *Children, the digital divide, and federal policy*. Retrieved from http://www.kff.org/entmedia/upload/Children-The-Digital-Divide-And-Federal-Policy-Issue-Brief.pdf.

The History Channel. (n.d.) *Leonardo da Vinci*. Retrieved from http://www.history.com/topics/leonardodavinci.

T.H.E. Journal. (2009, November/December). *Digital media benefits primary prep: Research reveals that exposing preschool children to educational videos and games helps them move on to K-12 with better literacy skills, 36*(6), 8.

The White House. (2012). *Change the equation*. Retrieved from http://whitehouse.gov/issues/education/k-12/educate-innovate.

Tu, J. I. (2011, September). Microsoft launches program to bridge digital divide for students; Seattle one of first cities to take part. *Seattle Times*. Retrieved from http://seattletimes.nwsource.com/html/microsoftpri0/2016261086_microsoft_launches_program_to_bridge_digital_divid.html.

United States Census Bureau. (2009). *American community survey, Table B16004*. Retrieved from http://factfinder.census.gov/.

United States Department of Commerce. (1996). *White Mountain Apache tribe project*. Retrieved from http://ntiaotiant2.ntia.doc.gov/top/details.cfm?oeam=046096059.

United States Department of Commerce. (1997). *Holland independent school district's central Texas collaborative: Access for one rural community*. Retrieved from http://ntiaotiant2.ntia.doc.gov/top/docs/nar/pdf/486095035.

United States Department of Commerce. (2000). *Falling through the net: Toward digital inclusion: A report on Americans' access to technology tools*. Retrieved from http://search.ntia.doc.gov/pdf/fttn00.pdf.

United States Department of Commerce. (2011). *Exploring the digital nation: Computer and Internet use at home*. Retrieved from http://www.ntia.doc.gov/files/ntia/publications/exploring_the_digital_nation_computer_and_internet_use_at_home_11092011.pdf.

United States Department of Education. (2004). *Office for Civil Rights Programs for English Language Learners*. Retrieved from www.ed.gov/about/offices/list/ocr/ell/edlite glossary.html.

United States Department of Education. (2012). *Infrastructure: Access and enable*. Retrieved from http://www.ed.gov/technology/netp-2010/infrastructure-access-and-enable.

United States Department of Education. (2013). *Office of Innovation and Improvement news*. Retrieved from http://www.ed.gov/oii-news.

United States Department of Education, Office of Educational Technology. (2010). *Transforming American education: Learning powered by technology.* Retrieved from www. ed.gov/sites/default/files/netp2010.pdf.

University of Oregon. (2004). *The technology access program for students with disabilities.* Retrieved from http://darkwing.uoregon.edu/~atl/tapstu.htm.

Urban Research and Outreach-Engagement Center (UROC). (2012). *Broadband access project.* Retrieved from http://www.uroc.umn.edu/programs/bap.html.

Vascellaro, J. E. (2006, August). Saying no to school laptops. *Wall Street Journal*, D1.

Vesely, P., Bloom, L., & Sherlock, J. (2007). Key elements of building online community: Comparing faculty and student perceptions. *Journal of Online Learning and Teaching, 3*(3), 234–246.

Voicu, J., (2004). From digital divide to global digital solidarity. *ABAC Journal, 24*(1), 1–46.

Volkman, E. (2012). *SSOCEM: A model for developing new online communities. Session 6, communication theory.* Retrieved from http://play-this-org/2012/02/13/ssocem-a-model-for-developing-new-online-communities-session-6-sommuication-theory/.

Wahl, L., & Duffield, J. (2005). *Using flexible technology to meet the needs of diverse learners: What teachers can do.* WestEd. Retrieved from http://www.wested.org/cs/we/view/rs/763.

Wang, L. (2005, May). The advantages of using technology in second language education. *Technology Horizons in Education Journal, 31*(10), 38–41.

Warschauer, M. (2002). Reconceptualizing the digital divide. *First Monday, 7*(7). Retrieved from http://firstmonday.org/htbin/cgiwrap/bin/ojs/index.php/fm/article/viewArticle/967/888#w4.

Warschauer, M. (2004). *Technology and Social Inclusion—Rethinking the Digital Divide.* Cambridge, MA: MIT Press.

Warschauer, M., & Matuchniak, T. (2010). New technology and digital worlds: Analyzing evidence of equity in access, use, and outcomes. *Review of Research in Education, 34*(1), 179–225.

Washuk, M. (2011, March 20). 10 years after laptops come to Maine schools, educators say technology levels playing field for students. *Maine Sun Journal.* Retrieved from http://www.sunjournal.com/state/story/988012.

Watson, J., Murin, A., Vashaw.L., Gemin, B., & Rapp, C. (2010). *Keeping pace with K-12 online learning: An annual review of policy and practice.* Evergreen. CO: Evergreen Education Group. Retrieved from http://kpk12.com/cms/wp-content/uploads/KeepingPaceK12_2010.pdf.

Watson, J., Murin, A., Vashaw, L., Gemin, B., & Rapp, C. (2012). *Keeping pace with K-12 online learning: An annual review of policy and practice.* Evergreen. CO: Evergreen Education Group. Retrieved from http://www.kpk12/com/cms/wp-content/uploads/KeepingPace2012.pdf.

Wenger, E. (2006). *Communities of practice: A brief introduction.* Retrieved from http://www.ewenger.com/theory/.

Wikipedia. (2012a). *Open-source movement.* Retrieved from http://en.wikipedia.org/wiki/Open_source_movement.

Wikipedia. (2012b). *Gamification.* Retrieved from http://en.wikipedia.org/wiki/Gamification.

Wikipedia. (2012c). *APP (Application software).* Retrieved from http://en.wikipedia.org/wiki/APP.

Wikipedia. (2012d). *Massive open online course*. Retrieved from http://en.wikipedia. org/wiki/Massive_open_online_course.

Wilhelm, T., Carmen, D., & Reynolds, M. (2002, June). Connecting kids to technology: Challenges and opportunities. *Kids Count Snapshot*. Retrieved from http://www. aecf.org/upload/publicationfiles/connecting%20kids%20technology.pdf.

Williams, R. (2011). Baby Boomers and technology. *Wired for Success*. Retrieved from http://www.psychologytoday.com/blog/wired-success/201101/baby-boomers-and-technology.

Willis, S., & Mann, L. (2000). *Differentiating instruction: Finding manageable ways to meet individual needs*. Retrieved from Association for Supervision and Development website: http://www.ascd.org/publications/curriculum-update/winter2000/ Differentiating-Instruction.aspx.

Wolk, R. (2010, April). Education: The case for making it personal. *Educational Leadership, 67*(7), 16–21.

Wolk, R. (2012). Common Core vs. common sense. *Education Week*. Retrieved from http://www.edweek.org/ew/articles/2012/12/05/13wolk_ep.h32.html?r=1532025728.

Wood, A. (2008). What is renewal? Why now? In J. I. Goodlad, R. Soder, & B. McDaniel (Eds.), *Education and the making of a democratic people* (pp. 29–45). Boulder, CO: Paradigm Publishers.

WSIS (World Summit of the Information Society). (2011). *Outcome document*. Retrieved from http://www.itu.int/wsis/index.html.

Wynne, M., & Cooper, L. (2007). *Digital inclusion imperatives offer municipalities new social and economic opportunities*. Retrieved from http://www.digitalaccess.org/pdf/White_ Paper.pdf.

Young, J. (2012). Blackboard buys 2 leading supporters of open-source competitor Moodle. *The Chronicle of Higher Education*. Retrieved from http://chronicle.com/blogs/ wiredcampus/blackboard-buys-2-leading-supporters-of-open-source-competitor-moodle/35837.

Zehr, M. A. (2007, January). Tussle over English-Language Learners. *Education Week, 26*(21). Retrieved from http://www.edweek.org/ew/articles/2007/01/31/21harrison. h26.html.

Zinth, J. (2012). *Individualized instruction: Faster. Cheaper. Smarter*. Denver, CO: Education Commission of the States. Retrieved from http://www.ecs.org/clearinghouse/01/00/ 28/10028.pdf.

Zucker, A., & Kozma, R. (2003). *The virtual high school: Teaching generation V*. New York, NY: Teachers College Press.

Index